THE INTELLIGENT
INVESTOR'S GUIDE
TO REAL ESTATE

Real Estate for Professional Practitioners
A Wiley Series
DAVID CLURMAN, Editor

THE INTELLIGENT INVESTOR'S GUIDE TO REAL ESTATE

DAVID W. WALTERS

JOHN WILEY & SONS

New York • Chichester • Brisbane • Toronto

This publication is designed to provide accurate and
authoritative information in regard to the subject
matter covered. It is sold with the understanding that
the publisher is not engaged in rendering legal, accounting,
or other professional service. If legal advice or other
expert assistance is required, the services of a competent
professional person should be sought. *From a Declaration
of Principles jointly adopted by a Committee of the
American Bar Association and a Committee of Publishers.*

Library of Congress Cataloging in Publication Data

Walters, David W

    The intelligent investor's guide to real estate.

    (Real estate for professional practitioners ISSN 0190–
1087)
    Includes index.
    1. Real estate investment. I. Title.

HD1375.W26   332.63′24   80–17718
ISBN 0–471–07874–3

Printed in the United States of America

10 9 8 7 6 5 4 3 2 1

SERIES PREFACE

Since the end of World War II, tremendous changes have taken place in the business and residential real estate fields throughout the world. This has been evidenced not only by architectural changes, exemplified by the modern shopping center, but also in the many innovative financing responses that have enabled development of new structures and complexes, such as multiuse buildings. It can be expected that real estate development will speed in new directions at an ever increasing pace to match the oncoming needs of our time. With this perspective, the Real Estate for Professional Practitioners series has been developed in response to professional needs.

As real estate professional activities have become divided into specialties, because of intensive demand for expertise at all stages, so has there developed an increasing need for extensive training and continual education for persons directly involved or dealing in business ventures requiring detailed knowledge of realty procedures.

Perhaps no field of business endeavor is more in need of a series of professional books than real estate. Working in the practical world of business and residential construction and space utilization, or at advanced levels of college training covering these areas, one is constantly aware that too little of existing creative thinking has been transcribed into viable books. Many of the books that have been written do not thoroughly enough encompass both the practical and theoretical aspects of complex subjects. Too often the drive for immediate answers has led to the overlooking of fundamental purposes and technical know-how that might lead to much more favorable results for the persons seeking knowledge.

This series will be made up of books thoroughly and expertly expounding existing procedures in the many fields of real estate, but searching as well for innovative solutions to current and future problems. These books are intended to offer a compendium of each author's wide experience and knowledge to aid the seasoned professional.

The series is addressed to professionals in all walks of realty endeavor. These include business investors and developers, urban affairs specialists, attorneys, accountants, and the many others whose work involves real estate creativity and investment. Just as importantly, the series will present to advanced students in many realty fields the opportunity to review professional thinking that will help to stimulate their own thoughts on modern trends in housing and business construction.

We believe these goals can be achieved by the outstanding group of authors who will create the books in the series.

DAVID CLURMAN

PREFACE

Individuals contemplating an investment in real estate are usually over-whelmed by three problems. The first problem is dealing with the incredible breadth and depth of knowledge required to make intelligent investments in real estate. No investment can be made in real estate without touching on such subjects as law, appraisal, finance, management, tax, and marketing. In addition, the amount of expertise required is substantial. It is not enough to know that promissory notes are frequently secured by mortgages or deeds of trusts; one must also know that such mortgages or deeds of trust often contain substantial restrictions on the borrower's right to deal with the property.

The second problem is the difficulty of selecting a single book to begin mastering the knowledge necessary to make intelligent real estate investments. For example, how is an investor to know whether a book about land investment is different from a book on investing in country land? Similarly, a book dealing with real estate investment strategy may not be different from one covering the real estate investment decision-making process.

The third problem frequently encountered by real estate investors is that most books about real estate are simply not written for the serious, intelligent investor. Many books contain collections of "war stories" or "how I made it big" tales with so-called rules of thumb that, if followed, certainly would bring wealth if only one could follow them in the real world. On the other hand, there are many fine books that extensively develop one particular aspect of real estate but ignore (of necessity) the whole picture.

The Intelligent Investor's Guide to Real Estate is a happy medium between the scholarly treatises covering a narrow and specific aspect of real estate investing and the popular but often merely entertaining collections of success stories frequently purchased by the novice real estate investor.

The first chapter of the book, "Introduction to Real Estate as an Investment," covers some of the popular conceptions (right or wrong) of the real estate game and whets the reader's appetite for more substantial real estate analysis techniques. The second chapter, "Techniques for Projecting and Analyzing Real Estate Cash Flows," jumps into some of the "technology" of real estate investment analysis and illustrates the state of the art pertaining to income property investment analysis. The third chapter, "Acquisition of Real Estate," examines how to "buy-low-sell-high" with other people's money and financing. The fourth chapter of the book, "Improving, Leasing, and Disposing of Real Estate," discusses what to do with real estate investments once they have been acquired. It covers the timing of the sale or other disposition of real estate investments and the taxation of gains from such sales or dispositions. The fifth chapter of the book, "Specific Real Estate Investment Opportunities," discusses the commonly encountered forms of real estate investments and specific tax and economic factors pertinent to each.

The book was assembled from my ten years of experience teaching real estate investment analysis to a variety of students (junior college, college, graduate, and professional groups) and is, in essence, the book I wish I had when I started my real estate career. I hope that you will find it useful and, having read it, you will become as excited about real estate investment as I.

DAVID W. WALTERS

San Francisco, California
September 1980

ACKNOWLEDGMENTS

This book is the result of my relationships with certain people who have, in countless ways, contributed to my life. In order of appearance:

Thanks to my parents, William C. Walters and Elizabeth Harvey Walters, who have always loved and supported me in every way.

Thanks to Marianne for always telling the truth.

Thanks to Mrs. Alexopolis, Mr. Poorman and Mrs. Myhre, who practiced the lost art of teaching in an age bygone.

Thanks to Peter O. Willauer and Outward Bound for giving me a taste of glory.

Thanks to Bea and Jim Herrick for providing Tania and me with an incredible role model for a marriage.

Thanks to Paul F. Wendt, PhD., M.A.I., for thinking I knew something about real estate.

Thanks to Tania for creating a supportive, nurturing, and inspiring relationship.

Thanks to Ruth Ann, Leo, Mike, Bill, and Nana for their encouragment.

Thanks to Jennifer for choosing me as her daddy.

And thanks to Werner Erhard and everyone in *est*.

D. W. W.

CONTENTS

CHAPTER 2

TECHNIQUES FOR PROJECTING AND ANALYZING REAL ESTATE CASH FLOWS   12

CHAPTER 3

CHAPTER 4

IMPROVING, LEASING, AND DISPOSING OF REAL ESTATE   104

CHAPTER 5

SPECIFIC REAL ESTATE INVESTMENT OPPORTUNITIES 151

APPENDIXES   247

THE INTELLIGENT
INVESTOR'S GUIDE
TO REAL ESTATE

CHAPTER 1

INTRODUCTION TO REAL ESTATE AS AN INVESTMENT

There are many ways in which money can be invested in real estate. Some investments involve direct ownership of real estate by the investor. Such investments include the following:

Passive ownership of real estate
    Residential home purchases
    Income property ownership
        Apartments
        Commercial property
        Offices
        Industrial property
        Special purpose property
    Speculation in land for future appreciation
Active ownership of real estate
    Subdivision of raw land for sale
    Rehabilitation of existing projects for resale

Money may also be invested indirectly in real estate, in which case the investor does not own real property in its own name, but owns interests in an entity or a fund, which, in turn, owns real estate. Examples of such investments include:

Real estate limited partnerships (syndicates)
Real estate investment trusts (R.E.I.T.s)
Pension and profit sharing plans

Money can also be invested in forms wholly unrelated to real property but which have derivative rights involving real estate. Examples of such investments include notes, in which case the investor's cash flow is secured by deeds of trust or mortgages on real estate, and insurance policies, in which case the assets of the insurance company are invested in real estate, and premiums may be based on the company's success or lack of success in real estate investing.

PECULIARITIES OF REAL ESTATE AS AN INVESTMENT VEHICLE

Real estate as an investment vehicle is typically regarded as having certain peculiarities that, for better or worse, distinguish it from other investments, such as stocks and bonds, and must be understood to invest successfully.

Size of Investment Required

Real estate investment must be made on a grand scale. Whereas one can usually buy a share of common stock for a few dollars, even the purchase of a single interest in a syndicate owning real estate may involve thousands of dollars. The large sums required usually necessitate substantial borrowing, and investment decisions are heavily influenced by the costs of such borrowings.

Length of Holding Period

Whereas stocks and bonds can be bought and sold quickly, the real estate marketing process and the legal requirements of real property transfers involve substantially greater amounts of time. Such time requirements make correction of errors more difficult and increase the investor's downside risk.

Complexity of Transfer Mechanism

Whereas an individual can usually open an account with a stock broker and begin trading in stocks or bonds very quickly, the purchase, sale, and financing of real estate usually involves numerous legal documents, financial institutions, governmental regulations, customs, and procedures. In addition, numerous other parties such as real estate appraisers, real estate brokers, insurance salesmen, attorneys, title companies, and escrow companies may be required to effect a real estate purchase.

Lack of Formal Market Structure

Many stocks, bonds, and commodities can be traded on organized, centralized exchanges, such as the New York Stock Exchange. In addition, there are numerous large, national brokerage houses organized to aid in the purchase and sale of such securities. However, similar institutionalized exchanges and large national brokerage houses do not exist to facilitate the sale or exchange of real estate, and real estate purchases and sales are usually handled on an individual basis.

Lack of Standardized Performance Information

Numerous statistics and averages are kept with respect to the performance of stocks and other similar investments. In addition, there are numerous, widely circulated publications reporting information relevant to investing in such investments. Information about real estate and the performance of such investments is more difficult to obtain, and generally reported on a less standardized and more irregular basis.

Individuality of Each Parcel of Real Estate

Each parcel of real estate is situated in a different location. Such differences in location make reliance on quantitative data, alone, dangerous, and may necessitate a personal visit to the proposed investment before any funds are committed.

Use of Asset During Holding Period

While an investment in stocks or bonds may provide the investor with periodic cash flows in the form of dividends or interest, an investor in such securities normally does not have the use of its investment. Real estate, however, in addition to providing a source of periodic cash flows from rents, may often be occupied, farmed, renovated, or otherwise used by its owner.

Entrepreneurial Potential

An investor's success in the stock market may reflect his or her efforts at astute economic analysis upon the initial purchase of the stock. Once the purchase is made, however, the stock market investor must remain relatively passive. However, in the case of a real estate purchase, the investor need not remain passive and can embark on additional activities with respect to the investment such as renovation, subdivision, rehabilitation, rezoning, use changes, or the implementation of new management and marketing plans.

Exposure to Changes in Laws and Governmental Regulations

While cash flows from all investments are subject to certain laws and governmental regulations (such as tax laws), real estate investments are often subject to numerous additional specialized laws and regulations. Such laws include rent control laws, land use regulations, property tax laws, and environmental control laws.

FACTORS THAT MAY MAKE REAL ESTATE A PARTICULARLY GOOD INVESTMENT VEHICLE

All investments have certain unique qualitative attributes that make them attractive to certain investors. For example, investments in most common stocks can be made relatively simply (a phone call to a broker) and do not normally involve additional inputs of money and management time. Similarly, investments in art or antiques permit the owner to enjoy and use his investment. Real estate investments are also characterized by many qualitative aspects that may make such investments more or less attractive to certain investors.

	Property A (*Unleveraged*)	Property B (*Leveraged*)
Purchase price	$50,000	$250,000
Mortgage	–0–	200,000
Net equity investment	50,000	50,000
Net income (10% of purchase price)	5,000	25,000
Less mortgage interest	–0–	<16,000>
Net income	$ 5,000	$ 9,000
Net income as a percentage of cash invested	10%	18%

An example of leverage potential (see page 5).

Leverage Potential

Investments in real estate are generally made with the use of considerable amounts of borrowed funds ("leveraging"). Assuming the cost of such funds is less than the return to be realized by the real estate investment, the ability to leverage the investment gives the investor additional returns on his invested capital ("equity") that would not otherwise be possible. An example of such leveraging is shown on page 4.

Favorable Tax Laws

Investments in real estate enjoy numerous favorable tax laws. Such laws provide for:

Deductibility of many expenses associated with the ownership of income property

Deductibility of real property taxes

Deductibility of interest charges

Limited applicability of investment interest limitations

Inclusion of borrowed funds in depreciable basis

Limited applicability of "at-risk" rules

Possible use of accelerated depreciation methods

Potential capital gains treatment of gains upon sales

Limited applicability of depreciation recapture rules

Tax-deferred exchange potential

Installment sales treatment potential

Deferral of gains on the sale of residences

While real estate investments may be advantageous apart from the above tax laws, the effect of such favorable tax laws should be appreciated. The table on page 6 shows the effect of disallowing a depreciation deduction and not permitting the investor to include borrowings in the depreciable basis.

Inflation Hedge

While funds invested in bonds or other investments with a relatively fixed return are subject to the effect of declines in the purchasing power of the dollar caused by inflation, funds in real estate are generally not so ex-

	With Favorable Tax Laws Permitting a Depreciation Deduction and the Inclusion of Borrowings in Depreciable Basis	Without Favorable Tax Laws
Purchase price	$100,000	$100,000
Mortgage	80,000	80,000
Net equity investment	20,000	20,000
Net operating income (10% of purchase price)	10,000	10,000
First year depreciation assuming 80% building to value ratio, 25-year life and using 200% double declining balance depreciation method	< 6,400>	<0>
Taxable income	3,600	10,000
Tax (@50%)	1,800	5,000
Net operating income	10,000	10,000
Tax	1,800	5,000
After tax income	$ 8,200	$ 5,000

posed. Commercial leases, for example, may contain clauses permitting the pass-through of increased costs and clauses increasing rents as the Consumer Price Index increases. In addition, real estate is a relatively scarce asset, and real estate prices often increase to adjust to declines in the purchasing power of the dollar.

Responsiveness to Entrepreneurial Efforts

Real estate, unlike typical securities investments, can be improved, renovated, and subdivided, and rents and sales prices can be affected by the owner's labor and capital inputs. For example, many real estate fortunes began with the purchase and restoration of a small "fixer-upper." Similarly, large amounts of money are currently being made by converting existing properties, such as an apartment building, to new uses such as condominiums.

Responsiveness to Creative Financing

While yields from investments in other forms can also be improved with creative financing and astute negotiating strategies, real estate affords a particularly good vehicle for the use of creative financing and acquisition techniques, such as wraparound mortgages, sales leasebacks, and ground leases.

Responsiveness to Personality Factors

Real estate cash flows are closely tied to rentals. Rentals, in turn, are tied to astute leasing practices and good tenant relationships. Real estate provides a place where an individual's skills in such areas may be rewarded with better leases, happier tenants, and fewer cash flow irregularities.

Forced Savings/Equity Buildup

While one usually purchases other forms of investments with a single payment, real estate purchases are usually made with borrowed funds requiring additional periodic mortgage amortization payments. Such mortgage may result in the eventual pay-down of the purchaser's loan, and upon the sale of the property may provide additional cash for reinvestment or other purposes.

Exchange ("Pyramid") Potential

Numerous real estate investors started their real estate fortune with a single small investment, made certain improvements justifying increases in rents, and then exchanged such investments, at little or no tax cost, into larger investments with additional opportunities for similar improvements. The opportunity to exchange ("trade-up") real estate is provided by specific *Internal Revenue Code* sections that do not generally apply to other types of investments.

Popularity

Real estate investing is the subject of numerous "How I Made A Million Dollars . . ." articles and books. Most individuals believe that real estate is a good investment and make their lifetime goal early retirement holding a portfolio of income-producing real estate projects. In addition, there are millions of real estate salesmen and real estate brokers espousing the virtues of real estate investments. The effect of such books, beliefs, and claims provides a continuous influx of buyers and may help to sustain real estate prices at relatively high levels.

RISKS OF REAL ESTATE INVESTMENT AND RISK REDUCTION TECHNIQUES

All investments are subject to risks. For example, stock investments are subject to swings in the market as well as the risk that the corporation owned will perform poorly. Similarly, an art collector is subject to the risk that his investment will suffer physical harm, be stolen, or lose popularity. Real estate, too, is subject to such risks and, in addition, is subject to certain risks unique to real estate as an investment vehicle.

Bad Purchase

A risk that always faces investors in real estate is that they simply paid too much for their investment. The lack of easily accessible market information, standardized indices, and universally accepted analysis techniques increases the risk of a bad purchase in real estate investing. The risk of a bad purchase can be reduced by improved negotiating skills, better market analysis techniques, and more extensive market information gathering systems.

Inflation

Dollars invested in any form of investment are subject to the risk that when those dollars are returned they will not have the same purchasing power as when they were invested. As previously indicated, real estate may produce a relatively good "inflation hedge" because it is a relatively scarce asset. In addition, the risk of inflation can be further reduced in real estate investments by inserting expense pass-through and escalator clauses in leases or providing for rentals based on increases in the tenant's gross sales. Further, keen market analysis may enable the investor to purchase property in areas where price increases exceed the rate of inflation due to increases in demand for real estate.

Business Failure

All business activities and investments in such businesses are subject to the risks of outright business failure. Business failures in real estate result from such things as changes (declines) in neighborhoods and functional and physical obsolescence of buildings and improvements. Careful market analysis can do much to reduce the risk of neighborhood declines, and close attention to consumer taste and creative renovations can reduce the risk of functional obsolescence. Adequate reserves and careful improvement analysis upon the initial purchase of a real estate investment can reduce the risk of physical obsolescence.

Exposure to Laws and Governmental Regulations

New laws or changes in governmental regulations under existing laws, such as tax laws, can alter expected investment returns from all forms of investment. In addition, real estate investments are subject to numerous other laws and regulations such as rent control laws, building moratoria, environmental protection acts, and condemnation powers. Good economic analysis and close attention to changes in political and social beliefs can help to reduce the adverse effect of such governmental action.

Illiquidity and Market Inefficiency

All investments suffer from some liquidity problems, and all investment markets suffer from some degree of inefficiency. For example, even trading in New York Stock Exchange listed stocks may be restricted if particularly unusual news hits the financial scene. Similarly, even the buying and selling of gold may involve assays and other formalities. However, investments in real estate are particularly illiquid, unless the sale is at a bargain price. For example, the purchase and sales transaction, itself, is usually time-consuming, burdensome, and complicated. Similarly, the real estate market is highly localized, and there is a lack of good standardized indices for performance analysis. In addition, financing for real estate is generally localized, and there is a limited secondary market for real estate financial instruments. Finally, most purchasers and sellers of real estate do so infrequently and are relatively uninformed. Diversification among various locations and among various sizes of investments can help reduce the effect of the risks of illiquidity and market inefficiency.

Long Holding Period

All investments involve a consideration of the optimum holding period for such investment. Real estate purchases and sales transactions are rarely made in expectation of short-term profits and cash flows, but with a view toward medium or long-term cash flows and property appreciation. This emphasis on returns in more remote periods adds additional uncertainty to the real estate investment game, since future reversionary values and alternative reinvestment opportunities are difficult to anticipate. The use of options, diversification of investments between property currently producing income and more speculative property, and refinancing as more and more appreciation is experienced by the property can help to reduce the problems associated with the long holding periods typically characteristic of most real estate investments.

MYTHS ABOUT POTENTIAL BENEFITS FROM REAL ESTATE INVESTMENTS

Although real estate can provide the investor with certain subjective and "qualitative" benefits, an investment in real estate is only advantageous if it ultimately produces cash in the pockets of the investor. Unfortunately, real estate is often sold only on the basis of its "qualitative" aspects. An understanding of the pitfalls of buying real estate solely on the basis of such qualitative aspects is essential to good real estate investor decision making.

Leverage

While real estate provides an excellent means of using borrowed funds to obtain large property holdings, high depreciation and interest deductions, and rapid profits from appreciation in investment value, the investor needs an ability to continue to make necessary interest and principal amortization payments during "difficult" times, or the investment as well as the investor's initial capital will be lost altogether. In addition, leveraging only works when the investment ultimately produces substantial cash flows and sales proceeds. A purchase of a particular piece of real estate on the basis of attractive financing without attention to its ability to produce cash flows is sheer folly. In short, leverage should only be a means to obtain fundamentally sound investments.

Tax Shelter

While real estate investment has been generally favored by tax laws, and many a bad investment has been saved because of its owner's ability to use its negative income to offset other outside income, the purchase of real estate solely because of its tax shelter potential is ill-advised.

Inflation Hedge

Real estate is commonly regarded as a good inflation hedge, and, indeed, has probably provided investors with better protection against loss of purchasing power than such investments as savings accounts and insurance annuities. However, real estate investments generally require the investment of large quantities of capital for long periods of time and the owner's ability to liquidate such investments depends at all times on the attractiveness, popularity, and marketability of his property. If consumer tastes or economic factors have shifted so that his property is no longer desirable, the investor's hoped-for "inflation hedge" may disappear.

Appreciation Potential

Undoubtedly many investors have made fortunes by the astute purchase of property in the fringes of a growing metropolitan area, or other improvable property, and the subsequent sale of such property at large profits as a consequence of land booms or wise anticipation of neighborhood resurgences. In addition, many investors have purchased real estate and watched the market bid the price of their property up and up as a consequence of additional population influxes in an area with limited new construction due to building moratoria, land shortages, or financial unfeasibility. However, not all geographic areas increase in value equally, and neighborhoods do decline as other more prestigious or better located areas compete for residents, workers, and businesses. Many investors have failed to anticipate neighborhood declines and have held on to their investments too long. Others have been unable to weather short setbacks and sold out too soon. Reaping the gains of appreciation in value from real estate requires careful study of which investments to make at the outset and an ability to anticipate the most advantageous moment to sell. Blindly purchasing just any piece of property because of stories of value appreciation in totally dissimilar areas can be disastrous.

Equity Buildup

The periodic payments necessary to amortize real estate loans may provide a source of additional equity when the property is sold. However, principal payments represent a current drain on cash available for other investments and the equity "buildup" by such payments is only available at the future date when the property is sold. In addition, unless the property is sold at a price in excess of the balance due on the investor's loan, the investor may not receive the benefits of such principal payments at all.

CHAPTER 2

TECHNIQUES FOR PROJECTING AND ANALYZING REAL ESTATE CASH FLOWS

While real estate investment is commonly regarded as a source of "equity buildup," "tax shelter," "appreciation," and as an "inflation-hedge," the returns from an investment in real estate consist of only two things: yearly net after tax cash flow ("Cash Flow") and a residual upon sale ("Residual"). "Equity buildup," "tax shelter," "appreciation" and "inflation-hedge" are merely terms traditionally used to define some of the factors that may produce Cash Flow and a Residual. Reliance only upon "equity buildup," "tax shelter," "appreciation," and "inflation-hedge" as justification for real estate investment may be dangerous.

COMPONENTS OF YEARLY NET AFTER TAX CASH FLOW

Each year investments in real estate produce Cash Flows consisting of the following elements:

Gross income	$ _____
<Vacancies and bad debts>	$<_____>
<Operating expenses>	$<_____>
Net operating income	$ _____

Net operating income	$ _____
\<Interest expenses\>	$\<_____\>
\<Depreciation deduction\>	$\<_____\>
Net taxable income \<loss\>	$ _____
Net taxable income	$ _____
\<Income taxes\> (+ tax savings)	$\< _____ \>
Net after tax income (\<loss\>)	$ _____
Net after tax income	$ _____
\<Loan amortization payments\>	$\<_____\>
Depreciation deduction	$ _____
Net after tax cash flow	$ _____

The use of this accounting outline can be illustrated as follows:

ASSUMED INVESTMENT

Purchase price	$100,000
Gross income	$ 15,300
Vacancy and bad debts	5% of gross
Operating expenses	$ 6,500
Investor's marginal tax bracket	38%
Loan	$ 80,000
Interest on loan	9% per year
Term of loan	25 years
Depreciable basis	$ 60,000
Method	150% declining balance
Life	25 years

COMPONENTS OF YEARLY NET AFTER TAX CASH FLOW
FOR FIRST YEAR

Gross income	$ 15,300
<Vacancy and bad debts>	< 765>
<Operating expenses>	<6,500>
Net operating income	8,035
Net operating income	$ 8,035
<Interest expense>	<7,164>
<Depreciation deduction>	<3,600>
Net taxable income (<loss>)	<2,729>
Net taxable income	$<2,729>
<Income taxes> (+ tax savings)	1,037
Net after tax income (<loss>)	<1,692>
Net after tax income (<loss>)	$<1,692>
<Loan amortization payments>	< 893>
Depreciation deductions	3,600
Net after tax cash flow	$ 1,015

Gross income should include the total actual rentals collected plus the market value of vacant space for the period it was vacant and should include uncollected rents from space actually occupied.

Operating expenses should include items such as payroll, supplies, electricity, water, gas, heating fuel, management, administrative costs, painting and decorating, maintenance and repairs, services, insurance, and real estate taxes. Operating expenses should not include interest charges, ground rent, depreciation allowances, principal amortization and investor income taxes.

Interest expenses should include all valid and deductible interest charges but not the principal amortization portion of the investor's periodic (monthly) payments on account of any borrowings related to the purchase and/or improvement of the property.

Depreciation deductions include such amounts as are permitted according to applicable tax laws and regulations pertaining to the property but should not include actual reserves for repairs or renovations.

Income taxes should include the additional Federal and state income taxes incurred as a result of the ownership of the property by the investor. Since various investors have different outside taxable incomes, the amount to be used for income taxes in the accounting outline may vary from investor to investor.

Tax savings should include the amount of income taxes saved, if any, as a result of the "tax shelter" provided by a negative net taxable income. As in the case of income taxes, the amount of tax savings will be dependent on the particular investor owning the property. Ideally the investor should calculate the exact differences in taxes due as a result of the ownership of the investment. However, such calculations may be difficult, and investors often approximate these tax savings by multiplying their marginal tax bracket times any negative taxable income. Such an approximation assumes that all tax savings are counted at the investor's top bracket and should not be relied upon if precision is important.

COMPONENTS OF RESIDUAL UPON SALE

When real estate is sold the residual is calculated as follows:

Gross sales proceeds	$ _____
<Selling expenses>	$<_____>
Net sales proceeds	$ _____

Net sales proceeds	$ _____
<Mortgage balance due>	$<_____>
<Taxes>	$<_____>
Residual	$ _____

The use of this accounting outline can be illustrated as follows:

ASSUMED SALE

Gross sales proceeds	$ 100,000
Selling expenses	7,000
Mortgage balance due	50,000
Taxes	30,000

RESIDUAL

Gross sales proceeds	$ 100,000
<Selling expenses>	< 7,000>
Net sales proceeds	93,000

Net sales proceeds	$ 93,000
<Mortgage balance due>	< 50,000>
<Taxes>	< 30,000>
Residual	$ 13,000

In the event that the sale involves installments to be paid in more than one year, the calculation of the Residual may involve more than one time period, and the Residual in periods other than the year of sale may not include all of the above elements.

In the event that the investor disposes of his property by means of a tax-deferred exchange there may not be a Residual. Rather, a new series of Net After Tax Cash Flows will be generated, which must be compared with the Net After Tax Cash Flows that would have been received by the old investment.

MULTIYEAR NET AFTER TAX CASH FLOWS

During each year the components of Yearly Net After Tax Cash Flow are constantly changing. For example, the amount of interest expense changes (usually downward) each year because the outstanding loan balance on which the interest charges are calculated changes. Similarly, the depreciation deduction under accelerated depreciation methods changes each year (usually downward) because the depreciable basis on which the depreciation deduction is calculated changes. In addition, most loan amortization schedules provide for larger and larger payments of principal over the life of the loan. Finally, the investor's other outside income may fluctuate, and the amount of income taxes or tax savings may vary from year to year. Thus, an accurate analysis of a real estate investment must account for changing period Cash Flows and Residuals occurring at different times in the future. The chart on page 17 outlines the components of periodic Yearly Net After Tax Cash Flows and Residuals.

TECHNIQUES FOR EVALUATING REAL ESTATE NET AFTER TAX CASH FLOWS AND RESIDUALS

Once the investor has determined the yearly Net After Tax Flows and Residual to be received by a particular investment he must then make a decision as to whether he should invest in that particular property. There are dozens of criteria and techniques by which Net After Tax Cash Flows and Residuals (or the components thereof) are evaluated. Some criteria and techniques are very simple, such as the gross income multiplier technique, which merely requires the calculation of the ratio between the sales price of the property and its first year gross rental income. Such criteria and techniques lack financial sophistication and accuracy, and may amount to little more than picking a basketball team only from persons taller than 7'3" in height. However, they are popular because of their simplicity and

$Year_{(1)}$
Gross income$_{(1)}$
$<$Operating expenses$_{(1)}>$
$<$Vacancy$_{(1)}>$

Net operating income$_{(1)}$

Net operating income$_{(1)}$
$<$Interest$_{(1)}>$
$<$Depreciation$_{(1)}>$

Net taxable income$_{(1)}$

Net taxable income$_{(1)}$
$<$Income tax$_{(1)}>$
$(+$Tax savings$_{(1)})$

Net after tax income$_{(1)}$

Net after tax income$_{(1)}$
$<$Amortization$_{(1)}>$
Depreciation$_{(1)}$

Net after tax cash flow$_{(1)}$

$+$

$Year_{(2)}$
Gross income$_{(2)}$
$<$Operating expenses$_{(2)}>$
$<$Vacancy$_{(2)}>$

Net operating income$_{(2)}$

Net operating income$_{(2)}$
$<$Interest$_{(2)}>$
$<$Depreciation$_{(2)}>$

Net taxable income$_{(2)}$

Net taxable income$_{(2)}$
$<$Income tax$_{(2)}>$
$(+$Tax savings$_{(2)})$

Net after tax income$_{(2)}$

Net after tax income$_{(2)}$
$<$Amortization$_{(2)}>$
Depreciation$_{(2)}$

Net after tax cash flow$_{(2)}$

$+ \cdots +$

$Year_{(n)}$
Gross income$_{(n)}$
$<$Operating expenses$_{(n)}>$
$<$Vacancy$_{(n)}>$

Net operating income$_{(n)}$

Net operating income$_{(n)}$
$<$Interest$_{(n)}>$
$<$Depreciation$_{(n)}>$

Net taxable income$_{(n)}$

Net taxable income$_{(n)}$
$<$Income tax$_{(n)}>$
$(+$Tax savings$_{(n)})$

Net after tax income$_{(n)}$

Net after tax income$_{(n)}$
$<$Amortization$_{(n)}>$
Depreciation$_{(n)}$

Net after tax cash flow$_{(n)}$

because the urgency of real estate dealings may not permit more precise techniques and criteria.

Other criteria and techniques may involve more complex mathematical equations as, for example, internal rate of return calculations. Such techniques and criteria are difficult to learn and understand and are often difficult to apply without the aid of computers. However, such techniques and criteria are mathematically more accurate than the other, simpler techniques, usually give a true picture of an investment's yield, and force the investor to investigate more closely the assumptions he is making about the components of Yearly Net After Tax Cash Flows and Residuals.

Rules of Thumb Commonly Used in Evaluating Real Estate Cash Flows

Numerous statistics (ratios, etc.) derived through mathematical operations on various components of the Yearly Net After Tax Cash Flow and/or Residual are commonly used by investors in evaluating real estate investment decisions. Most of these rules of thumb do not give an investor a completely accurate indication of an investment's yield since they usually do not take into account yearly variations in the components of the Cash Flow and are often based on the assumption of an infinite Cash Flow. In addition, most rules of thumb ignore the Residual. The following are examples of such rules of thumb:

CASH ON CASH

$$\frac{\text{Gross income} - <\text{Operating expenses}> - <\text{Principal payment}> - <\text{Interest expense}>}{\text{Down payment}}$$

TAX SAVINGS PLUS CASH FLOW

$$\frac{\text{Gross income} - <\text{Operating expenses}> - <\text{Principal payment}> - <\text{Interest expense}> + \text{Tax savings}}{\text{Down payment}}$$

EQUITY BUILDUP, TAX SAVINGS PLUS CASH FLOW

$$\frac{\text{Gross income} - <\text{Operating expenses}> - <\text{Interest expense}> + \text{Tax savings}}{\text{Down payment}}$$

PAYBACK

Buy investment that returns investment quickest.

BROKER'S NET BEFORE INTEREST DEPRECIATION AND TAXES

$$\frac{\text{Gross income} - <\text{Operating expenses}>}{\text{Down payment}}$$

RETURN-ON-INVESTMENT (VERSION 1)

$$\frac{\text{Average annual income}}{\text{Average investment}}$$

RETURN-ON-INVESTMENT (VERSION 2)

$$\frac{\text{Average annual income}}{\text{Original investment}}$$

MARGIN

$$\frac{\text{Debt service} + \text{Operating expenses}}{\text{Gross income}}$$

ACCOUNTING RETURN

$$\frac{\begin{array}{l}\text{Net after tax cash flow (year 1)} \\ + \text{ Net after tax cash flow (year 2)} \\ + \ldots \\ + \ldots \\ + \text{ Net after tax cash flow (year } n) \\ + \text{ Residual}\end{array}}{\text{Down payment}}$$

GROSS INCOME MULTIPLIERS AND CAPITALIZATION OF INCOME

Techniques

In addition to the use of the previous rules of thumb, real estate investors and appraisers also value income-producing property by means of "gross income multipliers" or the "capitalization of income." The following are formulas for each technique:

GROSS INCOME MULTIPLIER TECHNIQUE

$$V = I \times M$$

where $V =$ value
$I =$ income
$M =$ multiplier

CAPITALIZATION OF INCOME TECHNIQUE

$$V = \frac{I}{R}$$

where $V =$ value
$I =$ income
$R =$ capitalization rate

The techniques are related in that M and R are inverses. That is, $M = 1/R$, and $R = 1/M$.

Limitations of Gross Income Multipliers and Capitalization Techniques

Each technique, unless the multiplier and/or capitalization rate is chosen by means of very sophisticated techniques, suffers from serious defects. Among such defects are the following:

Both techniques assume a constant annual cash flow.
Both techniques assume an indefinite annual cash flow.
Neither technique accounts for a residual.
Neither technique accounts for loan amortization.
Neither technique accounts for interest payments on outstanding loans.
Neither technique accounts for a return on the owner's investment.
Neither technique accounts for a return of the owner's investment.

DISCOUNTED CASH FLOW

"Discounting a cash flow" describes the process whereby the "time value" of money is taken into account in evaluating a particular yearly Net After Tax Cash Flow and Residual to be received in the future. Discounting a Cash Flow is also commonly referred to as "present value analysis." The basic premise behind present value analysis is that a particular Cash Flow or Residual to be received in a future year can be replicated by an investment of some amount, today, at a specific interest rate. The amount required to be invested today (the "present value") is less than the amount to be replicated at a future time because of the effect of compound interest.

By adding up the present values necessary to replicate a particular future Cash Flow and/or Residual, real estate appraisers and investors are able to analyze more precisely a particular future Cash Flow and Residual than if they merely used the traditional rules of thumb, which do not consider the time periods in which Cash Flows or Residuals are to be received. For example, if the amount to be reserved in the future was to be $65.00 then the present value of such payment would be $50.70 ($65.00 × 0.78).

Sources of Data for Present Value Factors

Numerous tables have been published containing such present value factors. An example of such a table is as follows:

Present Value Factor/Discount Factor

Year	5%	6%	7%	8%	9%	10%
1	0.95	0.94	0.93	0.92	0.91	0.90
2	0.91	0.89	0.87	0.86	0.84	0.82
3	0.86	0.84	0.81	0.79	0.77	0.75
4	0.82	0.79	0.76	0.74	0.71	0.68
5	0.78	0.75	0.71	0.68	0.65	0.62

An example of the use of such a table follows:

ASSUME

Cash to be received in the future = $65.00
Discount rate = 9%
Year in which cash is to be secured = 4

CALCULATION

Present value factor = 0.71

Present value = (0.71) ($65.00) = $46.15

Present Value of a Series of Cash Flows

Discounting a single payment to be received in some future year involves the simple process of multiplying the future payment by the appropriate present value factor. For example, if the future payment is $10.00 and the investor expects to receive the payment in 5 years; the present value of such payment using a 5% discount factor is $7.80. (That is 0.78 × $10.00 = $7.80.) Discounting a series of payments merely consists of multiplying each yearly payment by the appropriate discount *rate* and adding all of the discounted yearly payments. The following is an example of discounting a series of payments:

	Year 1	Year 2	Year 3	Year 4
Cash flow	$10	<$5>	$25	$10
Discounted cash flow @ 5%	$10 × $0.95 $9.50	$<5> × 0.91 $<4.55>	$25 × 0.86 $21.50 Sum = $31.25	$10 × 0.82 $8.20
Discounted cash flow @ 9%	$10 × $0.91 $9.10	$<5> × 0.84 $<4.20>	$25 × 0.77 $19.25 Sum = $34.65	$10 × 0.71 $7.10

As this chart indicates, if the investor uses a "discount rate" of 9%, he should not pay more than $31.25 to purchase the investment.

Investment Analysis Using the Discounted Cash Flow Technique

Investment analysis using the discounted cash flow technique consists of picking an appropriate discount rate, generating accurate estimates of Cash Flows and the Residuals, taking the sum of the present values of such Cash Flows and Residuals, and comparing investments. The best investment is the one that has the highest discounted present value of the sum of the Cash Flows and Residual. The following is an example of investment analysis using the discounted cash flow technique:

ASSUME

Cash Flow Alternative *A:*

Year 1	Year 2	Year 3	Year 4
$10	$10	$10	$10

Cash Flow Alternative *B:*

Year 1	Year 2	Year 3	Year 4
$ 5	$ 5	$ 5	$27

Discount rate: 5%

PRESENT VALUE OF CASH FLOW ALTERNATIVE A

$$\$35.40 = \$10 \,(0.95) + \$10 \,(0.91) + \$10 \,(0.86) + \$10 \,(0.82)$$

PRESENT VALUE OF CASH FLOW ALTERNATIVE B

$$\$35.74 = \$5 \,(0.95) + \$5 \,(0.91) + \$5 \,(0.86) + \$27 \,(0.82)$$

Since Cash Flow Alternative B has the highest present value (at 5%) it should be selected.

Necessity for Accurate Calculation of the "Discount Rate"

In the previous example, the present value of Cash Flow Alternative B exceeded the present value of Cash Flow Alternative A if the discount rate of 5% is used. However, if the discount rate of 10% is used, Cash Flow Alternative A would then have a present value of $31.70, while Cash Flow Alternative B would then have a present value of $30.88; and Cash Flow Alternative A becomes a better investment. Thus, the investor must carefully select the "discount rate" he intends to use.

INTERNAL RATE OF RETURN ANALYSIS

Avoidance of Arbitrary Discount Rates

As the foregoing tables indicate, the present value of the sum of a particular series of Net After Tax Cash Flows and Residuals depends on the discount rate used. Unfortunately, selection of the appropriate discount rate is often done arbitrarily. An alternate analysis approach called "internal rate of return analysis" is available to real estate investors who are unwilling to make their investment decisions on the basis of arbitrarily selected discount rates.

Calculation of the Internal Rate of Return

Internal rate of return analysis is a process by which the investor fixes the present value of the sum of a particular series of Net After Tax Cash Flows and Residuals and then finds (often by trial and error) the discount rate that makes the sum of present value of the Cash Flows and Residual equal to the fixed present value. The fixed present value commonly used is the investor's equity investment (his down payment plus other out-of-pocket acquisition costs). The discount rate so determined is called the "internal rate of return" ("IRR") and is regarded by most financial analysts as a better indication of an investment's yield than the traditional rules of thumb.

The following analysis is an example of the Internal Rate of Return calculation process:

ASSUMPTIONS

Cash Flow

Year 1	Year 2	Year 3	Year 4
$10	$<5>	$25	$10

EQUITY REQUIRED (PRESENT VALUE) = $32.05

CALCULATION OF IRR

Discounted Cash Flow @ 7.0%

Year 1	Year 2	Year 3	Year 4
$10 × $0.93	$<5> × 0.87	$25 × 0.82	$10 × $0.76
$9.30	<$4.35>	$20.50	$7.60

Sum = $33.05; too large

Discounted Cash Flow @ 9%

Year 1	Year 2	Year 3	Year 4
$10 × $0.92	$<5>×0.84	$25 × 0.77	$10 × 0.71
$9.10	<$4.20>	$19.25	$7.10
		Sum = $31.35; too small	

Discounted Cash Flow @ 8%

Year 1	Year 2	Year 3	Year 4
$10 × $0.92	$<5> × 0.86	$25 × 0.79	$10 × 0.74
$9.20	<$4.30>	$19.75	$7.40
		Sum = $32.05; equality!	

The discounted present value of the Cash Flow @ 8% equals the equity required. Thus, the internal rate of return equals 8%, or the yield equals 8%.

RISK ANALYSIS

While present value analysis and internal rate of return analysis provide good methods for analyzing Yearly Net After Cash Flows and Residuals, the techniques do not account for uncertainties in the estimation of Cash Flows and Residuals. Sophisticated investment analysts are often unwilling to make such assumptions and have developed a variety of techniques for taking into account uncertainty in the estimation of Yearly Net After Tax Cash Flows and Residuals. An example of a simple risk adjustment technique applied to projected Cash Flows follows:

Hypothetical Data

Year	After Tax Cash Flow	Probability	Present Value Factor (12%)
1	$4,000	.30	0.89
	$5,000	.70	0.89
2	$6,000	.40	0.80
	$7,000	.60	0.80
3	$8,000	.50	0.71
	$9,000	.50	0.71

Risk Adjusted Present Value

($4,000) (.30) (0.89) = $1,068
($5,000) (.70) (0.89) = $3,115
($6,000) (.40) (0.80) = $1,920
($7,000) (.60) (0.80) = $3,360
($8,000) (.50) (0.71) = $2,340
($9,000) (.50) (0.71) = $3,706
                        $16,009

SOURCES OF DATA FOR CASH FLOW ANALYSIS

Projected Gross Income

Estimating gross income from real estate investments involves an analysis of the supply and demand for the particular project and can often involve sophisticated econometric models taking into account dynamic inter-relationships between numerous variables.

NATIONAL ECONOMIC FORECASTS. All estimates of the demand for real estate begin with some kind of measurement of the national economy. Factors usually measured and analyzed include such variables as the following:

Population and demographic variables

Population
Number of households
Population household formation growth rate
Age group distributions
Family size and composition
Migration trends
Population shifts
Employment rates
Characteristics of the labor force
Employment in durable goods industries
Employment in service industries

Economic and monetary variables
Gross national product

Per capita income
Per capita savings
Distribution of family spending
Bank deposits
Government reserves
Wholesale sales
Retail sales
Buying power index
Long-term interest rates
Short-term interest rates
Stock prices
Money supply
Capital investments
Inventories
Bank reserves
Labor costs
Commodities prices
New business formations
Housing starts
Federal housing policy

Analyses of the national economy vary widely in sophistication. Some discussions of the national economy merely note changes in the direction of certain variables (such as interest rates or population), do not attempt to describe the interrelationship between groups of variables, and merely let the user come to his own conclusions about the effect of such charges on property values. Such conclusions are all too often based on the investor's peculiar belief about the economy and not on any empirically proven economic models. Other analyses of the national economy focus the interreaction between the different variables and may contain conclusions involving complicated graphic and/or mathematical models of the national economic system. The practicalities of the smaller real estate transactions may not justify the use of such sophisticated models and data analyses techniques. However, as the size and complexity of the investment increases, as with new towns or large subdivisions, such modeling and analysis are often undertaken.

LOCAL ECONOMIC FORECASTS.   Once the national economy and its dynamics are described, analysis of the supply and demand for a particular project shifts to the local economy and local land development patterns. Analysis of the local economy usually involves consideration of the same variables as does the analysis of the national economy (such as population and household formation) but also considers the following additional types of variables:

Economic and monetary variables

Local economic base
Inventory of real estate
Foreclosures
Vacancies
Local taxes
Construction activity
Building costs
Land costs
Demolitions and conversions
Number and type of establishments in the central business district
Automobile registration

Consumer tastes

Locational preferences
Size, type and style preference
Amenities preferences
Schools
Government services

Population and demographic variables

In-migration/out-migration
Household income characteristics
Number of TV stations
Daily newspaper circulation
Employment in various economic sectors

Land use variables

Geographic limitations
Weather
Transportation patterns
Interstate connector routes

Travel times

Highest value of commercial land per square foot

Highest value of residential land per square foot

Highest residential rental rate per square foot

Shopping facilities location

Recreational uses

Social status

Zoning limits

Utilities

Soil conditions

As with the study of the national economy, analyses of data concerning local areas vary widely in sophistication. Often appraisers and investors are satisfied merely with simple textual descriptions and tables containing summaries of such data and leave the determination of the effect of changes in such variables up to the reader. Appendix A contains an example of such an analysis. Other analyses of local areas focus on the interrelationships among such data and may contain conclusions based on complicated graphic and/or mathematical models of the local or regional economic system. Appendix B contains an example of a sophisticated local area economic study. Appendix C contains an example of the use of readily available economic data for the analysis of a local area market demand for appliances.

SOURCES OF DATA FOR ECONOMIC FORECASTS. Specific quantitative data for national and regional market analysis are available from numerous sources. For example, the U.S. Department of Commerce publishes a *Directory of Federal Statistics for Local Areas*, which contains over 360 pages of data sources. The U.S. Department of Commerce publishes a *Guide to the Use of Federal and State Statistical Data*, which contains numerous examples of market analysis using readily available data. Good sources of information include:

U.S. Department of Commerce

The Bureau of the Census

The Federal Reserve Banks

The Department of Housing and Urban Development

The Federal Housing Administration

Research departments of banks, planning departments, The Urban Land

Institute (Washington), local newspaper research departments, tax assessors, title companies, local utilities, and local real estate boards also provide information concerning regional and local characteristics.

Operating Expenses

CATEGORIES. Operating expenses associated with real estate investments include the following:

Real estate taxes
>   Local real estate taxes, state real estate taxes, non-capitalized assessments

Maintenance and repairs
>   Interior
>   >   Noncapitalized replacement of floor coverings, draperies, heating, light fixtures, plumbing, electrical
>
>   Exterior
>   >   Landscaping, exterior painting and cleaning, elevator maintenance, boiler inspection and repair, air conditioning, fire extinguishers, plumbing, electrical, masonry, carpentry, roofing

Painting and decorating (interior)
>   Paint, wallpaper

Services
>   Window washing, extermination, rubbish removal

Insurance
>   Fire, liability, workers' compensation, fidelity bonds

Management
>   On-site, off-site, leasing or rental fees

Fuel
>   Oil used for heating, gas used for heating

Gas
>   Cooling, hot water

Water
>   Water costs, sewer charges

Electricity
>   Tenant and public areas, elevators, air conditioning, laundry

Supplies
>   Janitorial, light bulbs, uniforms

Payroll
    Janitors, doormen, elevator operators, taxes, welfare benefits

SOURCES OF DATA FOR OPERATING EXPENSE ESTIMATION. Data for operating expenses estimation are available from numerous sources concerning the prior experience of owners of various types of real estate. For example, the Institute of Real Estate Management (I.R.E.M.) publishes a yearly *Apartment Building Income—Expense Analysis,* which contains detailed breakdowns for various types of apartment buildings. Similarly, the National Association of Building Owners and Managers publishes a yearly *Experience Exchange Report* containing operation expense data for office buildings.

PITFALLS IN RELYING ON SELLER'S OPERATING EXPENSE DATA. Reliance on information supplied by property owners without independent verification can be dangerous. First, the owner may actually misrepresent the amount of expenses either by an outright fraud (such as purposely misstating an amount) or by an omission (such as a failure to state that invoices of only one of two suppliers of certain services are included in his information). In addition, property owners may not account for the value of their own management time and efforts or the costs of materials they can obtain below market prices. Finally, analyses of such data, even if accurate, may not indicate all of the qualitative and subjective aspects of the property such as different maintenance, low tenant morale, and functional and economic obsolescence and should never substitute for a personal visit to the property. The following example illustrates the potential problems of a typical expense statement:

Expense Items	Potential Problems
Real estate taxes	Real estate taxes may change on a sale and may not include improvement assessments.
	Some areas impose hybrid taxes (such as taxes on landlords based on tenant's operations) that may not be included in the owner's summary.
Maintenance, repairs, painting,	A personal visit must be made to determine if amounts expended are realistic.
decorating, services	Low figures may have been achieved by failing to expend funds for on-going maintenance and repairs and may indicate large deferred maintenance charges in the future.

Maintenance, repairs, etc.	Low figures may have been achieved at the cost of a bad reputation for the property, tenant dissatisfaction, and difficulty in re-renting as leases and rental agreements terminate.
Insurance	The amount necessary and costs thereof may change on purchase of property.
	Owners may have a blanket rate because of other buildings owned.
	Coverage may have deductibles or levels of personal liability protection inappropriate to new owner.
Heat, electricity, fuel, water, gas	The owner may have kept such expenses low at the expense of tenant satisfaction and the reputation of the property.
Payroll, management	The owner may have failed to include fair market value of the owner's time spent in managing the property.
	The owner may have skimped on services at the expense of future rerental potential and property reputation.

Interest

SIMPLE INTEREST.   Simple interest is computed entirely on the basis of the original borrowed funds (principal). To compute interest expense an investor must know how much money is borrowed, the rate of interest (rate) and the term of the loan (time). Simple interest is ordinarily computed by simply multiplying together the principal, time, and rate. This leads to the formula for simple interest:

$$I = PRT$$

where I = simple interest due in dollars
P = principal in dollars
R = interest rate to be paid per unit of time
T = time in units that correspond to the rate

The use of these equations can be illustrated by the following example:

ASSUME

$P = \$1,000$
$R = 5\%$
$T = 5$ Years

SIMPLE INTEREST DUE

$$\$250 = \$1,000 \ (0.05) \ (5)$$

COMPOUND INTEREST.   Compound interest is simple interest applied over and over to a sum that is increased by the simple interest each time it is earned. For example, an investment of $1,000 at 4% simple interest earns interest at $40.00 per year. However, if the interest as it is earned is added to the principal and the new principal then, in turn, earns interest, the investment increases more rapidly than will simple interest. Interest paid on an increasing principal in this way is known as compound interest. The following example shows the increases in an investment of $1,000 if the interest rate is 4% compounded annually:

Original principal	$1,000.00
Interest for first year @ 4%	40.00
Principal at the start of third year	1,081.60
Interest for second year @4%	41.60
Principal at the start of third year	1,081.60
Interest for third year @ 4 %	43.26
Amount at end of three years	$1,124.86

Thus, the compound interest earned on the original investment is $124.86 compared to $120.00 that would be earned at simple interest in the same length of time. The following equation can be used for determining the amount of principal and compound interest earned after a number of years:

$$S = P \ (1 + i)n$$

where S = the amount at compound interest ($)
P = the principal invested ($)
i = the interest rate per year (%)
n = the number of years (years)

The use of these equations can be illustrated as follows:

ASSUME

$P = \$1,000$

$I = 5\%$

$N = 5$ Years

AMOUNT ACCUMULATED AT COMPOUND INTEREST

$\$1,276 = \$1,000 \, (1.05) \, (1.05) \, (1.05) \, (1.05) \, (1.05)$

LIMITATIONS ON INTEREST DEDUCTIONS.   Interest expenses are generally deductible whether the debt is a business or personal expense. However, in order for the interest expense to be deductible, the expense must meet certain requirements including:

The expense must relate to a bona fide debt.

The indebtedness must be that of the taxpayer.

The expense must not be specifically disallowed.

The expense must be compensation for the use of money or forbearance of a debt.

The expense must not be specifically capitalizable by statute or regulation.

Principal Amortization

FORMULA.   The amount necessary to amortize a particular loan balance is calculated by means of the following formula (employing the compound interest formula):

$$R = \frac{P(1 + i)ni}{(1 + i)n - 1}$$

where R = periodic payment [interest and principal necessary to amortize a loan ($)]

P = principal balance at beginning of loan term ($)

n = term of loan (years)

i = interest rate on loan (%)

The use of these equations can be illustrated as follows:

ASSUME

$P = \$1,000$

$n = 5$

$i = 5\%$

YEARLY PAYMENT (INTEREST AND PRINCIPAL) NECESSARY
TO AMORTIZE THE LOAN

$$\$231 = \frac{\$1,000 \ (1.05) \ (1.05) \ (1.05) \ (1.05) \ (1.05) \ (1.05)}{(1.05) \ (1.05) \ (1.05) \ (1.05) \ (1.05) - 1}$$

TABLES. Numerous tables exist containing principal payments based on these equations. The following is an example of such a table:

Monthly Payment to Amortize Loan of $1,000 (Principal and Interest)

Term	Interest				
	8%	8½%	9%	9½%	10%
10 years	12.13	12.40	12.67	12.94	13.22
15 years	9.56	9.85	10.14	10.44	10.75
20 years	8.36	8.68	9.00	9.32	9.65
25 years	7.72	8.05	8.40	8.74	9.09
30 years	7.34	7.69	8.05	8.41	8.78

Since the amounts in this table are for loans of $1,000, an adjustment must be made if the loan being amortized is not exactly equal to $1,000. For example, a loan of $2,568 at 9% over 20 years would require a payment of $23.11. That is,

$$\$23.11 \text{ equals } \$2,568 \text{ times} \frac{1}{1000} \text{times } 9.00.$$

The amounts in such amortization tables usually include interest payments as well as principal payments. Tables are also available that break down such periodic payments into principal and interest. The following is an example of such a table:

$10,000 Loan @ 10% Interest:
10-Year Repayment Period—$132.15 Monthly Payment

Year	Balance	Principal	Interest
1	$9386.581	$ 613.418	$972.390
2	8708.930	677.651	908.157
3	7960.319	748.610	837.198
4	7133.320	826.999	758.809
5	6219.723	913.597	672.211
6	5210.460	1009.262	576.546
7	4095.514	1114.945	470.863
8	2863.819	1231.695	354.130
9	1503.149	1360.669	225.139
10	0.000	1503.149	82.659

Depreciation Deduction

CALCULATION PROCESS.   The process of calculating allowable depreciation deduction involves numerous steps including the following:

Determine the depreciable basis of the property.
Estimate the salvage value of the property.
Determine the useful life of the property.
Determine the allowable depreciation method.
Calculate the yearly depreciation deduction.
Keep records of accumulated depreciation.
Keep records of adjusted basis.

Each of these steps is discussed in later portions of the book.

LIMITATIONS ON DEPRECIATION DEDUCTION.   There are many limitations on a taxpayer's right to take depreciation deductions including:

Property.   The depreciation deduction must pertain to property subject to wear or tear, decay or decline from natural causes, exhaustion, or obsolescence that has a definitely limited useful life. Determining whether a particular expense incurred in connection with the acquisition of a piece of property may be depreciated is not always easy. For example, land is generally not depreciable, but certain costs associated with using land may be added to building construction costs and thereby depreciated. Similarly, it is not always easy to tell if a particular type of property may be depreciated in the first place. For example, tax regulations specify that avocado trees may not be depreciated because they have an undeterminable life, whereas lemon trees can be depreciated.

Taxpayer.   A depreciation deduction is only permitted by the party who sustains the economic loss from the investment. Determining who sustains the economic loss may not always be easy. For example, one need not necessarily be the legal title holder of property. Similarly, tenants, under carefully drawn lease clauses, may be able to depreciate real property that they merely lease.

Timing.   The deduction is only available when the asset is placed in service. Determining when or how much of the asset is placed in service may present problems in the case of buildings under construction.

Basis.   The deduction must be based on an establishable depreciable basis. Usually the initial basis is the investor's cost. However, property may be acquired by inheritance, gift, exchange, or in exchange for the cancellation of a debt, in which event, the basis may be calculated with reference to a previous owner's or property's basis.

Records.   Adequate records must be maintained to support the parameters used in calculating the depreciation deduction, such as the property's cost (or other) basis, data supporting the choice of useful lives, data supporting the salvage value used, and data supporting the value of various components of the property if the "component method of depreciation" is used. Taxpayers have been denied depreciation deductions on the basis of inadequate records.

Methods.   Depreciation methods are specifically prescribed for each type of property and may vary depending on the type of property and its date of acquisition.

Recapture.   All depreciation deductions taken in excess of straight-line are subject to recapture upon the sale of the property. The amount of recapture depends on whether the property was held less than 12 months, and the time period during which the excess depreciation was taken.

In addition to the foregoing elements of the depreciation deduction calculation, investors must take into account various other tax laws dealing with special rules for depreciation in the year of acquisition and/or sale, special rules and calculations for switching from one depreciation method to another, special rules governing the use of the component depreciation method, investment tax credit rules, rules for depreciation of special types of properties such as historical monuments, and, if the investor consists of a partnership, rules for allocating deductions among various partners.

CALCULATION OF AMOUNTS.   Once the real estate analyst has determined the appropriate parameters (basis, allowable depreciation method, useful life, salvage value) the exact amount of depreciation allowable for a particular year can be calculated with the following formula:

$$D = B \frac{(M)}{(L)} \frac{(1-M)^{N-1}}{(L)}$$

where $D =$ depreciation deduction for year N
$B =$ original basis
$M =$ method (1.25, 1.50, 2.00)
$L =$ life of asset
$N =$ year in which deduction is to be taken

The following is an example of the use of the above formula:

ASSUME

$B = 100$
$M = 150\%$ declining balance (1.5)
$L = 10$ years
$N = 7$

DEPRECIATION DEDUCTION YEAR 7

$$D = \$5.66 = \$100 \frac{(1.5)}{10} \frac{(1 - 1.5)^6}{10}$$

TABLES.   In addition to this formula, numerous tables exist for use in calculating depreciation. The following is an example of such a table:

10-Year Useful Life

Year	Straight Line	Declining Balance		
		125%	150%	200%
1	0.1000000	0.1250000	0.1500000	0.2000000
2	0.1000000	0.1093750	0.1275000	0.1800000
3	0.1000000	0.0957031	0.1083750	0.1280000
4	0.1000000	0.0837402	0.0921187	0.1024000
5	0.1000000	0.0732727	0.0783009	0.0819200
6	0.1000000	0.0641136	0.0665558	0.0655360
7	0.1000000	0.0560994	0.0565724	0.0524288
8	0.1000000	0.0490870	0.0480866	0.0419430
9	0.1000000	0.0429511	0.0408736	0.0335544
10	0.1000000	0.0375822	0.0347425	0.0266435

Tax Shelter

In the event a real estate investment has a positive net taxable income (and the investor is an individual or partnership), such net taxable income is added to the investor's other taxable income, and the investor must pay taxes on the total taxable income according to the applicable provisions of the *Internal Revenue Code* pertaining to individuals and/or partnerships. Where the investor is a corporation, the net taxable income is taxable to the corporation according to applicable provisions of the *Internal Revenue Code* pertaining to corporations, and subsequent distributions by the corporation to its owners will generally be taxable as dividends.

EXAMPLE OF TAX SHELTER POTENTIAL FROM REAL ESTATE. In the event a real estate investment has a negative net taxable income and the investor is an individual or a partnership, such loss may generally be used to offset other taxable income of the investor or partners in the partnership. The following is an example of the offset available:

ASSUME

Net taxable loss	=	<$40,000>
Income from other sources	=	100,000
Marginal tax rate	=	40%

TAX LIABILITY WITHOUT DEDUCTING REAL ESTATE NET TAXABLE LOSS

Other income	$100,000
Tax liability*	<50,500>
After tax income	$ 49,500

TAX LIABILITY AFTER DEDUCTING REAL ESTATE NET TAXABLE LOSS

Other income	$100,000
Real estate net taxable loss	<40,000>
Taxable income	$ 60,000
Tax liability*	<23,941>
Net after tax income	$ 36,000

TAX SAVINGS

Tax liability without offset	=	$ 50,500
Tax liability with offset	=	<23,941>
Tax savings		$26,559

If the investor is a corporation, any Net After Tax Losses from real estate generally cannot be passed through to the corporation's owners, and this offset may not be possible.

PROJECTED SALES PRICE

Estimation of the projected sales price is similar to the estimation of yearly gross incomes. Both processes involve measuring many variables affecting the supply and demand for real estate (such as population, disposable income, transportation costs, land availability, and credit costs), accounting for the interrelationships among those variables, and describing trends in the direction of such variables. Much of the previous discussion pertaining to the estimation of gross incomes is therefore applicable to the estimation of projected sales prices. Indeed, the two processes are closely related since the selling price of most real estate is closely tied to the property's gross income in the year of sale.

---

* Assuming a single taxpayer, using the 1979 Tax Rate Schedules, and assuming no other deductions.

Long-Term Trends Significant to Future Sales Prices

In estimating the projected sales price, more attention should be paid to changes in long-term trends and the factors that may radically change the supply and demand for real estate than is paid to estimating yearly gross incomes. In addition, more attention should be paid to the impact of the entrepreneurial activities of the investor with respect to the particular property. The following list gives examples of factors that may signficantly alter existing trends in the variables that influence supply and demand:

Changes in household formation rates
  Changes in childbearing expectations
  Changes in population age group distribution
  Changes in living-together arrangements
Changes in aggregate economic variables
  Employment rates
  Business cycle changes
  Saving/spending propensities
  Changes in employment among different industry classes
Changes in governmental regulations
  Zoning
  Environmental controls
  Taxation
  Development limitations
  Building regulations
Changes in consumer tastes
  Preferences for style
  Preferences for amenities
  Preferences for location
  Preferences for second homes
  Preferences for savings/spending
Changes in financing devices
  New secondary market devices
    Mortgage backed securities
  New capital raising devices
    Syndicates

New loan pricing devices
    Variable rate loans
Changes in local economic structure
    Shifts from durable goods to service industries
    Neighborhood decline/regeneration
Changes in the physical topography
    Urban renewal assemblage
    Bay fill
    Open spaces acts
Changes in transportation technology
    Rapid transit routes
    Airports
Changes in supply of social services
    Schools
    Transportation
    Fire, police protection

Entrepreneurial Activities

Examples of entrepreneurial activities that may significantly alter the demand for a particular site include:

Renovations, rehabilitations
Additions
Use changes
Obtaining subdivision, rezoning, etc.

Studies and Models of Future Value Changes

Sophisticated projections of selling prices of real estate in the future are often based on complicated, computerized, land use simulation models. An example of one such model was used in the *Bay Area Simulation Study* undertaken in 1968 by the University of California, Berkeley. That model involved a sophisticated computer program that evaluated input in the form of forecasts for national and state age, population, and financial variables and that produced population, employment, housing demand, and land use forecasts for seven counties located in the San Francisco area. An example of one such table produced by the *Bay Area Simulation Study* is as follows:

Population (1000s)	Forecast		
	1970	1980	1990
Alameda	1,115	1,357	1,583
Contra Costa	588	736	885
Marin	238	321	388
Napa	85	103	113
San Francisco	765	802	856
San Mateo	577	668	730
Santa Clara	1,042	1,134	1,523
Solano	190	295	436
Sonoma	220	312	427

Other similar studies are frequently undertaken by regional governmental agencies, universities, planning commissions, and financial institutions.

INCOME TAXES UPON DISPOSITION OF REAL ESTATE

Most investors understand that gains realized upon the sale of real estate are not taxed the same as earned income, but are taxed at "capital gains" rates and that losses upon the sale of real estate may be used to offset the owner's other ordinary income. However, the treatment of such gains and losses is considerably more complicated than such a general rule would suggest and depends on complicated rules and methods for determining the amount of gain or loss realized, the purpose for which the investment was held, the length of time the investment was held, the depreciation method used by the owner, the method of disposing of the real estate, and the method of making payments to the seller.

The Amount of Realized Gain or Loss

Obviously, there is no tax liability unless gain is realized by the disposition. The amount of gain realized may include items other than cash proceeds, such as the relief from liabilities, other property, or services and notes.

The Purpose for Which the Real Estate Was Held

Profits from the sale of certain types of real estate, such as lots produced by most subdividers, usually will not qualify for special capital gains treatment, although losses from the sale of such real estate can usually be deducted in full. On the other hand, profits from the sale of other types of real estate, such as raw land held by an investor for long-term appreciation, usually will qualify for capital gains teratment, but the deductibility of any losses as ordinary losses may be limited. Still other types of real estate, such as most rental property, may qualify for capital gains treatment of profits as well as full deductibility of losses as ordinary losses.

The Length of Time the Investment Was Held

The length of time the investment was held will determine whether any capital gains are short or long-term and the amount of any excess depreciation subject to recapture if the investment was owned prior to 1976.

The Depreciation Method Used by the Owner

If the owner used a depreciation method other than straight-line, some of the profits that might have otherwise qualified for capital gains treatment may be subject to special recapture rules and may be taxed at ordinary income rates. In addition, if the owner used an accelerated depreciation method rather than the straight-line method, the amount of remaining basis upon which taxable gain is based will be smaller, and potential taxable gain will be that much higher.

The Method of Disposing of the Real Estate

If the owner disposes of his property by means of a tax-deferred exchange, tax liability may be partially or totally deferred. Similarly, there are special rules for condemnation proceeds by which a taxpayer may avoid tax liability by prompt reinvestment of the condemnation proceeds.

The Method of Making Payments to the Seller

If the full purchase price of real estate is paid in cash in the year of sale the taxpayer will usually face liability for taxes on all of his profits in that year. However, if only a portion of the purchase price is received in the year of sale, the taxpayer may under certain circumstances, be able to spread his tax liability over several years.

CHAPTER 3

ACQUISITION OF REAL ESTATE

FINANCING REAL ESTATE PURCHASES

Investments in real estate require considerable sums of money, and the profitability of real estate investments depends in great part on the availability and cost of such sums.

Money for investment in real estate can be thought of as a commodity, like soap or coffee, that has an ultimate source and for which there is a market where suppliers and users interact to set prices.

The commodity, "money for investment in real estate," can take various forms such as:

30-Year FHA insured home loans

Equity participations in mortgage investment trusts

Short-term construction loans

30-Year "take-out" financing

5-Year home improvement loans

Equity participations in limited partnerships

Governmental interest payment subsidies

Governmental loan guaranty programs

Land warehousing

Equity participation in R.E.I.T.'s

In the case of the commodity called "money for investment in real estate," the ultimate source is earnings, profits, and taxes (production) that are not consumed, but set aside, and thus available for investment. Wage earners, businesses, and governments can set aside their earnings, profits, and tax revenues in a variety of ways, including:

Savings accounts
Pension fund contributions
Insurance policy payments
Taxes
Credit union deposits
Secondary mortgage market purchases
Stocks
Bonds
Mortgage backed pass-through certificates
Limited partnership interests
Thrift certificates
Real estate investment trust interests

In the case of the commodity called "money for investment in real estate," the marketplace is not as defined as the marketplace for soap or coffee (the local grocery store). In fact, while there are certain fixed locations where savers and borrowers transact business (such as mortgage companies acting as brokers between large-scale investors and large-scale lenders), the marketplace for real estate funds is very amorphous. In addition, savers and borrowers rarely transact business directly but act through intermediaries such as banks and savings and loan associations. Numerous Federal and private organizations publish data concerning the money market including:

Board of Governors, Federal Reserve System
(*Federal Reserve Bulletin*)
U.S. Department of Commerce
(*Survey of Current Business*)
U.S. Department of Housing and Urban Development
(*Housing and Urban Development Trends*)

Sources of Equity for Real Estate Investments

Most of the sources for real estate loans by policy or regulation, do not lend a borrower 100% of the cost of an investment. Thus, the first problem facing a real estate investor is to obtain the difference between the available loan funds and the project's cost. This difference is commonly referred to as "equity."

Equity funds for real estate investment other than from personal loans made to the investor and the investor's own savings generally come from a collective investment in the form of a partnership, trust, or corporation. Each form of collective investment has important differences in terms of taxation of profits and losses, liability of the investor, investor management rights, transferability of the investor's ownership interest, and ease of formation.

GENERAL PARTNERSHIPS. General partnerships enjoy complete pass-through of profits and losses and provide the investor with maximum participation in the business activities of the partnership. However, general partners are liable for the debts of the partnership, and a transfer of a general partnership interest usually results in a dissolution of the partnership.

CORPORATIONS. Corporations do not normally enjoy pass-through of profits and losses, and earnings of the corporation are taxed to the corporation and also to the owner(s) when distributed as dividends. On the other hand, since the corporation is usually a legal entity distinct from its stockholders, the stockholder's liability is limited. A corporation does not terminate upon the transfer of its stock, and corporate stock is usually more easily transferred than partnership interests.

LIMITED PARTNERSHIPS. Limited partnerships generally provide investors with pass-through of profits and losses and with limited liability for its limited partners. However, pass-through of profits and losses and limited liability can only be achieved by compliance with state limited partnership acts and Federal and state tax regulations that limit the ability of investors to participate in management decisions and to transfer their limited partnership interests.

R.E.I.T.'s. Real estate investment trusts also permit the pass-through of earnings (and tax losses not in excess of cash distributions), and provide the investor with limited liability. Tax regulations with respect to real estate investment trusts do not require restrictions on the transfer of the investor's interests. However, such regulations restrict the type of investments real estate investment trusts can make.

Securities Laws

Raising equity for real estate investments through any of the common forms usually involves the sale of a "security," and individuals forming such entities should be sure that they comply with the applicable provisions of Federal and state securities laws regulating the issuers' activities as well as the activities of salesmen or brokers selling the securities on behalf of the issuers.

REGISTRATION REQUIREMENTS OF THE SECURITIES ACT OF 1933 AND STATE "BLUE SKY" LAWS.   Under Section 5 of the Securities Act of 1933 every offer or sale of a security in interstate commerce must be registered with the Securities and Exchange Commission unless a specific exemption for the transaction can be found. Registration of an offering requires the issuer to prepare and file a detailed registration statement with the Securities and Exchange Commission, an integral part of which is a prospectus. Appendix D contains *Guide 60,* which contains the Securities and Exchange Commission's guidelines for disclosures to be made in a prospectus covering real estate limited partnerships. Most states have similar registration (or "qualification") requirements.

BROKER/DEALER REGULATIONS UNDER THE SECURITIES AND EXCHANGE ACT OF 1934.   Under the Securities and Exchange Act of 1934, brokers and dealers are subject to surveillance and regulation by the Securities and Exchange Commission. They must follow detailed rules regarding the securities in which they may deal and the manner in which they transact business with their customers. Subject to very narrow exceptions, no broker or dealer may engage in business without first registering with the Securities and Exchange Commission. Most states have similar regulations.

PRIVATE OFFERING EXEMPTION.   Fortunately, for most small-scale collective real estate activities there is a "private offering" exemption from the registration requirements of the Securities Act of 1933 and many states' "Blue Sky" laws. "Private offerings" involve the following types of limitations:

A limited number of offerees
A limited number of purchasers
Sophisticated investors
Previous relationships between the offeror and the investors
Access to information concerning the investment
Investment intent on the part of the investors
Securities containing unusual provisions
Limited amounts of money raised
No public advertising
Limited resale activities

Whether or not a particular offer and sale constitutes a private offering is often difficult to determine. For example, an offer to a single sophisticated investor may not qualify as a private offering unless it can be proven that the investor has access to the kind of information that a registration statement would disclose. Similarly, attorneys, doctors, and other professionals do not automatically qualify as sophisticated investors merely by virtue of their educational background or financial resources.

Since the burden of proof is on the issuer to show that the office of the security is exempt as a private offering, many issuers rely on the more objective criteria set forth in Rule 146 in determining whether their offer is a private offer in terms of Federal law. Such criteria include:

The Offeree must have "knowledge and experience in business and financial matters" or, in the alternative, he must be able to bear financially the economic role of the investment and must designate an "offeree representative" who has the requisite financial sophistication.

General advertising or solicitation, including seminars, meetings, letters, or offering circulars is not permitted.

Unless an offeree has access to the type of information that registration would disclose, he must be furnished that information.

No more than 35 purchasers of securities may be involved in the Rule 146 offering.

The issuer must exercise reasonable care to assure that all purchasers are making the investment for their own account and that resales are limited.

The issuer under certain circumstances must file a report with the Securities and Exchange Commission.

State "Blue Sky" laws may have similar "objective" criteria.

INTRASTATE EXEMPTION.   Under Section 3 (*a*) 11 of the Securities Act of 1933 any offering in which securities are offered and sold only to persons resident within a single state by an issuer resident or incorporated and doing substantially all of its business within that state is an exempt offering in terms of Federal law. Like the private offering exemption, a determination as to whether or not the exemption is available depends on numerous subjective circumstances, and like the "safe harbor" of Rule 146 with respect to the private offering exemptions, there is also a more objective set of criteria concerning the intrastate exemption contained in Rule 147. It should be noted that even if the requirements of Section

3(*a*)(11) of the Securities Act of 1933 are met, the issuer may still be subject to the registration requirements of the applicable state "Blue Sky" laws.

FULL DISCLOSURE.   While small-scale collective investments may be able to avoid the qualification and registration requirements of the various applicable Federal and state securities laws, such laws do not, generally, exempt the issuer from "full disclosure" requirements. "Offering circulars" or "private placement memoranda" are commonly prepared to supply investors with information concerning the proposed investment such as:

Risks of the investment
Sponsor's background
Sponsor's compensation
Use of proceeds
Assessments
Investment objectives and policies
Sponsor's track record
Management rights of the sponsor and investors
Investor's rights to reports
Taxation of the investment
Termination of the investment
Allocation of profits and losses
Conflicts of interest
Tax opinion

Appendix D (*Guide 60*) contains the Securities and Exchange Commission's guidelines as to full disclosure in registered offerings and provides a good beginning point for disclosure in exempt offerings.

The Four Major Sources of Debt Financing For Real Estate Investments

The most common sources of funds for debt financing are savings and loan associations, commercial banks, life insurance companies, and mutual savings banks. Together they furnish about 80% of all mortgage money. Each institution is subject to various regulations which, in large part, are primarily responsible for their differing lending policies. Appendix E contains a summary of the regulations affecting California savings and loan associations.

SAVINGS AND LOAN ASSOCIATIONS. Savings and loan associations are federally chartered and state chartered. Federally chartered savings and loan associations are regulated primarily by the Federal Home Loan Bank Board and indirectly by the Federal Savings and Loan Insurance Corporation. State chartered savings and loan associations are regulated primarily by state savings and loan departments and commissions and indirectly by the Federal Savings and Loan Insurance Corporation.

While there are some differences between the specific types of loans permitted by state and Federal savings and loan associations (for example, federally chartered savings and loan associations usually cannot lend as much on the same appraised value as state chartered savings and loan associations), both are similar in that they specialize in individual home loans, tend to lend more on older homes than banks, tend to have higher appraisals than banks, and tend to permit longer amortization periods. Their interest rates, loan fees, and prepayment penalties tend to be higher than commercial banks.

COMMERCIAL BANKS. Commercial banks consist of national banks and state chartered banks. National banks are regulated primarily by the Comptroller of the Currency and the Federal Reserve and indirectly by the Federal Deposit Insurance Corporation. State banks are regulated primarily by state banking departments or commissions and indirectly by the Federal Reserve, the Comptroller of the Currency, and the Federal Deposit Insurance Corporation.

While there are certain differences between the specific types of loans permitted by national banks and state chartered banks (for example, national banks may, under certain circumstances, make higher loan-to-value, unamortized loans than state banks), both are similar in that they tend to specialize in short-term commercial credit and construction loans, emphasize liquidity more than savings and loan associations, and tend to be more conservative in appraisals. Their interest rates and charges for loan fees and prepayment penalties are often less than savings and loan associations.

LIFE INSURANCE COMPANIES. Life insurance companies are chartered by various state governments whose regulations generally permit more flexibility in loans than is permitted for savings and loan associations and banks. Life insurance companies tend to concentrate their loans on larger commercial and income properties or to purchase batches of individual loans assembled by mortgage brokers. They often enter into joint ventures with investors. Life insurance companies typically make large loans through their home offices and make small loans through loan correspondents. A small loans correspondent may be a mortgage company or an individual who represents many different companies and who receives a finder's fee for each mortgage processed.

MUTUAL SAVINGS BANKS. Mutual savings banks exist primarily in the Northeast. They are regulated primarily by the state within which they are located. They tend to prefer loans on single-family dwellings with the larger mutual savings banks investing in apartment house, commercial, and industrial mortgages, and tend to be very conservative in appraisals and in lending policy.

PENSION FUNDS. Pension and profit-sharing funds are the most rapidly growing segment of the capital market. Often such pension plans are represented by banks, trust companies, mortgage correspondents, or special investment advisors. There are a number of private pension funds, established by high-income professionals who control their own investment policies, which have considerable flexibility in structuring an investment.

SOURCES OF INFORMATION CONCERNING LENDERS. There are numerous books and periodicals containing information about lenders and the availability of funds. The following is a partial list of some of the books and periodicals that may provide such information:

Crittenden Income Property Mortgage Directory
Crittenden Financing, Inc.
3300 West Coast Highway, Suite F
Newport Beach, CA

Federal Reserves Bulletin
Board of Governors of the Federal
Reserve System
Washington, DC 20551

Housing
McGraw-Hill, Inc.
P.O. Box 430
Hightstown, NJ 08520

Housing & Realty Investor
Audit Research Inc.
230 Park Ave, Suite 555
New York, NY 10017

Moody's Bank & Finance Manual
Moody's Investors Service, Inc.
99 Church Street
New York, NY 10017

The Mortgage Banker
Mortgage Banker's Assn.
1125 15th Street
Washington, DC 20005

The Mortgage and Real Estate Executives Report
Published by Warren, Gorham & Lamont, Inc.
210 South Street
Boston, MA 02111

The National Market Letter
Real Estate Research Corporation
72 West Adams Street
Chicago, IL 60603

National Real Estate Investor
Communication Channels, Inc.
6285 Barfield Road
Atlanta, GA 30328

Novicks' Income Property Finance Report
IPFR Publishing Corporation
60 East 42nd Street
New York, NY 10017

*Rand McNally International Bankers
Directory*
1st Edition, 1978
Rand McNally & Company
P.O. Box 7600
Chicago, IL   60680

Real Estate Investing Newsletter
Harcourt, Brace, Jovanovich, Inc.
306 Dartmouth Street
Boston, MA 02116

Real Estate Investors Report
Warren, Gorham, & Lamont, Inc.
210 South Street
Boston, MA 02111

Real Estate Newsletter
Published by Coopers & Lybrand
400 Renaissance Center
Detroit, MI 48243

Real Estate Newsletter
Published by Laventhol & Horwath
919 Third Avenue
New York, NY 10022

Real Estate Opportunities
Prentice-Hall, Inc.
Route 9W
Englewood Cliffs, NJ 07632

Government Sources of Money

Federal, state and local governments are an important source of funds, subsidies, guaranties, and backing for real estate development of all types. While the object of most programs ultimately is to increase the amount of housing and/or money available for loans, the programs usually (though not always) accomplish such ends indirectly rather than by direct construction or direct loans. Examples of the forms government programs can take include:

Method	Effect
Direct loans of government money (Cal-Vet programs)	Funds in the hands of the purchaser
Insurance of loans made by others (FHA 203(*b*) programs)	Reduced reluctance to lend to certain borrowers
Guarantees of loans made by others (VA loan programs)	Reduced reluctance to lend to certain borrowers
Subsidies of rental payments (FHA Section 8 programs)	Increased willingness of investors to supply housing to certain groups
Subsidies of owner interest payments (FHA Section 235–236 programs)	Increased ability to afford housing by certain groups
Purchase of loans made by others (FNMA, GNMA programs)	Increased willingness to lend to certain borrowers
Guarantees of investments in loan programs (mortgage backed security programs)	Increased funds in the housing loan segment of the capital market

FEDERAL AGENCIES PROVIDING FUNDS, INSURANCE OR GUARANTIES. There are a variety of Federal agencies directly involved in real estate finance and development. Some of the more commonly encountered agencies include the following:

HUD (U.S. Department of Housing and Urban Development). HUD is the cabinet department responsible for government housing programs. There are numerous subagencies in HUD including the FHA and GNMA. HUD programs are designed to deal with the problems of the inner cities, the secondary mortgage market, urban growth, new communities, interstate sales of land, and specialized housing programs.

FHA (Federal Housing Administration). FHA is a division of HUD that insures lenders against losses on a variety of loans. FHA is self-supporting through income derived from fees, insurance premiums, and investments.

FNMA (Federal National Mortgage Association). FNMA is a private corporation (federally sponsored) that buys and sells FHA and Veterans Administration mortgages.

GNMA (Government National Mortgage Association). GNMA is the division of HUD responsible for secondary market purchases of loans made pursuant to low and moderate income loan programs. GNMA also administers other government housing programs.

FMHA. FMHA is a division of the U.S. Department of Agriculture that makes direct housing and farm loans in rural areas.

VA (Veterans Administration). The Loan Guarantee Division of the Veterans Administration guarantees a portion of loans made by lenders to certain veterans.

Other Federal programs providing finance assistance include or have included: the RAA (Renewal Assistance Administration), which administers loans and grants to local housing authorities that provide low-rent housing; the SBA (Small Business Administration), which guarantees, as well as makes, loans to small businesses and insures rental payments to be made by small businesses; the NHC (National Housing Corporation), which is intended to serve as general partner in national limited partnerships that are to build housing units with subsidies under Federal programs; the EDA (Economic Development Administration), which is a part of the U.S. Department of Commerce and administers grants and loans to areas of high unemployment and economic disadvantage; and

Federal Land Banks, which are federally sponsored agencies that make loans on farms, ranches, rural houses, and farm related businesses.

FEDERAL AGENCIES INDIRECTLY AFFECTING THE AVAILABILITY OF FUNDS. Not all government agencies that affect the availability of funds for real estate loans and development do so directly by loans, subsidies, and/or guaranties. However, the impact of such agencies may be more significant than the direct lending subsidy and guaranty programs. Among the Federal agencies that affect the availability of money for real estate investment are:

Federal Home Loan Bank Board (FHLBB). The FHLBB charters Federal savings and loan associations and regulates state chartered savings and loan associations that are part of the FSLIC. It regulates the types of credit savings and loan associations can grant, and sets the maximum interest rates they can pay on deposits. It also loans funds to members to meet unexpected withdrawal demands, to provide seasonal liquidity, and to enable savings and loan associations to meet commitments in the event of a slowdown in deposits. It also regulates the reserve requirements of member associations.

Federal Reserve Board. The governors of the Federal Reserve Board, together with the presidents of Federal Reserve Banks, make decisions as to how much money will be added to or withdrawn from the supply of money. The Federal Reserve Board also regulates the reserve requirements of member banks.

Comptroller of the Currency. The Comptroller of the Currency regulates the lending activities of national banks.

Federal Deposit Insurance Corporation (FDIC). The FDIC insures deposits in member banks. Membership in the FDIC is contingent on compliance with its regulations, many of which contain numerous limitations on bank lending activities.

U.S. Treasury. The U.S. Government raises money in a variety of ways. One is by borrowing by the Treasury. Such borrowing competes with banks and savings and loan associations for savers' money and thus influences the amount of money available for loan by such institutions.

There are, obviously, numerous other agencies that significantly affect the availability of funds whose effect is even more indirect than those listed above. For example, by changing its audit emphasis concerning limited partnerships, the Internal Revenue Service may influence investor (saver) decisions on where to invest excess funds and may cause a shift in the supply of funds from one market (equity investments in, perhaps, questionable tax shelters) to another (for example, tax-free municipal bonds whose proceeds may be used to subsidize local rehabilitation programs). Similarly, the Securities and Exchange Commission, by promulgating new rules with respect to the "private offering" exemption, may reduce the number of tax shelter limited partnerships and thereby also cause a shift of funds to another market.

Other Sources of Financing

Acquisitions of real estate are often financed by means of more exotic arrangements than loans from banks or savings and loan associations. Indeed, there seems to be a certain pride in the real estate business in having come up with the most complicated, and "hidden" financing device.

PURCHASE MONEY LOANS.   Sellers can provide a source of "financing" in that they may agree to take the purchase price in the form of a note to be amortized (if at all) over a period of years. Tax considerations, such as the potential for installment sales treatment, may make a purchase money loan transaction attractive to a seller. In addition, purchase money obligations to sellers may be exempt from usury laws under the "time price doctrine." The seller may obtain a higher yield on his sales proceeds by allowing the purchaser to pay off the balance of the purchase price in installments that include a charge for deferring the payment of the sales price, rather than by loaning cash proceeds directly to other real estate investors.

TENANTS AND CONCESSIONAIRES.   Purchasers of certain buildings may be able, within the limits imposed by local landlord and tenant laws, to require prospective tenants to pay high "security deposits" to raise necessary capital or to pay the cost of interior renovation and improvements. In addition, certain tenants may be induced to make direct loans to landlords in partial consideration of their right to lease the landlords' space.

CONTRACTORS AND OTHER SUPPLIERS.   The use of deferred payment terms can provide necessary improvements without immediate cash outlays. Similarly, leasing equipment, such as elevators, escalators, and other electrical components, can be a way to obtain necessary building equipment on a deferred payment basis.

JOINT VENTURE ARRANGEMENTS.   Often lenders may not be willing to loan money at relatively low yields, but they will be willing to "joint venture" with the developer or investor. The form of such joint ventures varies considerably. Some "lenders" may enter into partnerships and fund the purchase of land and development expenditures in return for a portion of the profits. Other "lenders" may actually buy the land and contract with the developer for services and parcel out the potential profits to the developer. Either way, the developer has been provided with the opportunity to use his skills with the "lenders'" money.

TRUST ENDOWMENT FUNDS, CHARITABLE FOUNDATIONS. Trust endowment funds and charitable foundations can provide debt financing in real estate. Investment policies by such entities differ, and they may even be a source of equity financing.

Analysis of the Supply and Demand for Real Estate Funds

THE DEMAND FOR REAL ESTATE FUNDS. The demand for mortgage funds emanates from businesses and households desiring to make investments in real estate. There are many determinants of the demand for mortgage funds including:

Population
   Changes in household formation rates
   Changes in household characteristics
      Age distribution of members
      Size of households
   Changes in geographical distribution of households
Income and employment
   Changes in income level
   Changes in distribution of income
   Changes in savings
   Changes in location of employment centers
   Changes in wage structure
Housing and construction costs
   Changes in construction costs
      Materials
      Wages
      Land
   Changes in environmental regulations
   Transportation technology changes
   Changes in tax rates
   Changes in maintenance and utility costs

The supply of residential, commercial, industrial real estate
Completions
Removals
Demolitions
Conversions
Rental rates/prices
Consumer tastes
Construction starts
Governmental financing needs

THE SUPPLY OF REAL ESTATE FUNDS.   The supply of mortgage money for the purchase of a particular property by a particular borrower depends on a variety of macroeconomic and microeconomic factors.

Nationally.   At the national level, the supply of funds depends on such factors as:

The gross national product
The savings behavior of wage earners and businesses
Federal Reserve monetary policies
Federal, state and local tax policies
U.S. Treasury activities
Consumer expectations

Locally.   At the local level, the supply of funds will depend on such factors as:

The relative yields on investments made in various financial institutions
The current portfolio composition of financial institutions
Regulations of the various agencies responsible for Federal and state banks, savings and loan associations, insurance companies
The difficulty or ease with which financial institutions can enter capital markets
Governmental loan, insurance, and development programs
The difficulty or ease with which funds move between localities.

PRICE INDICATORS.   The price of mortgage money (interest rate charged on loans) is, obviously, determined by the amount supplied and demanded. Measures of the price of money include:

The Federal Fund Rate.   The rate charged by one bank to another for money loaned for short terms (24 hours).

The Treasury Bill Rate.   The rate paid by the Federal Government on Treasury bills.

The Prime Rate.   The interest rate charged by commercial banks to their most credit-worthy customers.

Qualifying for Loan Funds

While there are numerous potential sources of debt financing for real estate investments, not every investor will qualify for a loan. Lenders attempt to make their loans to investors who will be most likely to repay such loans, and they usually require collateral for such loans in the form of properties whose values will remain sufficiently high in the event of a foreclosure.

SOURCES OF CREDIT INFORMATION.   Analysis of borrowers by lenders begins with the collection of data concerning the prospective borrower. Such data can be in the form of a standard form loan application in the case of individuals, or balance sheets and profit and loss statements in the case of corporations. Lenders will also frequently require supporting data such as tax returns, deposit and employment verifications, and credit references.

Following the collection of such data, lenders will usually verify the information provided. Sources of such credit information include:

Credit reporting agencies
Public records
Borrower's bank
Trade suppliers
Employers
Landlords

SUBJECTIVE ANALYSIS OF BORROWER CHARACTERISTICS.   Analysis of the individual credit is usually done in terms of the following subjective criteria:

Credit characteristics of the mortgagor
    Character and business reputation
    Family life and community relationship
    Attitude toward obligations

Motivating interest in ownership of the property
   Motive for continuing ownership
   Motive for borrowing
Stability of effective income
   Stability of mortgagor's occupational income
   Stability of mortgagor's income from sources other than occupation
Adequacy of available assets for transaction
   Other obligations and risks to which property may be subject
   Sources of funds for acquisition of property

The first criterion focuses on the borrower's willingness to meet obligations under adverse circumstances and to curtail other expenditures in order to insure the quality of his credit record. The second criterion focuses on the investor's willingness to perform under the terms and conditions of the loan agreement in order to insure continual possession of the collateral pledged. The third criterion measures the ability of the borrower to continue to meet loan obligations over the whole term of the loan. The fourth criterion focuses on the likelihood that other commitments will take priority to the loan obligations.

OBJECTIVE ANALYSIS OF BORROWER CHARACTERISTICS. In evaluating individual borrowers, lenders consider numerous objective ratios including the following:

Ratio of total obligations to net effective income
Ratio of housing expenses and other recurring charges to net effective income
Gross income divided into home value
Earned income divided into home value
Ratio of loan to value
Ratio of monthly mortgage payments to monthly gross income
Ratio of value of dwelling to yearly income

Analysis of corporate borrowers usually involves an analysis of their financial statements in terms of the following ratios:

Current Assets to Current Liabilities. Widely known as the "current ratio," this is one test of solvency, measuring the liquid assets available to meet all debts falling due within a year's time.

$$\frac{\text{Current assets}}{\text{Current liabilities}}$$

Current assets are those normally expected to flow into cash in the course of a merchandising cycle. Ordinarily these include cash, notes and accounts receivable, and inventory and at times, in addition, short-term and marketable securities listed on leading exchanges at current realizable values. While some concerns may consider such items as cash-surrender value of life insurance as current, the tendency is to treat them as non-current.

Current liabilities are short-term obligations for the payment of cash due on demand or within a year. Such liabilities ordinarily include notes and accounts payable for merchandise, open loans payable, short-term bank loans, taxes, and accruals. Other short-term obligations, such as maturing equipment obligations and the like, also fall within the category of current liabilities.

Generally, it's considered advisable for a small business to maintain a current ratio of at least 2 to 1, or close to it, for the sake of sound cash flow and healthy financial condition. This is not necessarily a must—particularly if a major part of the current assets is in cash and readily collectible receivables—otherwise, "2 for 1," or better, is a pretty good idea.

Current Liabilities to Tangible Net Worth.   Like the "current ratio," this is another means of evaluating financial condition by comparing what's owed to what's owned. If this ratio exceeds 80%, it's considered a danger sign.

$$\frac{\text{Current liabilities}}{\text{Tangible net worth}}$$

Tangible net worth is the worth of a business minus any intangible items in the assets such as goodwill, trademarks, patents, copyrights, leaseholds, treasury stock, organization expenses, or underwriting discounts and expenses. In a corporation the tangible net worth would consist of the sum of all outstanding capital stock—preferred and common—and surplus, minus intangibles. In a partnership or proprietorship it could be made up of the capital account, or accounts, less the intangibles.

In a going business "intangibles" frequently have a great but undeterminable value. Until these intangibles are actually liquidated by sale, it is difficult for an analyst to evaluate what they might bring. In some cases they have no commercial value except to those who hold them: for instance, an item of goodwill. To a profitable business up for sale, the goodwill conceivably could represent the potential earning power over a period of years and actually bring more than the assets themselves. On the other hand, another business might find itself unable to realize anything at all on goodwill. Since the real value of intangible assets is frequently difficult to determine and evaluate, intangibles are customarily given little consideration in financial statement analysis.

Net Sales to Tangible Net Worth.   Often called "turnover of tangible net worth," this ratio shows how actively invested capital is being put to work by indicating its turnover during a period. Both overwork and underwork of tangible net worth are considered unhealthy.

$$\frac{\text{Net sales}}{\text{Tangible net worth}}$$

There is no particular norm for this ratio. Each line of business tends to establish its own, according to studies made by Dun and Bradstreet, Robert Morris Associates, trade associations, and others.

Net Sales to Working Capital.   Known as well as "turnover of working capital," this ratio also measures how actively the working cash in a business is being put to work in terms of sales. Working capital or cash is assets that can readily be converted into operating funds within a year. It does not include invested capital. A low ratio shows unprofitable use of working capital; a high one, vulnerability to creditors.

$$\frac{\text{Net sales}}{\text{Working capital}} = \frac{\text{Net sales}}{\text{Current assets–current liabilities}}$$

Deduct the sum of the current liabilities from the total current assets to get working capital, the business assets that can readily be converted into operating funds. A business with $900,000 in cash, receivables, and inventories and no unpaid obligations would have $900,000 in working capital. A business with $900,000 in current assets and $300,000 in current liabilities would have $600,000 working capital. Obviously, however, items like receivables and inventories cannot usually be liquidated overnight. Hence, most businesses require a margin of current assets over and above current liabilities to provide for stock and work-in-process inventory, and also to carry ensuing receivables after the goods are sold until the receivables are collected.

The importance of maintaining an adequate amount of working capital in relation to the amount of annual sales being financed cannot be overemphasized. And it is this degree of adequacy that the ratio of net sales to working capital measures.

Net Profits to Tangible Net Worth.   As the measure of return on investment, this is increasingly considered one of the best criteria of profitability, often the key measure of management efficiency. Profits "after taxes" are widely looked upon as the final source of payment on investment plus a source of funds available for future growth. If this "return on capital" is too low, the capital involved could be better used elsewhere.

$$\frac{\text{Net profits (after taxes)}}{\text{Tangible net worth}}$$

This ratio relates profits actually earned in a given length of time to the average net worth during that time. Profit here means the revenue left over from sales income and allowing for payment of all costs. These include costs of goods sold, write-downs and chargeoffs, Federal and other taxes accruing over the period covered, and whatever miscellaneous adjustments may be necessary to reduce assets to current, going values. The ratio is determined by dividing tangible net worth at a given period into net profits for a given period. The ratio is expressed as a percentage.

Average Collection Period of Receivables.   This ratio, known also as the "collection period" ratio, shows how long the money in a business is tied up in credit sales. In comparing this figure with net maturity in selling terms, many consider a collection period excessive if it is more than 10 to 15 days longer than those stated in selling terms. To get the collection period figure, get average daily credit sales, then divide into the sums of notes and accounts receivable.

$$\frac{\text{Net (credit sales for year)}}{365 \text{ days a year}} = \text{Daily (credit) sales}$$

$$\text{Average collection period} = \frac{\text{Notes and accounts receivable}}{\text{Daily (credit) sales}}$$

This figure represents the number of days' sales tied up in trade accounts and notes receivable or the average collection received. The receivables discounted or assigned with recourse are included because they must be collected either directly by borrower, or by lender; if uncollected, they must be replaced by cash or substitute collateral. A pledge with recourse makes the borrower just as responsible for collection as though the receivables had not been assigned or discounted. Aside from this, the likely collectibility of all receivables must be analyzed, regardless of whether or not they are discounted. Hence all receivables are included in determining the average collection period.

Net Sales to Inventory.   Known also as a "stock-to-sales" ratio, this hypothetical "average" inventory turnover figure is valued for purposes of comparing one company's performance with another's, or with the industry's.

$$\frac{\text{Net sales}}{\text{Inventory}}$$

A manufacturer's inventory is the sum of finished merchandise on hand, raw material, and material in process. It does not include supplies unless they are for sale. For retailers and wholesalers, it is simply the stock of salable goods on hand. It is expected that inventory will be valued conservatively on the basis of standard accounting methods of valuation, such as its cost or its market value, whichever is the lower.

Divide the average inventory into the net sales over a given period. This shows the number of times the inventory turned over in the period selected. It is compiled purely and only for purposes of making comparisons in this ratio from one period to another, or for other comparative purposes. This ratio is not an indicator of physical turnover. The only accurate way to obtain a physical turnover figure is to count each type of item in stock and compare it with the actual physical sales of that particular item.

Some people compute turnover by dividing the average inventory value at cost into the cost of goods sold for a particular period. However, this method still gives only an average. A hardware store stocking some 10,000 items might divide its dollar inventory total into cost of goods sold and come up with a physical average; this however, would hardly define the actual turnover of each item from paints to electrical supplies.

Fixed Assets to Tangible Net Worth.   This ratio, which shows the relationship between investment in plant and equipment and the owner's capital, indicates how liquid net worth is. The higher this ratio, the less the owner's capital is available for use as working capital to meet debts and payrolls, pay bills, or carry receivables.

$$\frac{\text{Fixed assets}}{\text{Tangible net worth}}$$

"Fixed assets" means the sum of assets such as land, buildings, leasehold improvements, fixtures, furniture, machinery, tools, and equipment, less depreciation. The ratio is obtained by dividing the depreciated fixed assets by the tangible net worth. Generally, it is inadvisable for a small business to have more than 75% of its tangible net worth represented by fixed assets.

Total Debt to Tangible Net Worth. This ratio also measures "what's owed to what's owned." As this figure approaches 100, the creditors' interest in the business assets approaches the owner's.

$$\frac{\text{Total debt}}{\text{Tangible net worth}} = \frac{\text{Current debt} + \text{fixed debt}}{\text{Tangible net worth}}$$

"Total debt" is the sum of all obligations owed by the company such as accounts and notes payable, bonds outstanding, and mortgages payable. The ratio is obtained by dividing the total of these debts by tangible net worth.

In this case, since there is no long-term debt, the result is the same as the ratio of current liabilities to tangible net worth.

Net Profit on Net Sales. This ratio measures the rate of return on net sales. The resultant percentage indicates the number of cents of each sales dollar remaining, after considering all income statement items and excluding income taxes.

A slight variation occurs when net operating profit is divided by net sales. This ratio reveals the profitableness of sales—that is, the profitableness of the regular buying, manufacturing, and selling operations of a business.

To many, a high rate of return on net sales is necessary for successful operation. This view is not always sound. To evaluate properly the significance of the ratio, consideration should be given to such factors as (1) the value of sales, (2) the total capital employed, and (3) the turnover of inventories and receivables. A low rate of return accompanied by rapid turnover and large sales volume, for example, may result in satisfactory earnings.

$$\frac{\text{Net profits}}{\text{Net sales}}$$

INSTITUTIONAL LENDING POLICIES. Most lending institutions adopt certain lending policies that may incorporate various provisions of applicable Federal and state regulations concerning loan procedures, as well as empirically derived screening criteria and documentation requirements. Appendix F contains a sample of such an institutional lending policy and procedure guide.

Laws Limiting Lender's Credit Analysis Procedures

Certain laws and regulations have been enacted that limit lender's credit analysis process. One such law is the Equal Credit Opportunity Act (commonly referred to as "Reg. B"), which is a Federal law prohibiting certain types of discrimination in credit transactions. Creditors subject to the provision of the Equal Credit Opportunity Act may not discourage an applicant from requesting credit on the basis of certain categories such as sex or marital status; may not ask certain questions such as birth control practices or childbearing expectations; may not take certain factors such as sex or marital status into consideration in a credit scoring system; and may not make inquiries concerning an applicant's spouse or former spouse except under very limited circumstances. The coverage of the Equal Credit Opportunity Act is extensive, penalties for violation are large, and few credit transactions are exempt from all of its provisions. Another Federal Act called the Fair Credit Reporting Act limits credit reporting agencies and provides borrowers with certain rights with respect to the data such credit reporting agencies may accumulate. Many states have acts similar to the Federal laws.

Lender Analysis of Loan Collateral

Lender analysis of the property to be pledged as collateral begins with an analysis of the neighborhood in which the property is located. Neighborhood analysis by lenders is similar to the analysis an investor might undertake and considers all of the factors previously described in predicting yearly gross income and projected sales prices.

ANALYSIS OF COMPARABLE SALES. In addition to an analysis of the neighborhood in which proposed collateral is located, lenders will collect data on recent sales of comparable properties in the area. Since no two properties are alike, adjustments are made to comparable sales data. Such adjustments include the following:

Date of sale
Square footage of building
Square footage of land
Age
Remaining economic life
Character of tenants
Quality of management

Facilities/amenities
Services provided by landlord
Location
Vacancy rate
Mortgage terms

RATIO ANALYSIS OF INCOME PROPERTY.   After adjusting each comparison point, lenders compare the various properties in terms of numerous ratios including the following:

Mortgage (loan) constant: Annual debt service divided by original loan amount.

Annual debt service: Loan amount multiplied by the loan constant.

Loan ratio: Loan amount divided by the sales price.

Breakeven (default ratio): Debt service plus total expenses divided by potential gross income (revenue).

Debt (loan) coverage ratio: Net income before recapture (NIBR) divided by debt service.

Minimum rent per apartment: Breakeven divided by 12 months divided by total number of apartments.

Minimum rent per room: Breakeven divided by 12 months (equals monthly breakeven) divided by total number of rooms.

Minimum rent per square foot—gross building area (GBA): Monthly (annual) breakeven divided by the square footage (GBA).

Minimum rent per square foot—net rentable area (NRA): Monthly (or annual) breakeven divided by the square footage (NRA).

Loan amount per apartment: Loan amount divided by the total number of apartments.

Loan amount per room: Loan amount divided by the total number of rooms.

Loan amount per square foot—GBA: Loan amount divided by the square footage (GBA).

Loan amount per square foot—NRA: Loan amount divided by the square footage (NRA).

Loan gross multiplier (potential): Loan amount divided by gross revenue (potential).

Loan gross multiplier (effective): Loan amount divided by effective gross revenue.

Leased space coverage: Actual lease rent divided by breakeven.

Major tenants coverage of breakeven: Major tenants coverage divided by breakeven.

Shortage: Breakeven minus the actual lease rentals.

Gross rent (income) multiplier—potential: Value and/or sales price divided by potential gross income.

Gross rent (income) multiplier—effective: Value and/or sales price divided by effective gross income.

Sales price or value: Gross income multiplied by gross income multiplier.

Expense ratio: Expenses (excluding real estate taxes) divided by potential gross income (PGI).

Total expense ratio: Total expenses (including real estate taxes) divided by PGI.

Tax ratio: Real estate taxes divided by potential gross income.

Categorical expense ratio: Operating expense (fixed, operating, etc.) divided by potential gross income (PGI).

Individual expense ratio: Each individual expense divided by PGI.

Average monthly apartment rental: Monthly gross rental divided by total number of apartments.

Average monthly room rental: Monthly gross rental divided by total number of rooms.

Operating cost per apartment per annum: Total expenses divided by number of apartments.

Operating cost per room per annum: Total expenses divided by total number of rooms.

Individual expense per room and/or per apartment per annum: Individual expenses divided by total number of rooms and/or apartments.

Appraised improvement value divided by total appraised value.

Value and/or sales price per unit: Value (sales price) divided by total number of units.

Value (sales price) per room: Value (sales price) divided by total number of rooms.

Original equity ratio: 100% minus loan ratio.

Original equity ratio: Down payment (equity) divided by sales price.

Cash flow: Net income before recapture (NIBR) minus debt service (also known as net cash flow, equity dividend, cash on cash, etc.).

Cash flow rate: Cash flow divided by down payment (equity); also known as equity dividend rate, equity return to investor.

Owner's appraised equity (equity reversion): Appraised value less loan amount (balance).

Return on owner's appraised equity: Net cash flow divided by appraised equity.

Terminal equity ratio: Net reversion divided by resale price or value at end of holding period.

Recapture rate: 1 divided by remaining economic life, or 100 divided by remaining economic life.

Additional ratios can be found in the January issue of the *Real Estate Appraiser,* p. 39.

Effect of Secondary Market on Credit Analysis Methods

Although there are differences among lenders in the evaluation of the data and ratios, some uniformity of analysis exists as a result of the entities that insure or purchase mortgages originated by such lenders. For example, lending guidelines of the Federal Housing Administration (FHA), which insures loans made by many lenders, provide that the total housing expense of a borrower should not exceed a specific percentage of the borrower's net effective income unless other favorable compensating factors are present. Similarly, the Federal Home Loan Mortgage Corporation (FHLMC), which purchases many loans made by lenders, will only purchase loans on two-, three-, or four-family dwellings where the loan-to-value ratios do not exceed a certain percentage. Thus, it is more difficult to get lenders to loan money for the purchase of a single-family house where the total housing expense of the borrower exceeds the FHA guidelines pertaining to the borrower's income or to loan money for the purchase of a duplex where the loan-to-value ratio exceeds the FHLMC guidelines unless other favorable compensating factors are available.

Loan Package Presentation

Obtaining funds from lenders requires the preparation and presentation to the lender of sufficient information about the borrower and any collateral to be pledged to enable the lender to analyze adequately his prospects for repayment by the borrower and the proceeds he might realize from any foreclosure on the collateral. At a minimum the lender should be provided with information such as the following:

Borrower general data
  Balance sheet
  Income statement

Borrower background data
    Investment experience
    Business experience
    Management experience
Borrower's real estate experience
    Other projects owned
    Other loans taken out
Financial and business references of borrower
Site plot plan
    Dimensions
    Location of buildings
    Topography
Building plans and specifications
    Photographs
    Renderings
Summary of major building features
    Parking
    Retail establishments
Preliminary title report/legal description
    Easements
    Restrictions
Area map showing location of site
    Neighboring uses
    Access
Summary of property revenues
    Minimum rents
    Percentage rents
    Cost of living increase
    Escalation clauses
    Security deposits
    Parking
Summary of property expenses
    Maintenance, repairs
    Management, personnel
    Heating, fuel, air conditioning, electrical, water
Summary of tax data
    Rate

Assessed value
Ratio of land to improvements
Summary of rental history
Vacancy rate
Lease-up times
Collection problems
Description of leases
Description of tenants
Rents
Terms and conditions
Options
Landlord's obligations
Summary of existing loans
Lender
Balances
Payments
"Lock-in" period
Tax or other impounds
Interest rate
Restrictions on sale or refinancing
Comparables
Location
Market value
Rental rates
Rental history
Features

Negotiating for loans also involves a certain degree of salesmanship. Lenders need to be shown that they will benefit from the loan. In addition, lenders may have to be convinced that they should overcome the inherent fear of lending and their preferences for certain types of loans when presented with an unusual type of loan. Similarly, lenders are subject to substantial regulatory agency review and need to be provided with facts to justify their loans in the event of an audit by such agencies. Finally, borrowers should understand that lenders are presented with many equally good loan opportunities and will make loans only when the combination of terms, conditions, profit potential, and personality factors best suit their needs.

REAL ESTATE ACQUISITION PROCEDURE AND DOCUMENTATION

Steps in the Typical Real Estate Transaction

The transfer of title to real estate from one living owner (grantor) to another (grantee) can usually be done by the simple execution and delivery of a document called a "deed." However, the typical real estate transaction consists of numerous other steps and documents including the following:

Event	Documentation
Seller lists property with real estate broker.	Listing agreement, agency agreement.
Purchaser makes offer to purchase property.	Deposit receipt, offer to purchase real estate.
Purchaser and seller enter into a contract for the purchase and sale of real property.	Deposit receipt and counter offers, real estate purchase and sale agreement, option agreement, exchange agreement.
Purchaser and seller authorize an independent party to handle the exchange of deeds and purchase consideration.	Escrow instructions.
Purchaser obtains funds for purchase.	Notes, deeds of trust, mortgages, installment land sales contracts.
Seller proves ownership of property to be conveyed.	Title abstracts, Title certificates, Title insurance policies.
Purchaser becomes owner of property subject to purchase money liens.	Deed, closing statement.
Purchaser becomes owner of the property free and clear of purchase money liens.	Deed of reconveyance.

Listing Agreements

A listing agreement is a contract between a seller and an agent in which the agent is authorized to seek a purchaser, and the seller is obligated to pay a commission if the agent is successful.

BROKER'S LEGAL RESPONSIBILITIES. Various state laws regulate the activities of real estate agents, and such agents may be liable to their principals for numerous acts including:

Fraud

Misrepresentation

Concealment

Negligent misrepresentation

Obtaining secret profits as a result of agency status

Conflicts of interest

Acting as a dual agent

Comingling funds

Failure to pursue agency duties with due diligence

Failure to use skill and care

BROKER'S RIGHT TO COMMISSIONS. The time at which a real estate agent earns a commission should be carefully negotiated. A real estate agent may be entitled to a commission upon the occurrence of numerous events including:

Event	Type of Listing
Commission due upon any sale of the property	Exclusive right to sell listing (obligation to pay commission conditioned on closing)
Commission due upon any sale of the property in which any real estate agent participated	Exclusive agency listing (obligation to pay commission conditioned on closing)
Commission due if agent provides a ready, willing and able buyer	Open listing (obligation to pay commission not conditioned on closing)
Commission due only if agent produces a ready, willing, and able buyer and closing occurs	Open listing (obligation to pay commission conditioned on closing)

DRAFTING LISTING AGREEMENTS. Since the real estate agent may be entitled to a commission when the agent obtains a party willing and able to purchase the property according to the terms and conditions set forth in the listing agreement, a listing agreement should carefully specify the seller's requirements including:

Property to be conveyed
    What real property is to be sold?
    What personal property is to be sold?
Method of payment of purchase price
    What deposits will be required of the purchaser?
        Cash
        Notes
    How much cash is to be paid upon closing?
    Will the seller take any purchase money notes?
        Amount
        Terms and conditions
    Will the purchaser be required to assume existing encumbrances?
        Amount
        Terms and conditions
Security for payment of purchase price
    Will the seller require a deed of trust?
        Covenants and conditions
        Events of default
        Remedies upon default
    Will the seller require a mortgage?
        Covenants and conditions
        Events of default
        Remedies upon default
    Will the Seller require the execution of an installment land sales contract?
        Covenants and conditions
        Events of default
        Remedies upon default
Condition of title to be conveyed
    What type of deed is to be provided to the purchaser?
        Warranty
        Grant
        Quit claim
    Will the seller give the purchaser a bill of sale to personal property?
    Will the seller provide a title insurance policy?
        Form

Coverage

Exclusions

What are the obligations of seller to remove defects?

Escrow, title companies

Proration and closing costs

What prorations will be made upon closing?

Taxes

Insurance

Rents

Security deposits

Salaries of employees

Who will pay closing costs?

Documentation

Escrow

Transfer taxes, charges

Delivery of possession prior to closing

Who will bear the risk of loss pending closing?

Are there any rights of existing persons whose possession will continue beyond closing?

Commissions

How much will be paid?

Which party is obligated to pay commissions?

Conditions in favor of the buyer

Is the purchaser's obligation contingent on his obtaining financing?

Time

Terms

Is the purchaser's obligation contingent on his inspection of the property?

Time

Right to cure defects

Is the purchaser's obligation contingent on his completion of the sale of other property?

Is the purchaser's obligation contingent on his participation in tax-deferred exchange?

Reservations of rights in seller

Will the seller retain any easements?

Will the seller retain any oil, gas, mineral rights?

Will the seller retain any leasehold interest?

Will the seller retain any water rights?

Warranties by seller

Will the seller warrant the condition of title?

Will the seller provide any warranties as to the condition of the property?

Will the seller provide any warranties as to the permitted uses of the property?

Will any warranties survive the closing?

Remedies in event of failure to close

Will the seller be entitled to retain any portion of the deposit?

Will the broker be entitled to any commission?

DEALING WITH REAL ESTATE BROKERS AND SALESMEN

Is a Broker Really Necessary?   Real estate brokers and salesmen can provide numerous services to sellers, including assistance in pricing the property, showing the property, investigating sources of financing, and closing the deal, and the right broker or salesmen will be worth every penny of commission paid. However, many of these services can be obtained from others (such as appraisers and attorneys), and the potential benefits of brokerage services should be carefully weighed against the costs of commissions that may be due upon a sale.

Should the Broker be Given an Exclusive?   If given the chance, brokers naturally prefer to have an exclusive right to sell the property they list. However, giving such a right is only justified if the broker will, in fact, actively market the property and has the resources to serve his client adequately. Wise investors carefully assess the real estate broker's capacities before granting an exclusive listing.

Has the Broker Defined the Services to be Provided?   The marketing of real estate involves many steps, including advertising, "open houses," collection of documents and information for review by prospective purchasers, and dealing with representatives of buyers. The seller's agreement with the broker should specifically define what steps the broker will take to promote the property. Wise investors define in advance the services that their agents will provide and evaluate the benefits of such services compared with their costs.

Has the Broker Fully Explained the Terms of His Employment? Listing agreements may contain automatic continuation clauses or clauses granting the broker a right to a commission at times other than the completion of a sale producing sufficient cash to pay such commissions. The listing agreement should fully set forth when commissions will be due, when his agency terminates, and under what circumstances he will be entitled to commissions for sales occurring after the termination of his agency.

Is the Broker Reputable? The business of real estate brokerage presents the real estate broker or salesman with many opportunities for unprofessional conduct. While most brokers will avoid such unprofessional conduct, experienced investors are aware of the pressures real estate brokers and salesmen may face. For example, brokers and salesmen may be tempted to represent that they have an offer on property in order to obtain a listing. A broker or salesman may be tempted to buy his client's property himself when his superior knowledge indicates that the seller has mispriced the property. Similarly, brokers and salesmen may be tempted to accept a client's listing, no matter how high the price, and then not actively market the property, planning, instead, to wait until the seller is desperate and forced to accept lower offers. In addition, brokers and salesmen are often tempted to turn their marketing and persuasion skills on their clients in order to obtain a quick commission when additional attention and effort might have produced a price or offer closer to the seller's desires.

Is the Broker Competent? Real estate brokers and salesmen occasionally take on assignments that require skills they do not necessarily possess (such as appraisals, document preparation, cash flow analysis, interpretation of title defects, and encumbrances) or that are more complex than their previous experience justifies (such as exchanges and sale-leasebacks). Experienced and reputable brokers, aware of the potential malpractice liabilities, will seek the advice of outside professionals whenever there is the slightest doubt that they have the necessary abilities. However, wise investors are always conscious of the temptation provided real estate brokers and salesmen to overextend themselves.

Real Estate Purchase and Sale Agreements

NEGOTIATING REAL ESTATE PURCAHSE AND SALE AGREEMENTS. Real estate transactions usually occur only after extensive bargaining between the parties and their representatives (brokers, attorneys, etc.) and when each side has convinced the other (or perhaps itself) that economically, legally, and psychologically it has obtained the best deal. Most of this book is concerned with the economic and legal aspects of the real estate transaction; however, experienced real estate dealers, their attorneys, and brokers are keenly aware of the psychological and tactical aspects of real estate acquisitions.

Bargaining Folklore for Buyers. The following list, without any guarantee of validity, gives some of the folklore concerning real estate bargaining that is particularly applicable to buyers:

Know the Owner's Motive for Selling. The ideal owner is "over a barrel," absent, in need of quick cash, fraught with personal problems.

Know the Prior History of the Building. A small equity may mean a recent purchase and a seller who may be more stubborn on price than one who has owned the building for a long period of time.

Know the Owner's Reputation. An owner may have personality traits that can be manipulated. An owner with a reputation for hard bargaining may require different negotiating strategy than a more straightforward owner.

Have Alternative Investments. An enthusiastic buyer or one "in love" with a project will be less able to negotiate the best price. Competition, whether real or not, puts pressure on a negotiator.

Be Prepared to Concede Something. The largest concessions are made early in the negotiations. Save something for each stage of the negotiations.

Don't Rush. Most buyers are too hasty in agreeing to a price after the seller has made the first concession.

Negotiate as a Team and Use Intermediaries. Use of a "Mutt and Jeff" routine, and the availability of a committee that must approve any decision the negotiator makes can help ferret out a seller's bottom-line position and avoid concessions in the heat of battle.

Know the Property's Defects. Bring out the most obvious defects as prelude to the initial offer. Save a few defects for later negotiations.

Anticipate Tricky Sellers. Owners may engage in a certain amount of "gamesmanship" for their own account such as phantom other offers, using your offer to squeeze other prospective buyers, relying on "asking-prices" of comparable properties rather than actual sales prices, and undertaking high-impact cosmetic improvements just prior to offering the property for sale.

Anticipate Broker's Sales Techniques.   Real estate brokers/salesmen may seek to influence the negotiations by interjecting various statements designed to encourage concessions at appropriate times. Such statements might include information about the property's unique attributes, imminent increases in financing costs, and imminent increases in the inflation rate.

Bargaining Folklore for Sellers.   The following list, without any guarantee of validity, gives some of the folklore concerning real estate bargaining particularly applicable to sellers:

Know the Property.   Large concessions usually come as a result of surprises (termites, imminent zoning changes, title defects, boundary problems, soil problems).

Be Objective about the Property.   Personal involvement usually results in unreasonable initial prices and emotional bargaining.

Price the Property Carefully.   Overpriced property will not be actively sold by brokers, and such brokers may be tempted to wait until time limits have reduced the seller's bargaining objectivity.

Get the Property in Good Marketing Condition Before Being Offered.   Minor cosmetic defects may provide buyers with ammunition for major bargaining concessions.

Anticipate that Every Defect in the Property Will be Brought Out as a Justification for Major Bargaining Concessions.   Buyers may point out such items as deferred maintenance and lack of amenities compared with other similar projects.

Anticipate Tricky Buyers.   Buyers may arrange for other parties to approach the seller to test out the seller's position. Buyers may use delaying tactics to reduce the seller's bargaining position.

Avoid Contingencies.   Although real estate deals may legitimately require certain reasonable contingencies, agreeing to numerous contingencies or contingencies that depend on the buyer's whims and not objective factors, can put the seller at the mercy of the buyer as the seller's time runs out.

Anticipate Pressure from Brokers and Salesmen.   In order to obtain commissions real estate brokers and salesmen may be tempted to pressure a client to close by statements designed to increase the seller's anxiety and willingness to take a sure thing. Such statements include such representations as: the effect of increasing interest rates on buyer's ability to close;

the effect of inflation on the property's operating expenses and the seller's ability to continue to hold the property much longer; and the possibility that the next offer could be lower.

Avoid Desperation.   Astute buyers will seek out any seller who is forced to sell and drive out such seller's bottom price.

Screen Buyers.   Entering into an agreement with a buyer who cannot obtain necessary financing, who does not have authority to act, or who cannot otherwise perform under the purchase and sale agreement can result in time delays and put the seller at the mercy of subsequent buyers.

Look at All Aspects of the Deal.   A large cash down payment or an offer at the seller's price may be accompanied with terms and conditions that are unworkable or unsuitable.

Know When and to Whom a Commission will be Due.   Sellers are often surprised at lawsuits claiming that they owe a commission on a deal that fell through or to brokers whom they did not originally contact.

Control the Closing Process.   Insufficient attention to closing dates, times by which contingencies must be satisfied, and times by which monies must be paid may leave the seller at the mercy of buyers as the seller's time runs out.

ADVANTAGES OF SHORT-FORM DEPOSIT RECEIPTS.   Prior to the time when purchasers and sellers exchange deeds and consideration, the parties usually set forth the terms and conditions of their agreement in a purchase and sale agreement. Such agreements can be in the form of standardized, preprinted "deposit receipts" (often prepared by local real estate agents' associations), or in the form of complex "purchase and sale agreements" prepared with the aid of attorneys and other experts.

Deposit receipts are typically employed in single-family home or small income property acquisitions. Deposit receipts contain relatively few terms and conditions, and leave much of the mechanics of the transactions to local law and custom. The major advantage in using standard form, preprinted deposit receipts is that the parties may be less apt to seek the involvement of other advisers when they believe that the terms and conditions of their transaction are standardized and customary. The input of such advisers may cause the parties to reconsider the proposed deal. However, in the event of an uncertainty or dispute not covered by the deposit receipt the parties may find that their transaction is subject to laws and custom with which they are not familiar and which is at variance with their wishes as to how the transaction was to have been consummated.

ADVANTAGES OF COMPLEX PURCHASE AGREEMENTS. Complex purchase and sale agreements are customarily used in acquisitions of larger income properties. The major advantage in preparing such purchase and sale agreements is that negotiations leading up to the preparation of such agreements usually force the parties to consider carefully all of the aspects of an acquisition transaction, and relatively little is left up to laws and/or custom with which the parties may not be familiar. However, such agreements usually involve additional costs and time and may result in such careful consideration of the proposed transaction that previously interested parties decide not to complete the acquisition.

AREAS TO CONSIDER IN DRAFTING PURCHASE AGREEMENTS. In the event the parties choose to negotiate carefully and prepare a purchase and sale agreement, the following areas should be considered:

Parties
>   Will seller permit purchaser to assign the contract?
>
>   If seller or buyer is a corporation, does other party want proof of valid organization?
>
>   If the buyer is a foreign corporation does seller want proof of authority to own real estate in seller's state?
>
>   If seller or buyer is a corporation, does other party want proof of signer's authority to act on behalf of such corporation?
>
>   If seller or buyer is a partnership, does other party want evidence of signer's authority to bind other partners?
>
>   If either party is an agent or attorney-in-fact acting on behalf of a principal, does other party want proof of such authority or status?
>
>   Does the seller want evidence of financial capacity?

Property to be conveyed
>   Real property
>>   Does purchaser want a survey?
>>
>>   Will seller be retaining rights?
>>>   Easements
>>>   Oil, gas, mineral
>>>   Leasehold
>>>   Water
>>
>>   Will the property be conveyed subject to any liens, encumbrances or other restrictions?
>>>   Obligations of seller

Tax liens

Assessments

Easements

Covenants, conditions, restrictions

Concessions and licenses

Encroachments

Zoning restrictions

Mineral rights

Drainage rights

Advertising leases

Other matters of record

Will the property be conveyed subject to leasehold interests?

Personal property

What personal property will be conveyed?

Fixtures

Tools

Air conditioners

Telephone systems

Machinery

Other

Will seller be required to repair damage caused by removal of personal property?

Does purchaser want bill of sale?

Are bulk transfer laws involved?

Is personal property subject to liens?

Purchase price

Amount?

Holding costs prior to closing

Method of payment of purchase price?

Does purchaser require earnest money deposit?

Method of payment?

Cash

Notes

Terms and conditions

Cash required to close?

Will purchaser permit seller to give purchase money notes?

Amount?
Terms and conditions?
   Interest
      Amount
      Prepaid
      Usury Laws
      Due Date
   Principal payments
      Amount
      Due date
      Prepayment rights
      Events of default
      Remedies upon default
Will purchaser assume existing encumbrances?
   Amount?
   Terms and conditions of assumption?
      Payment of assumption fees
      Liability for failure to make payments
      Release of seller from liability
Security for payment of purchase price
   Will the seller require collateral to be pledged as security for buyer's purchase money obligations?
   What collateral?
      Real property conveyed
      Other property
   Terms and conditions of security agreements?
      Description of property pledged
      Amount of debt secured
      Covenants and obligations with respect to collateral pledged
         Payment of obligations secured thereby
         Maintenance and care of collateral
         Payment of taxes and insurance
         Sale of collateral
         Further pledging of collateral
         Restrictions on leases
      Events of default

Breach of covenants

Breach of other obligations, contracts between buyer and seller

Purchaser's insolvency

Remedies of seller

Acceleration

Power of sale

Entry and possession

Rights of purchaser

Use of property

Further improvements

Alterations

Prepayment

Sale of collateral

Further encumbrances

Restrictions on seller in the event of default

Rights to cure defaults

Nonrecourse provisions

Subordination of security agreements to other pledges of the collateral

Types of loans

Limitations on use of proceeds

Release of portions of property from lien of security agreement

Sums payable prior to release

Amount of property subject to release

Formula for release

Warranties and representations

Does purchaser want specific warranties from seller?

Marketability of title

No undisclosed encumbrances or liens

No defaults on obligations secured by property

No restrictions on use of property

No assessments against property

No litigation involving property

No covenants, conditions, restrictions

No violations of housing codes

No violations of safety codes

No violations of zoning codes

No violations of fire codes

No violations of health codes

No violations of building codes

No defective conditions or improvements

No undisclosed leases or conditions giving tenants right to terminate lease

All information concerning property provided purchaser is accurate

Property will be maintained prior to closing

Approval of conveyance by underlying lenders has been obtained

Does seller want specific warranties from purchaser?

Authority to enter into agreement

Continued payment of assumed obligations

Indemnification of seller from liabilities resulting from purchase

Use of property prior to closing

Conditions upon parties' obligations

Does purchaser wish to condition performance upon any events?

Status of title

Availability of title insurance

    Form

    Coverage

    Exclusions

    Additional endorsements

Availability of purchase money financing

    Amount

    Terms and conditions

Availability of construction financing

    Permanent

    Take-out financing

Inspection of property

    Building

    Soil

    Topography

    Grading

Filling
Drainage
Survey of property
Examination and audit of seller's books
Examination and review of leases
Examination and approval of service contracts
Availability of public utilities, community services
Water
Electricity
Sewer
Gas
Schools
Transportation
Ability to change permissible uses
Zoning restrictions
Environmental restrictions
Regulatory approvals
Subdivision regulations
Local building code compliance
Building permits
Annexation
Termite, dry rot, and fungus inspection reports
Concurrent closing with other property
Issuance of business licenses
Does seller wish to condition performance on any events?
Purchaser's participation in tax-deferred exchange
Underlying lender's willingness to permit assumption/transfer
Qualification of sale for installment sales treatment
Closing within specific time limits
Underlying lender's willingness to permit prepayment
Will either party be able to waive the failure of a condition?
Closing procedure
Will an escrow be used?
Who will be escrow agent for the parties?
When will closing occur?
When are documents and monies to be put into escrow?

    Deeds
    Cash
    Notes
    Deeds of trust, mortgages
    Assumption agreements
    Lease assignments
    Subordination agreements
    Bills of sale
    Occupancy certificates
    Corporate resolutions
    Powers of attorney
    Financing statements
Who will pay closing costs?
    Escrow fees
    Document preparation fees
    Transfer taxes
Who will pay loan fees, appraisal costs?
Who will pay title insurance charges?
How will income and expenses be prorated?
    Taxes
    Rent
    Service contract charges
    Security deposits
Possession
    Does purchaser desire to occupy or use the property prior to closing?
    Right to conduct soil or other tests prior to closing
    Rent or adjustment to purchase price
    Will tenants be affected by transfer of title?
    Notice to tenants
    Assignment of leases
    Security deposits
Commissions
    Will purchaser and seller pay any commissions?
    To whom?
    How much?
    Method of payment?

Cash

Notes

Remedies in the Event of Failure to Close

Deposits?

Commissions?

Liquidated damages?

Exchange Agreements

Sellers of real estate often enter into agreements with other property owners whereby properties are exchanged. Such exchanges are advantageous in that gain recognized (taxed) is usually limited to the amount of cash and/or net mortgage relief. Exchange agreements usually resemble purchase and sale agreements, with each party being both a "seller" and a "purchaser." The portions of an exchange agreement covering the payment of the respective purchase prices should, of course, give credit for the respective properties transferred and obligations assumed. Careful attention should also be paid to the mechanics of the exchange process, particularly in multiparty or exotic exchanges, to insure that the transfer of properties will be treated as a tax-deferred exchange rather than a series of taxable sales. Although recent court cases are paying less attention to some exchange formalities, many of the court decisions in older cases dealing with multiparty, delayed, or other exotic exchanges have emphasized certain procedural requirements such as simultaneous closings, sequential deeding (rather than deeding directly to the ultimate recipient), and mutuality of conditions. Wise investors have their exchange agreements drafted by lawyers well versed in the current technicalities of exchange law.

Options

Options are agreements in which the seller gives the purchaser the right to acquire the property in consideration of the payment of an option fee. Purchasers often favor the use of an option rather than a purchase and sale agreement because an option enables them to tie up a particular piece of property long enough to determine if development is feasible without the corresponding obligation to purchase the property. Sellers often favor options because they are immediately entitled to the option fee whether or not the contemplated transfer of title actually takes place.

In order to have an enforceable option agreement, the parties must set forth the particulars of the proposed purchase and should cover all of the previously discussed elements of a purchase and sale agreement. In addition, an option agreement should address the following types of problems:

Parties
> Will the optionee have any assignment rights?
> Can the property be acquired by nominees?

Property subject to option
> What real property will be subject to the option?
> What personal property will be subject to the option?

Consideration for option
> Will the option fee apply to the purchase price?

Term of option
> Will the optionee have a right to extend the option period?
> Will the option continue if the seller goes bankrupt?

Manner of exercise of option
> What are the notice requirements?
> When must notice be given?

Optionee's rights during option period
> Does the optionee have the right to enter property?
> > Soil tests
> > Engineering studies
> Does the optionee have the right to record option agreement?

Risk of loss, condemnation during option period
> Is the optionee entitled to any insurance proceeds?
> Is the optionee entitled to any condemnation proceeds?

Seller's obligations during option period
> Will the seller be required to pay taxes?
> Will the seller be required to make payments on underlying obligations?
> Will the seller be required to keep the property free of additional liens?
> Will the seller be required to maintain the property?
> Will the seller be permitted to make lease alterations?

Terms of purchase upon exercise
> What will be the price of the property?
> > Amount
> > Method of payment

What will be the security for payment of purchase price?

Will the seller be required to make any warranties and representations?

What are the closing procedures?

Who will be entitled to commissions?

Optionees generally prefer to have their option rights recorded in the local records in order to insure that their rights are prior to any subsequent encumbrances and conveyances by the seller. Sellers are generally reluctant to permit the recording of options because they do not want the record clouded in the event the option is not exercised.

Escrow Instructions

While purchasers and sellers often meet at a single prearranged time ("closing date") and exchange deeds and money (a "closing") and thereby effect the transfer of real estate, many real estate transfers are accomplished through the use of an escrow agent who is instructed by each party as to how and when to turn over deeds, lease assignments, bills of sale, money, notes, deeds of trust, mortgages, and so on.

REGULATION OF ESCROW AGENTS.   Escrow agents may be independent entities or associated with title insurance companies or lenders, and are usually subject to numerous regulations.

ADVANTAGES OF FORM ESCROW INSTRUCTIONS.   Escrow instructions can be in the form of short preprinted standard instructions prepared by the prospective escrow agents or long detailed documents prepared with the assistance of the respective parties, attorneys, real estate agents, or other advisers. Preprinted standardized escrow instructions are advantageous when the parties wish to avoid additional delay, expense, and opportunities for "second thoughts" about the pending deal. However, in the event of a dispute the parties' rights and remedies may be subject to local custom and statutes unfamiliar to the various parties or to provisions designed to protect the escrow agent rather than to resolve disputes.

ADVANTAGES OF COMPLEX ESCROW INSTRUCTIONS.   Lengthy escrow instructions are advantageous where the parties are concerned about the occurrence of specific conditions and wish to insure that disputes are handled in a manner at variances with local custom or statutes. However, the deliberation necessary to prepare extensive escrow instructions may cause the parties to reconsider their deal.

EFFECT OF ESCROW INSTRUCTIONS ON PURCHASE AGREEMENT. Escrow instructions often provide a means whereby the terms and conditions of the parties' original purchase and sale agreement are altered, and purchasers and sellers should carefully examine each other's instructions prior to any agreement thereto.

Since the escrow holder will be acting as the agent of both parties in carrying out the terms and conditions of the closing, the escrow instructions should set forth or incorporate the terms and conditions of the purchase and sale agreement.

DRAFTING SELLER'S INSTRUCTIONS. In addition to the terms and conditions of the sale, the seller's escrow instructions should cover such items as:

The specific sums to be received

The form of notes, mortgages, deeds of trust, and other documents to be executed by the purchaser

Payments to be made out of cash proceeds

Return of deposits in the event of a failure to close

DRAFTING BUYER'S INSTRUCTIONS. In addition to the terms and conditions of the sale, the purchaser's escrow instructions should cover such items as:

The form of deed to be executed

The form of lease assignments, bills of sale, and other documents to be executed by the seller

Directions for forwarding documents after recording

Notes

When the purchase price of a particular real estate investment is not paid in cash at the time of the transfer of title, the seller will usually require that the purchaser execute a note memorializing the terms and conditions under which the remaining sums are to be paid.

DRAFTING NOTES. In drafting the note the parties should consider:

The date at which the principal is to be paid

The amount of interest to be charged the borrowe

The manner of calculating interest

The amount and number of principal payments

The amount and number of interest payments

The date on which principal payments are due

The date on which interest payments are due

Whether the obligation will be secured by the pledge of any property

Whether personal liability on the part of the purchaser should be waived

Whether the purchaser will be liable for a deficiency if the fair market value of any collateral exceeds the amount bid at the foreclosure sale by the seller

Whether the purchaser will be entitled to notice of any default

Whether the purchaser will be entitled to cure defaults within certain periods of time

Whether the seller will be required to resort to collateral pledged prior to a suit against the purchaser directly

Whether the note may be prepaid

Whether the purchaser may transfer or additionally encumber collateral pledged as security

Whether late payments will be permitted and, if so, whether late charges will be imposed

Mortgages, Deeds of Trust, Installment Land Sales Contracts

When real estate is transferred prior to the receipt of full cash payment, sellers often require the pledge of collateral as security for the purchaser's promise to pay the purchase price in full. The most common ways such promises are secured are by mortgages, deeds of trust, and installment land sales contracts.

MORTGAGES.   Mortgages are agreements in which the purchaser (or borrower) gives the seller (or lender) an "interest" in certain real property as collateral for a debt. The parties to a mortgage are usually referred to as mortgagor (purchaser or borrower) and mortgagee (seller or lender). In the event the mortgagor fails to pay off the note secured by the mortgage, the mortgagee, in compliance with local foreclosure laws may ultimately obtain title to the pledged property. In some states mortgages involve the outright conveyance of property to the lender (seller). In other states to secure the debt, the mortgage merely gives the lender (seller) a lien to secure the debt.

DEEDS OF TRUST.   Deeds of trust are usually agreements in which the purchaser (or borrower) conveys title to another party (the trustee) to be held in trust for the seller (or lender) to ultimately convey the property back to the purchaser (or borrower) if the note is paid as agreed or to be conveyed to the seller or lender if the note is not repaid as agreed (a "power of sale"). The parties to a deed of trust are usually referred to as the trustor (the purchaser or borrower), the trustee, and the beneficiary (the seller or lender).

INSTALLMENT LAND SALES CONTRACTS. An installment land sales contract (vendor's lien) is an agreement in which a seller agrees to convey title to a purchaser upon full performance of all of the terms and conditions in the installment land sales contract. The purchaser and seller are usually referred to as vendor and vendee, respectively, in such agreements. Title is not conveyed to the purchaser with a lien given to the seller, as in a mortgage, or to a third party, as in a deed of trust. Instead, title is retained by the seller as security for the performance of all terms and conditions in the installment land sales contract.

The rights and remedies of each of the parties under a mortgage, deed of trust, or installment land sales contract vary from state to state. In addition, there has been a hybridization of the various documents. For example, installment land sales contracts and mortgages frequently provide for the transfer of title to a third party with instructions as to how such title will be reconveyed in the event of default (a "power of sale"). Similarly, courts are increasingly providing defaulting vendees under installment land sales contracts with the same types of protection afforded by statutes protecting mortgagors (where there is a mortgage) and trustors (where there is a deed of trust).

DRAFTING REAL ESTATE SECURITY AGREEMENTS. In drafting mortgages, deeds of trust and installment land sales contracts, the parties should consider the following:

What property is to be pledged to the lender?
  Real property
  Fixtures
  Personal property
  Rents and profits from use of property
  Future acquisitions, additions, and improvements
Which obligations are to be secured by the pledge?
  Prior obligations, other loans
  Future advances
  Nonmonetary obligations

What covenants of borrower, purchaser will the creditor require?

Limitations on the use of the collateral

Restrictions on alterations and demolitions

Prohibitions against waste

Requirements as to maintenance and repairs of the collateral

Impound accounts

Requirements as to the payment of taxes

Payment deadlines, proof

Impound accounts

Requirements as to the payment of insurance

Type

Payment deadlines, proof

Impound accounts

Requirements as to the removal of liens

Requirements as to the maintenance of the borrower's financial condition

Which events will constitute a default?

Failures to perform agreed obligations

Note

Mortgage

Deed of trust

Installment land sales contract

Sales of the collateral

Future pledges of collateral

Breaches of other agreements

Notes

Mortgages

Deed of trust

What remedies will the seller, lender have upon a default?

Court foreclosure

Power of sale foreclosure

Receivers

Possession

What priority will the security interest have with respect to other liens pertaining to the collateral?

Subordination to other future liens

Subordination of prior liens

What rights will the borrower have to obtain the release of property from the pledge?

Sums required

Procedure

Order of release

Notice

Payment of costs

What limitations will there be on the seller's, lender's rights in the event of a default?

Sale of collateral prior to personal suit

Limitation of deficiency to difference between fair market value of property pledged and unpaid balance of note

Purchase money mortgage protections

Reinstatement rights

Redemption rights

Notice of default

Statutory foreclosure procedural requirements

Who bears the risk of loss of the property during the period it is pledged?

Insurance proceeds

Condemnation proceeds

Title Abstracts, Certificates of Title, and Title Insurance Policies

Prospective purchasers will usually require proof that the seller is the owner of the property to be acquired. Such proof is usually given in the form of a title abstract or certificate of title prepared by an individual or company in which the prospective purchaser has confidence and/or in the form of title insurance by which an individual company agrees under certain circumstances to protect the purchaser against subsequent claims against his title to the property.

While title abstracts, certificate of title, guarantees of title, and title insurance policies protect prospective purchasers against many title related risks, each form of protection is subject to many limitations with which an investor should be familiar.

TITLE ABSTRACTS.   Title abstracts represent summaries of the searches of the local records for conveyances, liens, encumbrances, and other matters pertaining to a particular piece of real property. The abstract usually contains only a compilation of the information discovered to be in the record and does not normally involve interpretation or discussion of the legal significance of the various items discovered. The liability of the abstractor is usually limited to mistakes based on negligence and to the actual loss occasioned by the error.

CERTIFICATES OF TITLE.   Certificates of title, while supposedly based on the issuer's study of all matters of record affecting a particular title, may not actually contain a summary of the issuer's search. The liability of an issuer of a certificate of title is usually limited to circumstances where the issuer has failed to exercise skill and care in studying the records and in reaching its conclusion as to the status of a particular title.

GUARANTIES OF TITLE.   Guaranties of title may provide an owner or prospective owner with protection against loss occasioned by causes other than breaches of the abstractor's duty to use due care and skill in searching the record. However, guaranties of title, as with title abstracts and certificates of title, usually only cover matters that are disclosed by an examination of the public records and not "hidden defects" such as fraud, incompetency of the grantor, or lack of delivery of a deed.

TITLE INSURANCE POLICIES.   A title insurance policy is a contract between a title insurer (usually a company) and an owner (or lender) whereby the insurer insures the owner against certain losses or damages, not exceeding the amount specified in the policy, and costs, attorneys fees, and expenses. Losses normally, but not always, covered include:

Title to the estate or interest insured being vested other than as stated by the title insurance policy

Any defect in or lien or encumbrance on such title

Unmarketability of such title

Lack of a right of access to and from the property

EVENTS NOT COVERED BY TITLE INSURANCE.   While the foregoing coverage is extensive there are many risks that are not normally included within the coverage of such policies. For example, many forms of title insurance policies do not protect against the following risks:

Taxes and assessments not shown as liens (proposed taxes or assessments)

Easements and encumbrances not disclosed of record (prescriptive easements, unrecorded vendor's liens)

Instruments not in the chain of title (wild deeds)

Rights of persons in possession (unrecorded installment land sales agreements, tenants)

Other matters disclosed by an inspection (power company easements, community driveways, possibilities of mechanics liens)

Physical characteristics of the land (encroachments, boundary defects)

Errors on recorded maps (incorrect original surveys)

Governmental acts and regulations relating to use (zoning, building codes)

Defects known to the insured

ENDORSEMENTS AND EXTENDED COVERAGE.   Where the coverage and limitations of the typical title insurance policy are not acceptable, extended coverage and/or special endorsements are available. The most familiar form of extended coverage policy is the American Land Title Association (A.L.T.A.) form of policy. The A.L.T.A. policy eliminates, where possible, the standard exceptions pertaining to off-record easements and liens, rights of persons in possession, and rights and claims that an inspection of the land or a correct survey would show. Numerous special endorsements are available that cover additional risks including:

Priority of lender's liens

Violations of Covenants, Conditions and Restrictions (CC&R's)

Violations of zoning ordinances

Encroachments

Mechanics liens

Deeds

A deed is a written instrument, executed and delivered, by which title to real property is transferred from one person, called the grantor, to another person, called the grantee. While there are usually few specific formal requirements, deeds must contain a sufficient description of the property to be conveyed, operative words of conveyance, and must be duly executed by a legally competent grantor. Deeds must also be delivered to and accepted by the grantee. In certain areas deeds must recite the consideration received for the conveyance, the grantor's source of title, the name and address of the draftsman, and whether or not the lien to secure the purchase price is involved. Investors buying properties in states with which they are not familiar should check local laws for specific requirements in drafting deeds.

Deeds vary in the expressed or implied covenants and warranties that are made by grantors. Among the possible warranties that grantors can make are:

That the grantor owns the estate he is purporting to convey

That the grantor has the power to convey the estate he is purporting to convey

That the title is free of and clear of all encumbrances

That the grantor will defend the title against the just and lawful claims of all persons

That the grantor will insure that the purchaser will not be disturbed in the future by the grantor or one with paramount claim

That the grantor will do, execute, or cause to be done or to be executed all such future acts, deeds, and things in order to more perfectly and absolutely convey and assure the lands and premises conveyed unto the grantee as the grantee may reasonably request.

Generally, a *warranty deed* contains most or all of the above covenants and warranties while a *quit claim deed* contains few, if any, of such covenants and warranties. Many states prescribe by statute the warranties and covenants made by use of certain types of deeds, such as *grant deeds*.

Rights and Remedies of Purchasers and Sellers Under Real Estate Purchase and Sales Agreements

When a purchaser and seller enter into a real estate purchase and sales agreement, the parties normally expect to ultimately transfer deeds and consideration and to part company as mutually satisfied businessmen. However, not all contracts for the purchase and sale of real property are consummated, and under such circumstances the parties may be left to the various remedies afforded by local statutes.

BUYERS.   Upon a failure to complete a real estate purchase and sale agreement a buyer may wish to seek (but is not always entitled to), the following types of damages and remedies:

Damage/Remedy	Nature
Specific performance	Require seller to convey property as agreed
Lost profits	Require seller to compensate buyer for amounts that would have been received (through resale, etc.) if the property had been conveyed as agreed
Benefit of bargain	Require seller to pay buyer the difference between the fair market value of the property (at the date of breach) and the contract price
Out-of-pocket costs	Require seller to reimburse buyer for expenditures made as a result of execution of contract (architectural plans, appraisals, etc.)
Rescission	Require seller to return all deposits and other monies paid seller on account of the contract

Whether a particular buyer will be entitled to any or all of these damages depends upon the local law where the property is located and whether the seller's breach was in bad faith. For example, lost profits traditionally have not been a remedy available to real estate purchasers (although there is a trend toward some liberalization of the traditional rules). Similarly, where the seller has not been guilty of bad faith, buyers may be limited to the return of monies advanced to the seller plus, under some circumstances, costs incurred as a consequence of entering into the contract. Obviously, any damages claimed must be proved by the buyer.

SELLERS.   Upon a failure of a buyer to perform a real estate purchase and sale agreement, sellers may wish to seek a variety of types of damages and remedies including:

Damage/Remedy	Nature
Specific performance	Require buyer to purchase property as agreed
Lost profits	Require buyer to compensate seller for amounts that would have been received (through investment of proceeds, etc.) if the property had been purchased as agreed
Benefit of bargain	Require buyer to pay the difference between the fair market value of the property (at the date of breach) and the contract price

Out-of-pocket costs   Require buyer to reimburse seller for expendi-
                             tures as a result of execution of contract (taxes,
                             insurance, refinancing charges, lost rent, broker's
                             commissions)
Liquidated damages   Require buyer to pay previously agreed upon
                             cash sums in event of breach; retention of de-
                             posit

Whether a particular seller will be entitled to any or all of these damages
may depend upon the local law where the property is located, whether the
buyer's breach was in bad faith, and whether the breach occurs in an appreciating real estate market. For example, most courts are reluctant to
award damages for lost profits because such damages are too speculative.
Similarly, in an appreciating real estate market, there may, in fact be no
"benefit of the bargain damages."

Rights and Remedies of Lenders and Borrowers

When a lender advances funds to a borrower or when a seller receives a
note as part of the purchase price of a real estate investment, the parties
normally expect payments of principal and interest to be paid as agreed.
However, defaults occasionally occur, and the parties may find themselves
subject to numerous statutes and regulations affecting their rights and
remedies.

LATE PAYMENT CHARGES, PREPAYMENT PENALTIES.   A lender (or seller
receiving a purchase money note) normally can expect prompt payments
of principal and interest when, and only when, due. Lenders frequently
require late payment penalties and special consideration if the borrower
wishes to repay a loan differently than agreed in the note. Statutes and
case law may limit a lender's ability to charge late payment fees and prepayment penalties in certain loan situations, such as residential loans.

USE OF COLLATERAL, IMPOUND ACCOUNTS.   When a borrower gives collateral for a loan, the lender may require that the collateral be maintained
in good repair, that impound accounts for insurance on the collateral be
established, that impound accounts for taxes assessed against the property
be established, that the property not be pledged as collateral for other
loans, and that the collateral not be transferred to others. New statutes and
case law may limit a lender's ability to require impound accounts for insurance payments and taxes, to prevent additional pledging of the collateral, or to prevent transfers of the collateral.

FORECLOSURE. When a borrower who has pledged real estate as collateral by a deed of trust or mortgage defaults in the performance of the obligations contained on the note or in the deed of trust, lenders expect to be able to sue the borrower for the monies due under the note, to require a court to foreclose upon any collateral pledged, or to be able to exercise a "power of sale" right that may be contained in the mortgage or deed of trust. However, there are many limitations on lender's rights including:

Procedural or Protective Provision	Nature
Notice requirements	Lenders may be required to notify (personally or by publication) the borrower of default, pending suit, elections to sell collateral, or other events within certain time periods.
Reinstatement rights	Lenders may be required to accept late performance within certain time periods.
Redemption rights	Lenders may be required to accept full payment of debt within certain time periods.
Sale of collateral prior to personal suit	Lender may be required to look to any collateral pledged prior to a personal suit against the borrower.
Purchase money security limitation	Lenders may not be permitted to sue the borrower, personally, if the note is executed as part of purchase price of real estate.
No personal action following exercise of power of sale right	Lenders may not be able to sue the borrower, personally, following the exercise of power of sale rights.
Fair value limitation	Lenders may be entitled to hold the borrower personally liable only for the difference between the principal and interest due and the property's fair market value.
One form of action in limitation	Lenders may be limited as to the procedures available to realize upon multiple collateral for the same debt.

CONSUMER LAWS. In addition to many protective laws and procedural requirements that may be available to borrowers, new consumer laws (as well as old laws relating to usury) may provide borrowers with counterclaims or separate actions against lenders. Among such laws are the following:

Law	Nature
Truth-in-Lending	Requires disclosure by "creditor" of certain elements of a loan transaction. May provide borrower with valuable rescission rights. Not applicable to loans for the acquisition of income property or for isolated loan transactions. Definition of "creditor" includes "arrangers" of credit, which, under come circumstances, may include investors or real estate agents. The Truth-in-Lending Act also requires a rescission period when certain liens are placed on residences and regulates credit advertising.
Real Estate Settlement Procedure Act	Requires disclosure (estimate) by "lender" of certain aspects of a real estate loan and closing (settlement) transactions. Requires disclosure by person conducting real estate closing (settlement) of costs of real estate loan and closing (settlement) transactions. The act is limited, generally(to "residential" transactions.
Equal Credit Opportunity Laws	Restrict the power of lenders to inquire about certain items and to deny credit on certain grounds.
Usury Laws	Limit the amount of interest chargeable on loans. Usury laws may provide for damage penalties if interest charges are excessive. Interest limits, definition of charges constituting interest, types of ex-

	empt lenders, and types of transactions that constitute loans vary from state to state.
Fair Credit Reporting Laws	Restrict the exchange of credit information upon which lending decisions are made.

CHAPTER 4

IMPROVING, LEASING, AND DISPOSING OF REAL ESTATE

As previously discussed, real estate investment is subject to many governmental regulations and restrictions. For example, the regulations of various governmental agencies affect the availability of money for real estate purchases, and numerous laws determine the rights and liabilities of real estate lenders and borrowers. In addition to the statutes and regulations already discussed, there are many other laws, regulations, and restrictions that directly affect the development, use, and disposition of real estate.

LAND USE RESTRICTIONS

Private Land Use Restrictions

TYPES. Private individuals can impose restrictions on the use of land by a variety of means including the following:

Conditions	Restrictions on the use of land imposed in the deed granting the estate in land whereby the property reverts to the grantor if the restriction is violated
Restrictions	Restrictions on the use of land imposed in the deed granting the estate in land whereby the grantor (or another) has the right to enforce the restrictions against the lot(s) so burdened
Covenants running with the land	Restrictions created by agreement between two or more landowners giving one or more of such landowners the right to enforce the restriction against the others

Subdivision restrictions	Restrictions created by declarations of covenants, conditions and restrictions, or recorded plot maps granting any lot owner the right to enforce the restriction against any other lot owner

LIMITATIONS ON ENFORCEABILITY OF PRIVATE RESTRICTIONS. Not all restrictions are enforceable, and in the event of litigation over a violation of a restriction courts may apply one or more of the following concepts to modify the operation of a restriction:

Minor violations, balancing of hardships	If an unintentional, minor violation has occurred, courts may "balance the equities" and not enforce the restriction.
Change in neighborhood	A court may refuse to enforce a restriction by injunction where the neighborhood has so changed in character as to make it unfair to continue the original use.
Abandonment or acquiescence	When property owners subject to restrictions have already violated the restrictions and the violations have been so general as to indicate an abandonment of the right to enforce the restrictions, or acquiescence to the violations, the restrictions will not be enforced.
Violations by party seeking to enforce restriction	One who violates a restriction himself may not be able to obtain an injunction restraining the violation of the restriction by others.

Public Control of Land Use

ZONING RESTRICTIONS. Zoning is the most common way governments regulate the specific use of land and buildings. Zoning is an exercise of the government's police powers and, as such, is subject to the following types of limits:

Zoning must be for the purpose of promoting health, safety, morals, and the public welfare.

Zoning must not be arbitrary, unreasonable, or discriminatory.

Zoning must not be a substitute for the government's condemnation power.

The zoning ordinance must be clear, unambiguous, and specific.

The administration of the zoning must be in compliance with state and Federal procedural requirements.

Interpretation of Zoning Laws. Most litigation over zoning law applications concerns claims that the local agency has exercised its zoning powers in excess of the limitations specified and that a particular use falls within that permitted by the zoning ordinance. For example, teaching of horsemanship was considered an educational function in one community, whereas use of a barn to teach and conduct classes in ballet and judo was held to not constitute a "private education institution" within the meaning of zoning ordinance in another community.

Variances and Exemptions. Zoning ordinances generally provide for variances or exemptions from the strict rule or literal enforcement of zoning laws as follows:

Nonconforming uses	Existing uses of land at time ordinance is passed will be permitted. The owner's right to expand such use or to repair damage or to reestablish the nonconforming use after it is discontinued may be subject to restrictions.
Variances	The right of an owner to petition to have his property exempted from some particular restriction applicable to the zone in which the property is located where the application of the zoning law creates a particular hardship to the owner.
Special use permit	The power of the local zoning administrative body to issue special permits for uses when it finds that public convenience and welfare will be substantially served by such uses.

Factors Local Agencies Consider in Granting Variances. In granting variances local agencies are required to consider such factors as the following:

Whether the hardship affecting the property is special and peculiar to the property or applicable to all property in the district

Whether the hardship was created by the owner

Whether there are any reasonable alternative uses permitted by the zone that will permit a reasonable use of the land and return on the property

Whether the proposed alternative use will be consistent with the general character of the neighborhood

Tactics to Obtain Zoning Changes and Variances.   Often a developer's ability to obtain zoning changes depends on his presentation and tactics more than the benefits of his project. For example:

Developers should be aware that local residents may regard them with considerable mistrust. They will usually be introducing new people into the area, altering the environment, and any proposed change may arouse deep-seated fears.

Developers should appreciate that any new project will create new public costs such as additional police, educational, and fire costs. Developers should be able to establish that their project will, in fact, benefit the neighborhood and not create unusual burdens on the community.

Developers should appreciate the fact that local politics may be involved and that local board members may have peculiar positions about certain issues. Often it may help to include local planners, counsel, and interest groups in the developer's plans and orient any presentations toward solving particularly pressing local problems.

Developers should appreciate the fact that local residents, interest groups, and local planning authorities may not look at problems and issues in the same way as they do. Any presentation in support of the proposed development should deal constructively with such residents', interest groups', and authorities' views and should not assume that such views are any more invalid or unreasonable than those of the developer.

BUILDING CODES.   Most cities have adopted building codes specifying various requirements in great detail as to the construction of buildings including:

Materials
Structural design minimums
Size and location of rooms
Location of exits, windows, ventilation
Electrical installation
Chimneys
Heating
Mechanical refrigeration
Illumination of exits
Plumbing

Compliance with building codes upon the construction of new real estate improvements is usually signified by the issuance of a building permit, which may require the examination of plans and specifications by numerous agencies such as fire and health departments. A building permit may require commencement of construction within certain specified time limits.

Compliance with building codes after initial construction is completed is sometimes accomplished by annual inspections by local agencies or the issuance of certificates from local agencies upon any conveyance of the property.

SUBDIVISION REGULATIONS.   The subdivision of parcels of land and improvements is frequently subject to regulation of subdivision map acts. The purposes of such regulations is usually to coordinate lot design, street patterns, rights of way for drainage, and sewers with the community pattern and plan as laid out by local planning authorities. Such regulations also are intended to insure that the areas dedicated for public purposes by the filing of subdivision maps, including public streets and other public areas, will be properly improved initially by the subdivider so that they will not become an undue burden in the future on the general taxpayers of the community. "Subdivisions" to which such regulations apply often include:

Divisions of property for sale
Divisions of property for lease
Divisions of property for financing

Exemptions.   Numerous exemptions are often incorporated into such acts including:

Exemption if less than a certain number of parcels are subdivided
Exemption if the size of each parcel exceeds a certain minimum
Exemption for, or expeditious handling of, certain types of subdivisions

Conditions on Approval of Maps.   Local agencies frequently impose numerous conditions before approving subdivision map filings. Examples of such conditions include:

Dedication of streets to the locality
Dedication of parks to the locality
Payment of sums of money to local school boards

Dedication of land to local school boards
Payment of sums of money for local drainage facilities
Installation of water mains
Dedication of land for local playgrounds
Payment of license tax on development business
Securing performance bonds

Other local agencies, such as sewer districts and municipal water districts, also impose similar conditions on the granting of permits.

NATIONAL AND STATE ENVIRONMENTAL PROTECTION ACTS. The National Environmental Policy Act (NEPA) directs all Federal agencies to prepare environmental impact statements (E.I.S.) for all major Federal actions significantly affecting the quality of the human environment. Many states have similar acts requiring similar environmental impact reports (E.I.R.) or statements. Litigation over the application of the provisions of NEPA or similar state statutes has centered around:

The nature and degree of Federal or state involvement in a project that is required to make the project a federal or state action
Whether the action is "major"
Whether the action will have significant impact on the environment
What changes in the proposed project may be required to mitigate the environmental effects
What specific social, economic, or other considerations justify approval of a project with environmental effects
What procedural safeguards must be provided during the E.I.S. or E.I.R. review process.

OTHER STATE AND FEDERAL ACTS. Many other acts and regulations affect the use and development of land. Included in those that directly affect land use are:

The Rivers and Harbors Act
National Housing Act of 1934
U.S. Housing Act of 1934
Federal Water Pollution Control Act
Federal Planning Assistance Program
Clean Air Act

Federal Highway Aid Act
Airport and Airway Development Act
Air Quality Act
National Environmental Policy Act
Water Quality Improvement Act
Noise Pollution and Abatement Act
Noise Control Act
Coastal Zone Management Act
Flood Disaster Protection Act
Federal Land Policy and Management Act

CONSTRUCTION CONTRACTS

The basic requirements of construction contracts do not differ from other types of contracts. For example, the parties must reach a mutual agreement that is supported by consideration. However, the contractor-owner relationship created gives rise to many special legal problems.

Negotiating Construction Contracts

Building contracts may be entered into after negotiations between specific parties or following the submission of bids by interested contractors.

Usually the request for bids is merely an invitation for offers, and the owner can reject any offer without liability. Invitations to bid should contain at least the following types of information:

Name and location of project
Names and addresses of owner and architect
Date, time, and place for receiving bids
Type of bid opening
Requirements, if any, for the posting of bidders' bonds or other bid security
Description of project, including type of construction and basic materials and systems
Type of contract

Places and procedures for examining and obtaining bidding documents
Statement of time of completion and liquidation damages

Drafting Construction Contracts

To be enforceable, a construction contract must contain information including:

The name of the owner
The name of the contractor
The identity of the property
A description of the work to be done

While highly detailed specifications of the work to be done and surveys of the property to be improved are not necessary for a construction contract to be enforceable, the chances of disputes are reduced as the specificity of construction contracts is increased. In addition to the above minimum provisions, construction contracts should cover the following:

Parties
   Proof of capacity to contract
   Proof of corporate, partnership existence
Description of work
   Labor
   Materials
   Specifications
   Plans
   Quality of workmanship
Duties of contractor
   Supervision of contractor
   Chain of command
Payment
   Stipulated or lump sum (contractor's risk)
   Cost plus fee (owner's risk)
   Guaranteed maximum (owner's risk up to certain point)
   Target price (owner and contractor share risk)
Method
   Progress payments

Conditions on final payment
Joint checks to contractors and subcontractors
Risk of inaccurate surveys, engineering reports
    Owner
    Contractor
Time for start and completion
    Adjustments for delay due to weather, and so on
Risk of delay
    Owner
    Contractor
    Damage for delay
    Owner's right to discharge contractor
    Penalties for delay
Drawings, specifications, permits
    Bearing of costs
    Ownership
Risk of failure to pay for labor and materials
    Withholding progress payments
    Indemnification of owner
    Bonds
    Letters of credit
Extra work, changes, deletions
    Written modifications
    Right to additional compensation
    Sharing of cost savings
Possession
    Conditions
    Certificate of completion
Insurance
    Owner's insurance
    Contractor's insurance
Guaranties
    Work
    Material
Arbitration of disputes
    Disputes covered

Method of selecting arbitrators
Method of voting
Contractor's right to stop work if not paid
Resolution of conflicts between documents
Corrective work and repairs
Conditions on contractual obligations
Financing
Material and labor availability
Waiver of mechanics' lien rights
Right to make claims concerning work after payment of final purchase price
Liability for disturbance of neighboring land
Warranties of contractor
Completion of building free of all liens
Work quality
Materials used
Payments to subcontractors
Compliance with codes
Warranties of owner
Plans
Engineering reports
Ownership of land
Surveys
Zoning

Avoiding Construction Contract Disputes

Construction seems to involve more litigation than other business contractual relationships, and such litigation usually involves numerous plaintiffs and defendants, including: owners, lenders, architects, contractors, subcontractors, suppliers, sureties, and bonding companies. Some suggestions follow for avoiding disputes at the various stages of the construction process.

Bidding process
Clearly establish that none of the bids has to be accepted.
Clearly establish that lowest bids do not have to be accepted.

Clearly specify the work, plans, specifications, materials, and other parameters on which bids are to be based.

Clearly specify whether additional, post-bidding negotiations will take place.

Clearly specify whether the owner can accept nonresponsive (alternative) bids.

Clearly specify whether the owner can accept late bids.

Clearly specify that bids can be withdrawn prior to acceptance.

Construction process

Clearly establish what standards will be used to resolve questions of adequate performance.

Custom and usage

Architect arbitration

Clearly establish who will supervise and who has the ultimate authority for determining completion.

Architect

Owner

Contractor

Lender

Subcontractor

Clearly establish the procedure for modifying the contract.

Bearing of extra work costs

Determining what work is covered by the contract

Rights to withhold contract price payments

Right to stop work

Validity of oral modifications

Notice requirements

Rebates for cost savings

Effect of acts of God

Effect of unforeseen economic hardship

Interpretation of ambiguities

Bearing of costs of mistakes

Clearly specify the method of payment and the purposes for which funds disbursed may be used.

Conditions on progress payments

Joint checks

Diversion of funds for other projects' kickbacks

Waiver of mechanics' lien rights by endorsement of payment check

LEASING REAL ESTATE

Landlord and Tenant Law

Landlord-tenant rights depend on a combination of property law, tracing back to Anglo-Saxon England, and modern contract law, interspersed with an increasing number of statutory rules designed to provide certain tenants with additional rights.

CREATION OF LEASEHOLD INTERESTS. The most common way a landlord and tenant relationship is created is by a lease. Under statutes of frauds applicable in most states, an agreement to lease real property (usually for more than 1 year) is invalid unless it is in writing and signed by the party to be charged. Usually such written agreements must contain at least the following provisions:

A description of the property leased
A definite term
A definite rent and the time and manner of payment
The identity of the parties

Lease agreements usually contain numerous other clauses defining the parties' rights and obligations, and, under certain circumstances, courts will imply additional covenants in the event of controversies between the parties.

RENT. Leases normally provide for the express duties of the tenant to pay rent. However, a tenant is obligated to pay the reasonable value of the premises even where there is no express promise to pay rent.

LEASE DEPOSITS. Lease provisions commonly require tenants to make some sort of advance payment at the time the lease is executed to assure the tenant's performance. In the event the tenant defaults, the right of the parties to the deposit depends on the following factors:

Whether the deposit is a bonus for executing the lease
Whether the deposit is prepaid rent
Whether the deposit is a security deposit
Whether the deposit is a penalty
Whether the lease is subject to statutory provisions with respect to the treatment of deposits

POSSESSION AND USE.   At the beginning of the tenancy the landlord has the duty of transferring to the tenant the legal right to possession and, in most states, actual possession of the real property. During the existence of the lease there is an implied covenant of quiet enjoyment by which a landlord warrants not to interfere with the tenant's possession, use, and enjoyment of the leased premises. Where there is a substantial interference with the tenant's possession, use, or enjoyment of the premises, the tenant may terminate the lease.

TENANTABILITY.   Until recent years a landlord had no duty to deliver the premises in any particular condition, and there was no implied covenant that the premises were fit for the intended use (caveat emptor). Certain exceptions evolved where there was a lease of a furnished house, where there were hidden defects known to the landlord and not discoverable by the tenant, or where a building was under construction at the time the lease was executed.

In recent years, the traditional rule of caveat emptor has been substantially changed. For example:

Courts have held that there is an implied covenant of initial habitability in leases of urban dwellings.

Courts have held that there is a covenant of initial suitability for the contemplated use in commercial leases.

Statutes have been enacted that impose on landlords affirmative duties to put residential premises in a tenantable condition prior to leasing them.

LANDLORD'S DUTY TO REPAIR.   Until recently landlords had no duty to repair the premises unless the landlord specifically agreed to make repairs. However, even then, the landlord's duty was usually regarded as independent of the tenant's covenant to pay rent, and if the landlord failed to make repairs, the tenant could not refuse to pay rent.

Recently, the traditional rule has been substantially changed. For example:

Courts have implied a continuing covenant by the landlord of liability to repair.

Courts have held that a covenant to pay rent is dependent on any covenant to repair.

Statutes have been enacted imposing a duty to repair on landlords.

Statutes have been enacted permitting tenants to repair damages and deduct the cost of such repairs from rent.

Statutes have been enacted permitting tenants as a group to escrow rents for purposes of repairs.

Statutes have been enacted that prohibit the waiver of landlord's duties to repair.

TENANT'S DUTY TO CARE FOR PROPERTY.   A tenant is liable to a landlord for damages caused by the tenant. Tenants may also expressly agree to repair and maintain the premises, in which event, failure to so repair and maintain the premises would be a breach of the lease. Statutes may also specify certain duties of tenants to keep the premises clean and sanitary.

LANDLORD'S LIABILITY TO TENANT'S GUESTS.   Until recently the duty to keep the premises safe rested primarily on the person who had occupancy or possession of the premises (the tenant). Certain exceptions existed, including liability for injuries caused by concealed defects of which the landlord had actual knowledge or reason to know of such defects, liability for negligently made repairs, and liability for injuries occurring in common areas.

In recent years the traditional rule has been substantially changed. For example:

Implied warranties of liability applicable to both tenants and their visitors have been imposed on landlords by courts.

Statutes imposing duties of repair and maintenance have been applied to impose liability for injuries to tenants' visitors.

Local building codes have been held to imply a duty to tenants' visitors.

ASSIGNMENT AND SUBLETTING.   In the absence of a provision to the contrary, leases are usually assignable, and tenants may sublease portions of the premises. Where there is an assignment the new tenant becomes directly liable to the landlord. However, when there is merely a sublease, the new tenant is usually not directly liable to the landlord. Many leases contain covenants against transfers by tenants. However, such covenants are strictly construed, and covenants not to assign may not prevent tenants from subleasing. Similarly, covenants against subleasing may not prevent assignment. In addition, courts frequently find that landlord's powers to prevent assignment or subleasing are waived.

TAXES.   When land is leased the lessor normally has the duty to pay taxes assessed against the property. However, some leases contain a lessee's covenant to pay taxes or assessments. Such covenants must be carefully drafted since a covenant to pay "taxes" may not be construed to cover special assessments and taxes levied in lieu of property taxes.

OPTIONS TO RENEW.   Landlords often give tenants an option to renew the lease. In such options investors should be careful not to confuse first rights of refusal with absolute options and should be careful not to provide for agreements to agree ("upon terms to be mutually agreed upon"). Options to renew must be exercised in accordance with their terms, and failure to comply exactly will justify a landlord's refusal to extend the term of the lease.

OPTIONS TO PURCHASE.   Landlords also frequently give tenants an option to purchase the leased property. As with renewal rights, investors should be careful not to confuse a first right of refusal with absolute options and should be careful not to provide for agreements to agree ("upon terms and conditions to be agreed upon"). Such options must also be exercised in accordance with their terms, and failure to comply exactly will justify a landlord's refusal to convey.

TERMINATION OF TENANCY UPON TENANT'S BREACH.   Most leases contain provisions permitting landlords to terminate the lease upon a breach of the tenant's obligations thereunder. The provisions for such forfeitures must be drafted carefully and clearly, and the landlord must strictly comply with any notice requirement or "cure" provisions, and forfeiture rights may be waived by the acts of the landlord. A forfeiture clause does not generally empower the tenant to end the lease at will by failing to perform.

LANDLORD'S REMEDIES UPON TERMINATION OF TENANCY.   When a tenant abandons the premises, the landlord usually has two options. He may do nothing, not relet the premises, and sue as each rent installment comes due. Or, he may reenter the premises and relet it to another tenant. Certain state statutes obligate the landlord to relet the premises and do not permit the landlord to let the premises lie idle. When the landlord relets the premises, statutes in a few states construe such an action as terminating the tenant's obligations to pay rent. Similarly, some state statutes provide that any revenues received by the landlord upon such reletting in excess of the rent due by the tenant belong to the tenant. In certain other states landlords have an additional remedy consisting of the right to sue for the present value of the full amount of the rent owed over the remainder of the lease.

Negotiating Real Estate Leases

The landlord and tenant relationship may come into existence without a written agreement at all, and many written lease agreements leave much of the specifics of the landlord and tenant relationship to custom, usage, or statutory presumptions. However, landlords and tenants, where possible, should carefully define the parameters of their relationship in formal lease agreements. In negotiating such leases the following areas should be discussed:

Parties
>What proof of authority of officers, partners, trustees, cotenants to execute on behalf of their respective entities will the parties require?
>>Statutory requirements
>>Resolutions
>>Statutory presumptions
>>Powers of attorney
>Are the individuals executing leases legally entitled to contract?
>>Minors

Description of premises
>What premises will be leased?
>What appurtenances are to be included?
>Is the tenant's premise subject to easements?
>Is the tenant entitled to parking?

Term of lease
>Are there any statutory limits on the length of leases?
>Will the tenant be entitled to any renewal rights?

Rent for premises
>Is the rent fixed?
>Will the tenant be required to pay cost of living increases?
>>Method of calculating tenant's share
>>Definitions
>>Base year
>Will the tenant be required to share in costs?

    Operating expenses
        Definitions
        Base year

Taxes

    Will the tenant be required to pay all or a portion of the taxes and assessments?

    What are the penalties for nonpayment?

        Interest

    What is the definition of taxes and assessments?

        Charges imposed in lieu of taxes

        Local business taxes

    Will the tenant have the right to contest additional assessments?

Insurance

    What insurance will be required on the land and improvements?

        Liability

        Fire

    What insurance will be required on fixtures and personal property?

    What type of policies and insurance companies will be acceptable to the landlord?

    What amount of insurance will be required?

Security deposits

    How much will the landlord require?

    What are the tenant's rights to interest on security deposit?

    Are there any restrictions on the landlord's use of security deposits?

    What events will entitle the landlord to the deposit?

        Failure to pay rent

        Liability to return

        Failure to perform other covenants

    Who owns the security deposit upon transfer of property?

        Old landlord

        New landlord

    Does the tenant have any liability to replenish the deposit if any expenditures are made by the landlord?

Utilities

    What are the minimum utilities to be supplied by landlord?

        Type

        Hours

Is the landlord liable for failure to supply?
Can the landlord charge for additional services?
    Costs to be charged tenant
What is the landlord's liability for tenant's failure to pay suppliers?
    Limitation on tenant's use of unusual apparatus
Use of premises
    Are there any limitations on tenant's use?
        Any lawful purpose
        Single-purpose buildings
        Restrictions on services/products
            Antitrust laws
        Zoning, local ordinances
    Are there any rules and regulations applicable to the premises?
        Flexibility
    What advertising and signs may tenant place on the property?
    What acts constitute prohibited waste and nuisance?
        Disturbance of other tenants
Repairs
    What are landlord's obligations?
        Time
        Notice
        Compliance with health and safety law
        Liability to third persons
        Liability disclaimers
        Remedy for breach
            Terminate lease
            Offset rent
    What are the tenant's obligations?
        Time
        Notice
        Covenants to repair
            Damage not the fault of tenant
            Arbitration of disputes
        Indemnification of landlord
        Remedies for breach
Fixtures

Does the tenant have any rights to remove fixtures at the termination of the lease?

Who has ownership of fixtures not removed?

Alteration and restoration

Are there any statutory limits on tenant's rights to alter the premises?

What alterations are authorized?

What rights does the landlord have to approve contractors performing work?

What are the tenant's duties to restore premises upon termination?

What steps has the landlord taken to secure the performance of tenant's duties?

Who has the liability for alterations required by law?

Destruction of the premises

Will there be any options to terminate the landlord-tenant relationship upon destruction of premises?

What are the landlord's covenants to repair?

Does the tenant assume the risk of destruction?

Are there any tenant's covenants to rebuild?

How will the insurance proceeds be used?

Condemnation

Will the landlord-tenant relationship continue upon condemnation of premises?

Partial taking

Total taking

Do the parties have any rights to terminate lease upon partial taking?

Will there be any rent reduction upon partial taking?

Who will have the use of condemnation proceeds upon partial taking?

Will there be an apportionment of condemnation damages?

Transfer of the parties' interests

What are the tenant's rights to assign or sublet?

Circumstances under which landlord must consent

Standards for exercise of consent

Circumstances under which assignment or subletting can take place by operation of law

Bankruptcy

Tenant's right to assign or sublet to subsidiary, affiliates, parent, or upon reorganization

    Corporate reorganization

What are the landlord's rights to convey property?

    Release of landlord upon sale of property

    Transferee's right to terminate lease

What are landlord's rights to assign rental payments?

    Tenant's right to set-off with respect to assignee

Renewal

    Is additional rent required?

    Does any renewal incorporate existing lease provisions?

    Is the renewal provision an option versus merely first right of refusal?

    Is the lease automatically renewed unless timely notice is given?

Default and remedies

    What events will result in a default?

        Monetary obligations

            Rent

            Share of costs

        Nonmonetary obligations

            Use of premises

            Repairs

    Are there any notice requirements?

    Does the tenant have any rights to cure?

    Are there any rights of third parties to cure?

        Mortgagees

        Sublessees

    What remedies will the landlord have in the event of a default?

        Past rent

        Present value of future rent

        Reentry, reletting

        Ownership of rental from reletting

        Ownership of property upon abandonment

    Is there a right to arbitration?

        Procedure for selecting arbitrators

        Matters subject to arbitration

        Decision making procedure

           Baseball arbitration
           Time limitations
           Allocation of costs
       What happens upon termination of tenancy?
         Tenant's obligation to restore premises
         Tenant's obligation to remove fixtures
         Ownership of tenant improvements
         Ownership of tenant's fixture
       Does the tenant have to indemnify the landlord?
         Circumstances under which tenant will indemnify landlord
           Tenant's negligence
           Third parties
       What miscellaneous matters are covered by the lease?
         Attorney's fees
         Governing law
         Incorporation of other documents
           Master leases
           Covenants, conditions, and restrictions
         Guaranties of tenant's performance
         Incorporation of rules and regulations
         Landlord's right to show premises prior to tenant's termination of lease

Managing Real Estate

THE BUSINESS OF INCOME PROPERTY OWNERSHIP. Unlike "passive" investments such as stocks and bonds, income property ownership involves substantial management activities. Management activities for an apartment project, for example, include:

    Leasing/marketing
        Analyzing competitive units (market surveys, amenity comparisons)
        Obtaining tenant prospects (ads, signs)
        Preparing units for rent (cleaning, refinishing)
        Marketing units (showing vacancies, answering questions)
        Screening tenant prospects (completion of rental agreements, verification of data)

Administration/record keeping
  Banking (rental deposits, reconciling bank accounts)
  Filing governmental reports (taxes, lender's compensation)
  Tenant records keeping (lease expiration, deposits)
  Personal property records keeping (furniture, recreational equipment)
Cleaning/maintenance
  Interior common areas (floors, walls, equipment)
  Landscaping (watering, trimming)
  Exterior areas (painting, plastering)
  Tenant units (preleasing refurnishing, appliance maintenance)
Repairs/renovation
  Exterior areas (equipment, common area facilities)
  Tenant units (appliances, heating/air conditioning)
Tenant relations
  Enforcement of rules and regulations (noise, use of facilities, guests)
  Rent collection (records, delinquency follow-up)

LAWS APPLICABLE TO INCOME PROPERTY MANAGEMENT. The business of managing income property investments may involve numerous laws covering such areas as:

State laws
  Labor laws
  Minimum wage laws
  Disability insurance laws
  Worker's compensation laws
  Unemployment insurance laws
  Fair housing laws
  Business license laws
Federal laws
  Federal Insurance Contributions Act (FICA)
  Income tax withholding laws
  Equal employment opportunity laws
  Fair labor laws
  Federal unemployment tax
  Economic stabilization acts
  Fair housing laws

PROFESSIONAL PROPERTY MANAGEMENT. Many investors hire professional property managers to perform all or part of the numerous business activities required in connection with income property ownership.

Nature of the Relationship. The relationship between the property owner and the property manager usually takes the form of employer and employee, principal and agent, or owner and independent contractor. While most of the services rendered by property managers can be performed in any one of these roles, different rights and obligations are attached to the parties if the relationship is one of employer or principal and agent than are imposed if the relationship is one of owner and independent contractor.

For example, if the relationship is one of employer and employee or principal and agent, the property owner is normally obligated to pay contributions to various governmental bodies such as unemployment funds or workers compensation funds; the property owner is usually liable for torts committed by the employee or agent in the performance of his duties; and the property owner is usually subject to applicable labor and fair employment practices laws.

On the other hand, if the relationship is one of owner and independent contractor, the owner is not normally required to make contributions to unemployment funds or workers compensation funds and is not usually liable for the negligence of a contractor performing work for him. In addition, if the relationship is one of owner and independent contractor, the property owner is normally not subject to labor and fair employment practices laws.

It is not always easy to tell the difference between an employee, an agent, and an independent contractor. The distinction between an independent contractor and an agent is based on many factors including, most importantly, the amount of supervision provided and the nature of the tasks to be performed.

An independent contractor normally performs tasks with little or no supervision and usually has a distinct skill needed on an infrequent basis. On the other hand, an employee or agent is usually closely supervised in the performance of tasks and is usually hired as part of the regular business of the employer.

The distinction between an agent and an employee is usually based on the amount of authority given the agent to act on behalf of the principal. The agent is usually granted broad authority to act on behalf of the principal and to represent the principal.

The relationship between the property owner and the property manager is most often one of principal and agent because the property manager is usually hired to provide a broad range of services on a continuing basis and because of the broad authority property managers are given for such things as rent collection, leasing, and contracting for outside services.

In the event the parties wish to create an owner and independent contractor relationship rather than a principal and agent relationship, they should carefully structure their agreement so that the characteristics of the principal and agent relationship are avoided. The parties should itemize the specific results to be performed and define the specific fees and compensation to be paid for each result. In addition, the property manager should be given maximum discretion in the performance of services and tasks leading to such results; control over the property manager in the performance of such services and tasks should be minimized. The parties should avoid contractual provisions calling for a specific number of hours to be worked. The parties should also avoid contractual provisions calling for overtime wages or bonuses.

Finally, the authority of the property owner should be carefully defined on a result-by-result basis; the property manager should not be considered as the owner's stand-in with respect to each and every aspect of the property's ownership, operation, maintenance, and management.

Duties and Authority of the Property Manager. The property owner and property manager should carefully define the areas where the property manager's services are to be rendered and describe the duties, responsibilities, and authority to be given to the property manager in each area. While detailed consideration of specific duties and responsibilities can be time-consuming and uncomfortable to parties who may be used to dealing in terms of "gentlemen's agreements" and "custom," there are advantages to clarifying responsibilities carefully and setting limits on authority.

From the property owner's point of view, a detailed consideration of the services to be provided can facilitate the selection of the most suitable property manager and property management services and enable the property owner to make arrangements for other parties to fill any gaps in service. From the property manager's point of view, a detailed consideration of the services to be provided can help to avoid future claims of misfeasance or fee disputes. In addition, a detailed consideration of the property manager's authority can serve to reduce the possibility that the property manager will be held to be personally liable on a contract executed on behalf of the owner.

If the property manager is hired to show and rent spaces in the property, all duties and authority should be specified in considerable detail. Duties and authority to be considered include: (*a*) conducting market surveys to determine appropriate rent levels; (*b*) drafting legal documents necessary for leasing or renting the space in the property; (c) advertising to procure tenants; (d) screening prospective tenants; (e) negotiating leases or rental agreements with prospective tenants; (f) entering into leases or rental agreements; and, (g) reviewing or extending leases or rental agreements.

If the property manager is hired to maintain the owner's property, all duties and authority should also be specified in great detail. Duties and authority to be considered include: (a) inspecting the property to de- of emergency repairs, maintenance, or renovating; and, (f) performing or contracting for the performance of large-scale improvement, renovation, or refurbishing; (d) purchasing or contracting for the purchase of supplies, tools, and materials; (e) performing or contracting for the performance of emergency repairs, maintenance, or renovating; and, (f) performing or contracting for the performance of repairs or maintenance or renovations ordered by governmental authorities.

If the property manager is hired to deal with other personnel who may also be rendering services to the property, all duties and authority should be carefully specified. Duties and activities to be considered include: (a) performing periodic surveys to determine necessary staffing or employment requirements; (b) recruiting and screening prospective employees; (c) contracting with employees for services to be rendered; (d) supervision of employees; (e) paying and remunerating employees; and, (f) discharging employees.

If the property manager is hired to contract for the supplying of services to the property, all duties and authority should be specified in considerable detail. Duties and authority to be considered include: (a) periodic surveys to determine service necessary for the operation and maintenance of the property; (b) negotiating for services necessary for the operation and maintenance of the property; (c) verification of the performance and quality of services necessary for the operation and maintenance of the property; (d) paying for services necessary for the operation and maintenance of the property; and (e) resolving disputes as to the quality, quantity, or cost of services necessary for the operation and maintenance of the property.

If the property manager is hired to manage the fiscal affairs of the property, all duties and authority should be carefully specified. Duties and authority to be considered include: (a) receiving rent or other revenue due to the property owner; (b) paying expenses associated with the operation and maintenance of the property; (c) paying certain expenses or charges associated with the property in preference to other expenses or charges that may also be due and payable; (d) making mortgage or other payments due as a result of encumbrances secured by the property;

(e) paying taxes, assessments, and other governmental charges associated with the property; (f) preparing income and expense reports; (g) preparing operating budgets and income forecasts; (h) preparing reports due governmental authorities; (i) opening bank accounts; (j) contracting with accountants or other professionals; and (k) providing access to all records to the owner.

If the property manager is hired to procure or monitor the adequacy of insurance necessary for the maintenance and operation of the property or the protection of the owner, his duties and authorities should also be carefully specified. Duties and authority to be considered include: (a) obtaining recommendations as to insurance needed to protect adequately the property and the owner and to comply with the applicable laws; (b) selecting suitable insurance companies with which to carry necessary insurance; (c) procuring and paying for necessary coverage; (d) supplying the owner with proof of coverage; (e) investigating accidents or claims for damage relating to the ownership, operation, and maintenance of the property; and (f) filing reports with insurers and cooperating with insurers.

Compensation.   The types of compensation a property manager may receive can vary from a fixed salary or fee to a variable commission or percentage of income with living expenses and fringe benefits.

In negotiating the form of compensation, the property owner and property manager should consider the type of compensation to be paid for each specific service rendered. Where the service is one that requires a fixed expenditure of time and money on the part of the manager and where an incentive of extraordinary effort is not necessary, compensation in the form of a fixed salary or fee might be appropriate and desirable to both parties.

For example, bookkeeping is usually an area where the property manager incurs fixed and predictable costs and where the property manager's extraordinary efforts are not likely to provide the property owner with any particular gain. It would be appropriate to provide that the property manager's compensation for such services is a fixed fee or that a fixed salary be paid for such service.

However, where the service is one that requires a variable amount of time or money on the part of the property manager and where additional incentive for extraordinary effort is appropriate, variable compensation in the form of a commission or a percentage of rent might be beneficial to both parties.

For example, where the property manager is hired to lease or rent space, the property manager's costs are not as fixed or predictable, and extraordinary efforts on the property manager's part can result in direct financial gain to the owner. It would be appropriate to provide that the property manager's compensation for such services be based on a commission or a percentage of income produced.

In discussing the form and amount of compensation to be paid the property manager, the parties should also consider such factors as expense reimbursements, fringe benefits, cost of living increases, and periodic compensation evaluations. Often, as the relationship progresses, the duties and responsibilities change so that previously agreed to forms of compensation are not appropriate and do not provide sufficient incentive for proficient performance.

Duration of Relationship and Rights to Terminate by Both Parties. There is usually no limitation on the length of time for which the parties can contract. However, some state labor laws limit the enforceability of employment contracts against employees beyond a certain number of years and thus most contracts do not extend for unusually long periods of time.

An employment contract that contains no specified term may usually be terminated at the will of either party on notice to the other. Thus, if the property owner or property manager desires additional certainty as to the relationship, a specific term should be specified.

The power of the parties to terminate the relationship should be considered at the beginning of the relationship, and the property owner and property manager should specify the circumstances under which it may be terminated and the means of termination in great detail. In discussing the rights of the parties to terminate, the property owner and property manager should consider the amount of expenditures to be made by the property manager at the outset of the relationship for record keeping and operations setup and preliminary analysis of the property's needs.

The parties should also consider the needs of the property manager for time to prove his abilities. Where the property manager will be asked to expend considerable time and money to set up a system of records or to analyze the property's staffing or maintenance needs, sufficient time should be provided for the property manager to recoup his investment. Similarly, if the property has been badly managed prior to the hiring of the property manager, some time must be allocated to turning the property's performance around, and the property manager should be given sufficient time to demonstrate his abilities without the inertia of previously implemented policies or procedures.

TAXATION OF REAL ESTATE CASH FLOWS

The tax treatment of a particular investment in real estate depends on numerous tax statutes, regulations, and cases that define, limit, and characterize each and every element of an investment's yearly net taxable income (or loss).

Gross Income

Gross income is the starting point in determining tax liability. The *Internal Revenue Code* defines gross income to include all income from whatever source derived and includes rents as one of the specific items to be included in gross income. However, the landlord-tenant relationship often involves other payments, events, and activities beside the payment of rent, including:

Event	General Rule
Prepaid rent	Taxable when received.
Security deposits	Not taxable where landlord strictly accountable and must return upon completion of lease.
Tenant improvements	Not taxable, either at time made, or at end of lease unless specifically made a substitute for rent.
Payment of landlord's expenses	Taxable income to landlord.
Lease option payments	Payments to landlord may, under certain circumstances constitute return of capital or capital gain.

Certain tax law concepts have evolved to handle payments and events such as those listed including:

Concept	General Rule
Realization of income (appreciation in value, lessee improvements)	Gains must be realized before they are taxable income. Appreciation in value alone is not income or gain. Bargain purchase at arm's length is not income or gain.
Return of capital (proceeds upon foreclosure of loan)	Repayment of taxpayer's capital investment does not constitute realized income.
Claim of right (security deposits, option payments)	Under certain circumstances, amounts received constitute income in the year of receipt in spite of the fact that the taxpayer's use of the funds may be subject to claims and that the taxpayer might be required, ultimately, to restore an equivalent amount.

| Constructive receipt (last month's rent) | Income, although not actually reduced to a taxpayer's possession, is constructively received by him in the taxable year during which it is credited to his account, set apart for him, or otherwise made available so that he may draw upon it at any time. |
| Recognition of income (exchanges) | Not all realized gains are taxable. |

Operating Expenses

DEDUCTIBLE EXPENSES.   Expenses are classified by the *Internal Revenue Code* as either (*a*) expenses incurred in the taxpayer's trade or business; (*b*) expenses incurred for the production or collection of income or for the management, conservation, or maintenance of property that is held for the production of income; or (*c*) expenses that are purely personal. The *Internal Revenue Code* allows the deduction of the first two expenses, while the third type of expenses, with a few exceptions, is not deductible.

TESTS FOR DEDUCTIBILITY.   In order for an expense to be deductible as a business expense certain tests must be met including:

The expense must be incurred in an activity entered into with a good-faith expectation of profit.

The business must be engaged in regularly and continuously.

The purpose of the expenditure must have a direct and proximate relationship to the trade or business.

The expense must be ordinary and necessary (reasonable and customary).

The expenditure must not be a capital investment.

The expenditure must not violate public policy.

The expenditure must be paid or incurred in the taxable year.

The first requirement substantially limits the ability of "gentlemen farmers" to deduct expenses associated with such investments as race horse ranches and rural hunting estates. The third and fourth requirements are aimed at the "three martini" lunch. Whether a particular expenditure qualifies as a deductible business expense or a capital expenditure depends on numerous factors including:

Whether the expenditure increases the value of the property

Whether the expenditure appreciably prolongs the useful life of the property

Whether the expenditure makes the property adaptable for a different use

Whether the expenditure is substantial in amount

Whether the expenditure is performed pursuant to a specific plan of rehabilitation and improvement

Whether the replacement material is superior to the old material

Property Taxes

State, local, and foreign real property taxes are deductible whether or not the taxpayer is in a trade or business with respect to the real estate. However, in order for such taxes to be deductible as taxes, the tax must meet certain requirements including the following:

The tax must be a genuine tax and not a regulatory fee.

The liability must be that of the taxpayer.

The first requirement is aimed at such charges as water taxes or sewer taxes levied by some localities, which are not actually taxes, but fees for supplying certain commodities to the property owner. The second requirement is important in the case of so-called "triple-net leases" where the tenant agrees to pay the landlord's taxes. In such a case the expense is not deductible by the tenant as a tax, but only as an operating expense.

Interest

Interest expenses are generally deductible whether the debt is a business or personal expense. However, in order for the interest expense to be deductible:

The expense must relate to a bona fide debt.

The expense must not be specifically disallowed.

The expense must be compensation for the use or forebearance of money.

The expense must not be specifically capitalizable by statute or regulation.

The expense must not result in a material distortion of income.

The first requirement is aimed at certain "tax shams." The second requirement relates to borrowings to purchase exempt bonds and to so called "investment interest" limitations. The third requirement relates to charges such as loan origination fees, loan placement fees, and appraised costs that may be associated with borrowing but which may not necessarily be deductible as interest. The fourth requirement relates to such interest charges as construction period interest. The last requirement relates to certain prepaid interest charges that are not based on any valid business needs, but are merely tax avoidance shams.

Depreciation Deduction

While the *Internal Revenue Code* permits taxpayers to deduct a reasonable allowance for the exhaustion, wear, and tear on property used in a trade or business or held for the production of income, there are numerous rules governing the amount of such deductions.

DEPRECIABLE BASIS. Cost. The basis of property obtained by purchase is its net cost plus certain costs associated with its acquisition such as title charges, broker's commissions, tax stamps, option payments, attorneys' fees, appraisal costs, and surveys.

Indebtedness. When real property is acquired subject to an indebtedness, the depreciable basis generally includes the amount of the unpaid liability. Examples of such indebtedness include a purchase money mortgage and existing mortgages on the property. The fact that the taxpayer does not personally assume liability for the debt does not usually affect its inclusion in the basis. However, newly enacted "at-risk" rules may limit the ability of certain entities to include mortgages in the depreciable basis.

Exchanges. The basis of property received in a tax-deferred exchange is determined by reference to the basis of the property exchanged. Where there is no boot involved (other property, cash, or net relief of liabilities), the basis of the property received is the same as the adjusted basis of the property transferred. If cash or other property is received, or if there is net relief of liabilities, the basis is decreased by such cash, property, or net relief of liabilities and increased by recognized gain.

Land. Since land is, generally, not depreciable, calculation of the depreciable basis of real property requires apportioning the property's basis among land and depreciable real property (buildings, fixtures, etc.). An allocation between depreciable and nondepreciable property must be made based on the ratio of the respective fair market values at the time of acquisition. In allocating the purchase price between several items of property, the evidence most acceptable to the Internal Revenue Service is the value determined by independent appraisers.

Building and Personal Property.   Once the purchase price or other basis of a real property investment has been allocated between nondepreciable assets (land) and depreciable assets (buildings and personal property), a further allocation is required of the depreciable assets between real property assets and personal property assets. Such an allocation is required because of different tax treatments afforded real property versus personal property. For example, investments in personal property may be subject to special investment tax credits and different recapture rules.

USEFUL LIVES.   The Internal Revenue Service (IRS) in *Rev. Proc. 62–21* published useful lives for various types of real estate. While taxpayers frequently use shorter lives, and courts have sustained the use of substantially shorter lives than those set forth in *Rev. Proc. 62–21,* the burden of proving the validity of such shorter lives is on the taxpayer.

Guidelines.   The following are examples of the lives allowed by the IRS in *Rev. Proc.* 62–21 and the courts:

Types of Real Estate	IRS	Courts
Apartments	40 years	33 years
Office buildings	45 years	50 years
Stores	50 years	25 years

Component Lives.   A taxpayer may, under certain circumstances, segregate and separately depreciate the components of a structure over their respective individual useful lives (the "component method"). Use of the component method may increase the allowable depreciable deduction. For example, while a $1,000,000 depreciable basis depreciated over a 25-year period would (using the straight-line method) result in a yearly depreciation deduction of $40,000, use of the component method could provide for additional depreciation as follows:

	Useful Life (Years)	Cost	Straight-Line Depreciation
Building (shell)	40	$ 480,000	$12,000
Wiring	15	90,000	6,000
Plumbing	15	120,000	8,000
Roof	10	60,000	6,000
Heating	10	80,000	8,000
Paving	10	20,000	2,000
Ceiling	10	40,000	4,000
Air conditioning	10	20,000	2,000
Elevator	15	90,000	6,000
		$1,000,000	$54,000

SALVAGE VALUE. Depreciation deductions are allowed only on the excess of the depreciable basis over estimated salvage value unless a declining balance method or the IRS ADR Guidelines are used. Even when a declining balance method is used, an asset may not be depreciated below its salvage value. Probable salvage value of a depreciable asset must be estimated when it is first depreciated. The IRS provides little guidance in selecting salvage values with the following general exceptions:

Salvage value shall not be changed at any time after the determination made at the time of acquisition merely because of changes in price level.

Salvage value may be reduced by removal costs.

A taxpayer may, with respect to personal property, reduce the amount taken into account as salvage value by an amount that does not exceed 10% of the basis of such property.

DEPRECIATION METHODS.   The depreciable basis of real estate may be deducted over its useful life under a variety of allowable methods. One method is the straight-line method. Under this method the basis of the property, less its anticipated salvage value, is deducted in equal amounts over its useful life. Another method is the declining-balance method. Under this method, an initial depreciation rate is calculated by dividing the useful life into 100. The rate so determined is then multiplied by an allowable factor (125%, 150%, or 200%) to arrive at the declining balance rate. This declining balance rate is then multiplied by the undepreciated basis at the beginning of each period to arrive at each period's depreciation deduction.

The *Internal Revenue Code* contains rules as to which methods can be used for various types of real estate. Allowable depreciation methods are as follows:

Type of Property	Date of Construction or Acquisition	Maximum Write-Off Permitted
Residential real estate		
New property	1954 and subsequent years	200% Declining balance or sum-of-years' digits method
Used property	Prior to 7/24/69	150% Declining balance method
Used property	After 7/24/69	125% Declining balance method
Non-residential real estate		
New property	1954 and subsequent years through 7/24/69	200% Declining balance or sum-of-years' digits method
New property	After 7/24/69	150% Declining balance method
Used property	Prior to 7/24/69	150% Declining balance method
Used property	After 7/24/69	Straight-line method only

TIMING THE SALE OF REAL ESTATE

Factors Influencing the Sale Decision

The determination of the optimum time to sell real estate involves a consideration of numerous factors including:

The investor's personal needs and desires
  Cash for retirement
  Cash for vacations
  Cash for education
The economy and the real estate market
  Relative attractiveness of other investment vehicles such as stocks, bonds, or precious metals
  Proposed adverse economic changes
  Imminent local area decline
  Imminent changes in the availability and cost of credit shifts in government tax, housing, and fiscal policies
The competitive status of the investor's project
  Alternatives for other real estate investments
  The project's ability to command high gross revenues
  Increasing operating expenses
  Impending deferred maintenance charges
The ability of the project to provide "tax shelter"
  The remaining depreciable basis
  The proportion of loan payments constituting deductible interest expense
  The applicability of depreciation recapture regulations
  Changes in taxation of revenues
  Changes in deductibility of expenses
  Changes in treatment of gains on sale

While an analysis of many of these factors does not lend itself to quantitative techniques (such as an analysis of the investor's need for vacation cash), certain techniques are available to quantify certain aspects of the sale decision. Two commonly used techniques are "sensitivity analysis" and "reinvestment rate analysis."

Sensitivity Analysis in Real Estate Decisions

In analyzing a real estate investment, it is important to know how the investment's yield (IRR) is influenced by changes in the various components of the Yearly Net After Tax Cash Flow and/or Residual upon Sale. The systematic process of changing the components of the Yearly Net After Tax Cash Flow and/or Residual upon Sale, one by one, to determine the investment's sensitivity to such changes is referred to as "sensitivity analysis."

The process of sensitivity analysis can be illustrated as follows:

ASSUMED INVESTMENT

Cost	$440,000
Gross income	$ 60,000
Operating expenses	$ 24,000
Depreciable basis	66% Of cost
Depreciation method	125% Declining balance
Depreciable life	33 Years
Mortgage financing	70% Of cost
Interest on mortgage	8% Per year
Mortgage term	27 Years
Growth rate	2% Per year
Selling expenses	6% Of sales price
Owner's tax bracket	30% Marginal tax bracket
Holding period	9 Years
Internal rate of return	9.85% Per year

SEQUENTIAL CHANGES (+10%)

Variable	Changed to	Increase in IRR
Cost	$396,000	20.3%
Gross income	$ 66,000	30.3%
Operating expenses	$ 21,000	11.9%
Depreciable basis	72% Of cost	1.1%
Depreciation method	137% Declining balance	2.2%
Depreciable life	36 Years	1.0%
Mortgage financing	77% Of cost	11.8%
Interest on mortgage	7.2% Per year	12.7%
Mortgage term	30 Years	2.6%
Growth rate	2.2% Per year	5.0%
Selling expenses	5.4% Of sales price	5.0%
Owner's tax bracket	27% Marginal tax bracket	1.6%
Holding period	8.1 Years	0.5%

USE OF SENSITIVITY ANALYSIS TO DETERMINE OPTIMUM HOLDING PERIOD.
As the sensitivity analysis indicates, the rate of return on the project increases if the property is held for 8.1 years rather than 9 years. If another sensitivity analysis were done on the project at, for example, a
holding period of 7.3 years (an additional 10% shorter holding period);
and, if the rate of return decreased, the investor could conclude (assuming
all other variables did not change) that the optimum holding period was
close to 8.1 years. Computer programs are available that make the
numerous calculations of yields easy, and sophisticated investors often
make such calculations to determine the optimum holding period of an
investment prior to any acquisition.

Reinvestment Rate Analysis

Sensitivity analysis can be a useful tool in analyzing an investment prior
to acquisition and to determine, absent significant change in assumed
variables, the optimum holding period of the investment. However, additional techniques are necessary to determine whether an investment should
be abandoned in "midstream" and proceeds therefrom invested in an
entirely different investment. The following formula can be used to give
a good approximation of the return that must be realized from a new
investment to justify termination of an old investment:

$$R = \frac{\text{equity} - \sum\limits_{t=1}^{T} \frac{\text{NCF}_t}{(1+r)^t} - \frac{\text{NRC}}{(1+r)^s}}{\sum\limits_{t=T+1}^{s} \frac{\text{NRC}}{(1+r)^t}}$$

where: NCF_t = yearly after tax cash flow from
existing investment

S = total number of years existing investment
was to have been held

T = year in which reinvestment opportunity occurs $(1 < T > S)$

r = internal rate of return that would have been earned on existing investment if held as originally planned

equity = original equity invested

NRC = amount of cash available if the investment is sold (after taxes, loan pay off, etc.)

R = the rate that would have to be earned on a new investment if the original investment is sold and the proceeds (NRC) reinvested

Σ = mathematical symbol which means here "the sum of."

The following is an example of the use of the reinvestment rate formula to determine if an investment should be sold and the funds reinvested at a different rate R.

ASSUME:

NCF =	Year 1	Year 2	Year 3	Year 4	Year 5
	$6,000	$6,000	$6,000	$6,000	$6,000

$S = 5$ years; $T =$ year 3; $r = 10\%$; equity $= \$22,745$; NCR $= \$7,000$

CALCULATION OF REINVESTMENT RATE:

$$R = \frac{\$22,745 - \left[\dfrac{\$6,000}{[(1+0.10)^1} + \dfrac{\$6,000}{(1 \mid 0.10)^2} + \dfrac{\$6,000}{(1+0.10)^3]}\right] - \dfrac{\$7,000}{(1+0.10)^5}}{\dfrac{\$7,000}{(1+0.10)^4} + \dfrac{\$7,000}{(1+0.10)^5}}$$

$$R = \frac{\$22,745 - \left[\dfrac{\$6,000}{1.10} + \dfrac{\$6,000}{1.21} + \dfrac{\$6,000]}{1.33}\right] - \dfrac{\$7,000}{1.61}}{\dfrac{\$7,000}{1.46} + \dfrac{\$7,000}{1.61}}$$

$$R = \frac{\$22,745 + \$5,455 + \$4,959 - \$4,511 - \$4,347}{\$4,795 + \$4,347}$$

$$R = \frac{\$3,473}{\$9,143}$$

$$R = 38\%$$

Thus, the investor would have to earn 38% to justify selling and reinvesting in a new investment. As the formula indicates, where R is greater than r, abandonment of the current investment is not advised. Where R is less than r, the change of investments is advised.

TAXATION OF PROCEEDS UPON DISPOSITION OF REAL ESTATE

Amount of Gain or Loss

The amount of gain or loss realized on the sale of real estate is the difference between the proceeds from the sale and the adjusted basis of the property. The proceeds from the sale include such items as cash payments, purchase money notes, the fair market value of negotiable notes, and liabilities of the seller assumed by the purchaser. Expenses of selling the property, such as brokerage commissions, and legal fees relating to the transfer are deductible from the sales price in determining the amount of gain or loss realized. The adjusted basis of property is usually the cost of the property (cash plus indebtedness incurred or assumed by the owner) less accumulated depreciation deductions.

Character of Gains or Losses

Real estate may be held for personal use, for investment or the production of income, for use in a trade or business, or for the sale to customers in the ordinary course of business.

PERSONAL RESIDENCE. If the real property is held for personal use (such as a residence), net gain on the sale will usually be taxed at capital gain rates, and a net loss will be deductible only pursuant to the limitations contained in Section 1221 of the *Internal Revenue Code*. An exception to the taxation of gains upon the disposition of a residence is provided by Section 1034 of the *Internal Revenue Code* which permits deferral of tax on gain realized on the disposition of a principal residence if (among other requirements) the proceeds are reinvested in another principal residence, which the owner buys within 18 months, or builds within 24 months.

PROPERTY USED IN TRADE OR BUSINESS.   Section 1231 of the *Internal Revenue Code* contains provisions that provide for special tax treatment for real and depreciable property held for more than 12 months and used in the taxpayer's trade or business. In such a case, net gains from sales are taxed at long-term capital gains rates, and net losses are fully deductible from ordinary income. The capital gains treatment of net gains from the sale of real and depreciable property held for use in the taxpayer's trade or business is modified by the recapture rules contained in Sections 1245 and 1250 of the *Internal Revenue Code.* The determination of whether or not a particular piece of income property is held for use in a trade or business depends on a variety of factors such as the owner's intent upon acquisition, the number of rental properties held by the owner, and the extent of his participation in their management.

PROPERTY HELD FOR SALE.   Where the real estate is held for sale to customers in the ordinary course of business by, for example, a developer, net gains on the sale of such real estate are taxed at ordinary income rates, and net losses are deductible from ordinary income. An exception to this rule is provided by Section 1237 of the *Internal Revenue Code* which provides for capital gains treatment upon a subdivision of land for sale if (among other requirements) the property has been held for more than 5 years and no more than five lots are sold in the year of sale.

PROPERTY HELD FOR INVESTMENT.   Where the real estate is held for investment, net gains on the sale of such real estate are taxed at capital gains rates, and net loss may be deducted only as permitted by the capital loss limitations contained in Section 1221 of the *Internal Revenue Code.*

Recapture

The general rule that gain on the sale or exchange of real property (other inventory of a "dealer") qualifies for capital gains treatment is modified by Section 1250 of the *Internal Revenue Code,* which provides that under certain circumstances such gain will be taxed (recaptured) as ordinary income. The basic rule of Section 1250 is that, with the exception of certain specific types of property, any excess of accelerated depreciation over straight-line depreciation taken on property held more than 1 year taken in any year beginning on or after January 1, 1976 will be subject to recapture on sale (not to exceed realized gain). The rule of Section 1250 is actually more complicated because the recapture rules have changed two times since 1963, and, where a property was purchased prior to 1969, three different recapture rules apply to excess depreciation deductions. For example:

If the property was held 12 full months or less, all depreciation taken (not just excess) is recaptured.

All post-1975 excess depreciation taken (or gain if less) will be recaptured in full.

All post-1969 (but pre-1975) excess depreciation (or remaining gain if less) will be recaptured in full unless the date when such property was held for 100 months occurred between January 1, 1970 and December 31, 1975, in which event the percentage of excess depreciation taken during such period to be recaptured will decrease by an amount equal to the number of months the property was owned in excess of 100.

All post-1963 (but pre-1969) excess depreciation (or remaining gain if less) will be recaptured in full unless the date when such property was held for 20 months occurred between January 1, 1964 and December 31, 1969, in which event the percentage of excess depreciation taken during such period to be recaptured will decrease by an amount equal to the number of months the property was owned in excess of 20.

For example, assume a $100,000 residential rental property acquired new on January 1, 1968 has been depreciated by the 200% declining-balance method over 40 years (no salvage). If it was sold on January 1, 1980 (a 144-month holding period), depreciation recapture would be computed as follows:

DEPRECIATION TABLE

Year	Actual Depreciation Taken	Straight-Line Depreciation Allowable	Excess Depreciation
1968	$* 5,000	$ 2,500	$ 2,500
1969	4,750	2,500	2,250
1970	4,512	2,500	2,012
1971	4,287	2,500	1,787
1972	4,073	2,500	1,573
1973	3,869	2,500	1,369
1974	3,675	2,500	1,175
1975	3,492	2,500	992
1976	3,317	2,500	817
1977	3,151	2,500	651
1978	2,994	2,500	494
1979	2,844	2,500	344
	$45,964	$30,000	$15,964

GAIN ON SALE

Sales proceeds = $100,000
Adjusted basis = ($54,036)
$ 45,964

EXCESS DEPRECIATION

Post-1975 excess: $ 817
651
494
344
———
$2,306.00

Post-1969/pre-1976 excess: $2,017
1,787
1,573
1,369
1,175
992
———
$8,913.00

Post-1963/pre-1970 excess: $2,500
                               2,250
                                              $4,750.00

DEPRECIATION RECAPTURE

Post-1975:   Lesser of gain or
                          excess depreciation
                          times 100% $2,306.00
Post-1969/pre-1976:   Lesser of
                          remaining gain
                          ($45,964 less $2,306)
                          or excess deprecia-
                          tion ($8,913) times
                          56% (100% less 44%) $4,991.00
Post-1963/pre-1970:   Lesser of
                          remaining gain
                          ($45,964 less $2,306
                          and less $8,914)
                          or excess deprecia-
                          tion ($4,750) times 0%
                          (100% less 144% but
                          not less than zero) $ 0
Total $7,218.00

Method of Payment of Purchase Price

The method used to pay the sales price will also affect the taxation of
the proceeds from the sale of real estate.

INSTALLMENT METHOD. While net gain is generally taxed in the year of
sale, taxpayers may, under certain circumstances, elect to report gain on
the installment method and thereby spread the recognition of gain over
several years.

To qualify for installment treatment, "payments in the year of sale"
must not exceed 30% of the "sales price." "Payments received in the
year of sale" do not include evidences of indebtedness of the purchaser and liabilities assumed (or taken subject to) except to the extent
they exceed the seller's basis in the property. Payments in the year of
sale also do not include seller's obligations that are merely "wrapped-
around" regardless of whether or not they exceed the seller's basis. On

the other hand, payments in the year of sale do include principal payments made by the buyer during the year of sale on a purchase money mortgage, a buyer's note which is payable on demand or which becomes due during the year of sale, and property given by the buyer in payment such as promissory notes of a third party. "Sales price" equals the total consideration received including any liabilities assumed by the purchaser, plus the amount of any mortgage on the property, whether or not assumed by the purchaser.

As an example of the calculations necessary to determine if the installment method is available, assume a project sold for $280,000, which consisted of cash payment of $70,000, a purchase money note in the amount of $30,000, and the assumption of the seller's mortgage in an amount equal to $180,000. Assume further that the property had an adjusted basis of $160,000. The transaction could not qualify for installment sales treatment since the amount of payments received in the year of sale exceeded 30% of the sales price. That is:

PAYMENTS IN YEAR OF SALE

Cash	$70,000
Excess of mortgage over basis ($180,000 less $160,000)	20,000
	$90,000

RATIO OF PAYMENTS IN YEAR OF SALE TO SALES PRICE

$$\$90,000/\$280,000 = \$32.1\%$$

If the installment method is available, the taxpayer may spread the recognition of gain over the life of the debt with each payment being apportioned to taxable gain, according to the ratio of gross profit on the sale over the total "contract price." For purposes of such allocation, "contract price" equals the selling price, less any liabilities assumed by the purchaser and less any mortgage on the property, except to the extent the aggregate liabilities or indebtedness exceeds the basis of the property sold.

As an example of the calculation of the portion of each payment to be treated as taxable gain, assuming the sale qualifies for installment sales reporting, assume a project sold for $250,000, which consisted of a cash payment of $70,000, a purchase money note in the amount of $30,000, and the assumption of the seller's mortgage in an amount equal to

$150,000. Assume further that the property had an adjusted basis of $160,000. The gain to be recognized in the year of sale is as follows:

GROSS PROFIT

Sales price less basis	$250,000
	<160,000>
	$ 90,000

CONTRACT PRICE

Sales price less liabilities assumed	$250,000
by buyer	<150,000>
	$100,000

RATIO OF GROSS PROFIT TO CONTRACT PRICE

$$\frac{\text{Gross profit}}{\text{Contract price}} = \frac{90,000}{100,000} = 90\%$$

GAIN TO BE RECOGNIZED IN YEAR OF SALE

$$90\% \times 70,000 = \$63,000$$

In calculating the taxation of sales proceeds using the installment method, consideration must also be given to future dispositions of the installment obligation. Certain dispositions may result in the recognition of all of the income in the year of such dispositions. Consideration must also be given to the imputed-interest rules under Section 483 of the *Internal Revenue Code,* which may reduce the "sales price" for purposes of determining if the 30% test is met. Finally, sellers should provide that installment obligations are not prepayable (at least during the first year) to insure availability of the installment election.

Manner of Disposition

The final important consideration in determining the taxation of real estate dispositions is the manner of the disposition. Real estate can be transferred as a result of a variety of transactions such as a sale, exchange, condemnation, and involuntary conversions (fire, etc.) or foreclosures. Where the transfer is by sale, the taxation of the gains or losses follows the pattern discussed. However, special considerations or sections of the

Internal Revenue Code cover exchanges, condemnations and/or involuntary conversions, and mortgage foreclosures.

EXCHANGE.   Tax on the transfer of real estate in exchange for other real estate can, under certain circumstances, be deferred. The requirements of such "tax-free exchange" treatment include the following:

Purpose of Ownership.   The property to be exchanged must have been held for productive use in a trade or business, or for investment, and must be exchanged for other property to be held for productive use in a trade or business or for investment. Whether or not a particular property has been held for productive use in a trade or business or for investment depends on numerous factors including the investor's intention upon acquisition, the extent of development activities with respect to the property, and the circumstances surrounding the exchange. Investors who acquire property for the purposes of quick turnaround or for conversion to cooperative or condominium units should carefully plan their acquisitions and activities with competent tax counsel in order to minimize the risk that they will be considered dealers.

Like Kind Property.   The property to be exchanged and the property to be acquired must be "like kind." Tax laws and regulations are quite liberal with respect to fee ownership interests in real estate and permit the exchange of very diverse types of property such as raw land for improved property or foreign real estate for U.S. real estate. However, tax laws and regulations are less clear or liberal with respect to exchanges of more exotic ownership interests and rights to real estate. Investors considering the exchange of options, leasehold interests, or promises to locate and acquire property in the future should consult with tax counsel concerning the latest regulations and court cases applying Section 1031 to such interests and rights.

Not Specifically Excluded.   The property must not consist of stocks, bonds, notes, choses in action, certificates of trust or beneficial interest, or other securities or evidences of indebtedness or interest.

Exchange.   The transaction in which the properties are conveyed between the respective parties must be an exchange. The tests applied by the courts in determining whether the transaction is an exchange or merely a sale and reinvestment of funds include: whether or not the respective closings were mutually contingent; whether or not there was sequential deeding (did the parties requiring real estate from transferors deed properties to such transferors); and, whether or not the closings were simultaneous. Recent court decisions are changing many of the traditional views about the necessity for simultaneous closings and sequential deeding, and wise investors should consult with competent tax counsel as to the proper way to structure exchange transactions.

Exchanges may also involve cash or nonqualifying property ("boot"); in which event, gain is recognized to the extent of any boot received. Similarly, property may be transferred subject to a mortgage, in which event the net relief of mortgages is treated as the receipt of boot. Where both cash and mortgages are involved, cash given can offset net relief of mortgages.

CONDEMNATION.   In general, the destruction, theft, or condemnation of property is a taxable event, and the receipt of proceeds in the form of a condemnation award or insurance may produce taxable gain. The *Internal Revenue Code* (Section 1033) provides that, at the election of the owner, gain realized on such an involuntary conversion shall not be recognized if the property converted is replaced within specific time periods by the purchase of like-kind property.

FORECLOSURE.   When property is transferred as a consequence of the default in obligations secured thereby, the transfer may result in taxable gain to the mortgagor even though he receives no cash for his interest. Generally, the amount of gain will be the difference between the mortgage and the taxpayer's adjusted basis. The character of the gain may depend on whether transfer is pursuant to a court foreclosure, a transfer in lieu of foreclosure, or an abandonment.

CHAPTER 5

SPECIFIC REAL ESTATE INVESTMENT OPPORTUNITIES

KNOW THYSELF

Not all real estate investments are good for all types of investors, and not everyone should invest in real estate.

Survival Versus Investing

Most investment analysts suggest strongly that no investment should be made in any type of investment with the investor's last dollar. If the investor cannot afford to lose the investment, perhaps the investment is not appropriate.

Different Types of Investors

There are many differences among various investors including:

Individual investors
    Assets available for investment
    Outside "other" income and need for tax shelter
    Available time for analysis and management
    Preference for safety over risk

Time within which returns are needed
Corporate/institutional investors
Assets available for investment
Yield requirements
Acceptable risk level
Available staff
Time within which returns are needed
Regulatory environment

CRITERIA BY WHICH VARIOUS FORMS OF INVESTMENT DIFFER

While all real estate investments are similar in many respects, there are numerous differences between specific types of real estate investments. For example, the cash flow to be expected from an investment in raw land to be held for long-term speculation differs from the cash flow to be expected from an investment in a 12-unit apartment house in an established residential area. Similarly, changes in economic and population variables do not necessarily affect hotel and motel properties in the same way as such changes affect cash flows from industrial property. A partial list follows of the areas in which specific types of real estate investments may differ from each other:

Cash flow pattern
Appreciation potential
Tax shelter potential
Liquidity
Portfolio flexibility/diversity
Safety of initial investment
Safety of annual earnings
Management time and skill requirements
Availability of and restrictions on financing
Supply and demand determinants
Investment scale required
Sensitivity to government regulations
Optimum investor types

SINGLE-FAMILY HOMES

Advantages and Disadvantages of Owner-Occupied Single-Family Home Investment

The purchase of a single-family home for occupancy is usually the first investment a real estate investor makes. Such an investment has the following advantages over other types of investments:

Low initial investment
Ease of financing
    High leverage
    Long mortgage terms
    Less stringent borrower requirements
    Liberal appraisals
Legal environment favorable to home investors
    Tax laws
        Interest deductions
        Capital gains on sale
        Special gains deferral rules
    Lender-borrower regulations
Responsive to entrepreneurial efforts
    Rehabilitation, renovation
High liquidity
    Refinancing for other purchases
    Refinancing for other purposes
Market participants not sophisticated
Good appreciation potential
Higher safety of initial investment

While an owner-occupied family home has been traditionally considered a good investment, there are certain disadvantages including:

Limited tax shelter potential
    Operating expense deductions not allowed
    Depreciation deductions not allowed
Limited yearly cash flow potential
Limited economies to scale
    Management costs

Advantages and Disadvantages of Investor-Owned Rental Single-Family Home Investment

Some of the factors that make a single-family home an attractive investment vehicle for the owner/occupier also apply in the case of the investor-owned rental single-family unit. Additional potential advantages include:

Portfolio flexibility/diversity if many homes owned
Tenant stability
Minimal management time and effort

In addition to some of the disadvantages listed for the owner-occupied home, investor-owned rental single-family home investments have the following additional disadvantages:

Volatile market
Speculative market
High sensitivity to vacancies
Low yearly cash flow yield
Inefficient use of land

Feasibility Analysis for Single-Family Home Investment

PECULIARITIES OF SINGLE-FAMILY HOUSING DEMAND. The demand for owner-occupied and rental single-family housing is closely tied to all of the economic, monetary, population, and land use variables previously discussed. However, analysis of the competitiveness of a particular residential site involves an additional consideration of variables associated with the renter's or purchaser's "consumer preferences" including:

Commute times and distances
Access to and availability of shopping facilities
Access to and availability of recreational and cultural amenities
Prestige of the community
Quality of schools
Risk of assault, robbery, and so on
Population density
Homogeneity of population
Property tax rates
Quality of community facilities and services

Analysis of the factors listed must not merely include a quantification of the attributes, but should include a consideration of the relative weight renters and purchasers place on the various variables. For example, experienced developers and residential landlords have found that:

Purchasers and renters may prefer a poorer house in a better neighborhood to a better house in a poorer neighborhood.

Purchasers and renters may prefer a better interior to a better exterior for the same price.

Purchasers and renters may prefer better schools to lower taxes.

Purchasers and renters may prefer neighborhoods with fewer children.

Purchasers and renters may prefer better neighborhoods to ease of accessibility.

SINGLE-FAMILY HOME MARKET SEGMENTS. The demand for single-family housing can be broken down into various markets including:

Market	Important Amenities
Singles	Living room area and master bedroom
Young couple, working wife planning a family	Kitchen, master bedroom, secondary bedrooms
Young couple, working wife, no plans for children	Living room/dining room combo, decoration
Divorcees, children at home	Family room, master bedroom
Established family	Formal dining area, separate master bedroom suites
Professional established family	Formal entry/dining areas, guestroom, privacy, and secretary
Empty nesters	Maintenance free, intimate patio deck
Active retired	Secondary bedrooms for hobbies, formal orientation of house

EVALUATING COMPARABLE SALES. Determining whether a prospective purchase is a good bargain involves an analysis of comparable sales within the same area. Data collected should be adjusted for variations in the properties studied including:

Differences in the enclosed spaces
    Room type
    Room sizes
    Room layout
Differences in the land on which the improvement is located
    Size
    Topography
    Soils
    Mineral rights
Difference in access
    Work
    Schools
    Shopping
    Churches
Differences in community services
    Police
    Fire
    Recreation
    Trash removal
Differences in purchaser and seller motivations
    Forced sale
    Estate sale
    Speculative purchaser
    Conversion motivation
Differences in costs to own
    Property taxes
    Commute costs
Differences in legal restrictions
    Zoning
    Easements
    Deed restrictions
Financing
    FHA

Assumable loans

Nature of money market at time of purchase

ANALYSIS OF SINGLE-FAMILY HOME SITES.   The property should be free of hazards like subsistence, flood erosion, and other hazards that could affect the health and safety of the occupants or the structural stability of the building. Potential dangers to be investigated include:

Periodic area and property flooding potential	Site should be free from dangers of flooding associated with streams, watercourses, ocean tides, and street drainage.
Storm drainage flooding	Site should not be near drainage catch basins or drainage channels with histories of overflowing.
Subsistence	Site should not be subject to unusual plot or building settlement.
Erosion	Site should not be subject to erosion from storm water runoff.
Topography	Site should not be adjacent to any unusual land hazards.
Inharmonious uses	Site should not be mixed in with commercial or industrial uses.
Access	Site shall be accessible from public streets. If street is private there should be a recorded maintenance agreement.
Traffic exposure	Site should not be on major arterial highways.
Zoning	Site should not be in an area permitting higher usages.
Common well	Common wells may foretell future difficulties in collecting payments for replacements and in preventing overuse.
Common private sewer line	Common private sewer lines may foretell future difficulties in collecting payments for repairs.

ANALYSIS OF THE PHYSICAL CONDITION OF SINGLE-FAMILY HOMES.   No investment of any type should be made without carefully determining the physical condition of the buildings to be acquired. A partial list follows of things to be checked in inspecting the physical components of a proposed single-family house investment:

Basement
  Walls
    Are there visible signs of water stains?
    Are walls damp?
    Insulation adequate?
  Floors
    Is there evidence of flooding?
    Is there evidence of settling?
  Structural supports
    Are there visible signs of termite damage?
  Stairs
    Are stairs safe?
    Are stairs lighted?
Plumbing
  Fixtures
    Are the fixtures new or in good condition?
    Does each fixture have an accessible cutoff valve?
    Does each fixture work?
  Pipes
    Are pipes free of buildup residue?
    Can all showers, dishwashers, clothes washers, sinks be operated at the same time?
    Are pipes all of uniform material?
    Are connections of pipes with different material specifically insulated to prevent deterioration?
  Sewers
    Is the sewage disposal system connected with a public system?
Electrical system
  Fixtures
    Are fixtures new or in good condition?
    Does each fixture work?
  Wiring
    Does each fixture have a separate switch?
    Is the system able to carry numerous modern appliances?
    Is 220-volt power available?
    Is the wiring up to code?

Is there a circuit breaker system?

External electrical system

Is there outside lighting?

Is there a working doorbell?

Heating

Type/adequacy

Is the heating a central system that is properly ventilated?

Is the heating system adequate, or will dangerous space heaters be required?

Storage for fuel

If heating system requires oil or butane, is the storage capacity sufficient for one full season?

Exterior building components

Foundation

Is the foundation firm and not crumbling?

Is there drainage away from the foundations?

Is the foundation free from sagging and cracks?

Is there foundation shrubbery planting?

Walls

Are wooden walls free from curling or twisting?

Are wooden walls free from termites?

Are wooden walls free from cracks?

Are wooden walls free from dry rot?

Is stucco firm and tight to walls?

Is mortar firm and in place?

Paint

Is paint free from blisters or curling?

Windows

Is there caulking around windows to keep out rain and dust?

Are there awnings or shutters to diffuse sunlight?

Are there screens for windows?

Roof

Is the roof adequately vented?

Is the roof free from cracks and signs of recent repairs?

Is insulation adequate?

Are downspouts adequate to carry away roof water?

Are roof ridges straight?
Chimney
Are chimneys straight?
Are masonry cracks filled?
Are smoke pipe connections rotted or unsafe?
Landscaping
Are there outside faucets?
Is there access to all planted areas?
Is there an outdoor storage area?
Interior building components
Living room
Is there adequate light?
Is there adequate wall space?
Are floors level?
Do floors need refinishing?
Do windows open easily and close tightly?
Are there adequate electrical outlets?
Is there sufficient privacy?
Is there accessible storage?
Is there adequate heating?
Is traffic flow acceptable?
Is shape of living room acceptable?
Is size of living room acceptable?
Dining room
Is there adequate light?
Is there adequate wall space?
Are floors level?
Do floors need refinishing?
Do windows open easily and close tightly?
Are there adequate electrical outlets?
Is there sufficient privacy?
Is there adequate heating?
Is access to living room and kitchen acceptable?
Is there storage for dishes, linens, and such?
Is shape of dining room acceptable?
Is size of dining room acceptable?

Bedrooms

Is there adequate light?

Is there adequate wall space?

Are floors level?

Do floors need refinishing?

Do windows open easily and close tightly?

Are there adequate electrical outlets?

Is there sufficient privacy?

Is there adequate heating?

Is access to bathrooms acceptable?

Is there adequate closet space?

Is there adequate insulation from noise?

Bathrooms

Is there adequate light?

Is there adequate wall space?

Are floors level?

Will floors resist wetness and moisture?

Do floors need repair?

Can floors and fixtures be cleaned easily?

Do windows open easily and close tightly?

Are there adequate electrical outlets?

Is there an electrical outlet near the wash basin?

Is there sufficient privacy?

Is there adequate and safe heating?

Is access to other rooms acceptable?

Is there storage for linens?

Is there a separate shower?

Can all bathroom fixtures be used without affecting use of other fixtures?

Is there a medicine chest?

Are there adequate towel racks?

Is bathroom noise insulated from the remainder of the house?

Do all drains work?

Kitchen

Is there adequate light?

Do windows open easily and close tightly?

Is there adequate ventilation?

Is there adequate wall space?

Are floors level?

Will floors resist wetness and moisture?

Do floors need repair?

Can floors and appliances be cleaned easily?

Are appliance and fixture types acceptable?

Are fixtures and appliances adequate?

Can all plumbing fixtures be used without affecting the use of other fixtures?

Do all drains work?

Are there adequate electrical outlets?

Is location of electrical outlets acceptable?

Is there adequate heating?

Is access to other rooms adequate?

Is location of sinks, appliances, work areas acceptable?

Is there storage space?

Are the size, location, and condition of cabinets acceptable?

Are work surfaces acceptable?

Is there sufficient space for additional appliances?

Are the size and layout of eating spaces and nooks acceptable?

Garages

Is size of garage adequate?

Is access to garage acceptable?

Is garage sufficiently maintained?

Is garage adequately secured?

Stairways

Are stairways sufficiently wide?

Is lighting in stairways adequate?

Are stairways safe?

Single-Family Home Lease Negotiations

While the previous discussion of landlord-tenant law and lease negotiations generally applies to single-family home leases, single-family home leases differ in certain areas such as:

Single-family lease negotiations tend to be informal, and outside professionals are not normally involved.

Single-family landlords and tenants tend to be unsophisticated with respect to their legal rights and economic conditions, generally, and enter into such transactions on an infrequent basis.

The basic single-family rental agreement is frequently not memorialized in a written document, and much of the landlord-tenant relationship is left to local statutes, common law, and custom.

Single-family leases tend to be standardized, form documents.

Tax Factors Pertaining to Single-Family Home Ownership

While much of the previously discussed material concerning taxation of cash flows and residuals applies to single-family home ownership, there are certain tax laws specifically applicable to or highly relevant to single-family home investments.

TAX INCENTIVES FOR HOME OWNERSHIP. The *Internal Revenue Code* contains numerous provisions aimed at facilitating the ownership of homes including:

Interest deductions
Property tax deductions
Deferral of gain on sale
Casualty loss deductions

DEFERRAL OF GAIN UPON SALE OF RESIDENCE. If a homeowner sells a principal residence and within the 18-month period before or after the sale buys a new home, the gain is recognized only to the extent that the adjusted sales price of the old residence exceeds the cost of the new one. For example, assume a home is purchased in 1973 for $35,000 and sold in February 1979 for $60,000. Assume further that a new home was bought in July 1979 for $60,000 and is occupied as the principal residence of the purchaser. The $25,000 gain will not be recognized.

Cost. The cost of a new residence includes: cash payments; the amount of any mortgage or other debt to which the new residence is subject, whether or not the taxpayer assumes the debt; the face amount of any liabilities of the taxpayer that are part of the consideration for the purchase; commissions and other purchasing expenses paid by the taxpayer; and construction and replacement costs.

Adjusted Sales Price.   The adjusted sales price of the old residence is the amount realized reduced by "fixing-up" expenses. Fixing-up expenses are those expenses that:

Are not otherwise deductible personal expenses
Are not capital expenditures
Are paid within 30 days of the sale
Are incurred for work done during the 90 days ending on the day the contract to sell the old residence is made

$100,000 ONE-TIME EXCLUSION.   The *Revenue Act of 1978* grants home-owners 55 years of age and older a once-in-a-lifetime opportunity to exclude up to $100,000 of the gain realized on the sale of a principal residence. There are certain limitations on the exclusion opportunity including:

The taxpayer must be at least 55 years of age before the date on which the residence is sold.

The taxpayer must have owned and used the residence as his or her principal residence for periods totaling at least three years during the 5-year period ending on the date of the sale.

The exclusion may be taken only for the taxpayer's principal residence.

The taxpayer must elect to take the exclusion within 3 years from the date the return for the year in which the residence was sold is due.

APARTMENTS

Advantages and Disadvantages of Apartment Investments

A small or medium-size apartment is usually the next type of investment a real estate investor undertakes. Such an investment has the following advantages over other types of investments:

Relatively stable cash flows
Higher loan-to-value loans available
Good resale market
Less sophistication required
Broad rental market

Efficient use of land

Variety of sizes and prices

Rapid depreciation write-off and high tax-shelter potential

Availability of rehabilitation expenditure deductions

Responsiveness to entrepreneurial efforts

Investments in large apartment complexes may have even additional advantages over investments in smaller apartment units because of decreases in per unit operating costs (due to scale economics) and ease of renting due to the additional amenities (pools, tennis courts) such large apartments may provide.

An investment in an apartment may involve some or all of the following disadvantages:

Relatively low yearly cash flow potential

Higher demands for management time, skill and money

Greater exposure to government regulations

Transient tenants

No key tenants

Low diversification potential

Exposure to shifts in consumer tastes

Exposure to overbuilding and swings in residential construction cycles

Feasibility Analysis for Apartment Investment

DEMAND ANALYSIS.   The demand for apartments is, in many respects, closely tied to the same economic, monetary, and consumer variables affecting the demand for single-family homes. However, there are certain important differences between the characteristics of apartment renters and home renters including:

Apartment renters are more sensitive to commute distances.

Apartment renters are more sensitive to access to public transportation.

Apartment renters are more mobile and willing to move to more attractive, newer, or popular apartments.

Apartment renters are more sensitive to distances to shopping facilities, recreational, and cultural amenities.

Apartment renters are more sensitive to amenities and building age.

Apartment renters' incomes are more vulnerable in periods of recession, and loss of jobs is more frequently experienced by apartment renters than single-family home renters.

Apartment renters tend to be in the lower and upper age brackets.

SUPPLY ANALYSIS.   Because of the effect of consumer tastes, an analysis of the supply of rental apartment units involves more than a mere counting of competitive units, and the analyst must evaluate the qualitative aspects of competing rental units including:

Unit mix
    Adults only
    Number of bedrooms and baths
    Size of units
Amenities available
    Exercise room
    Pools
    Tennis courts
    Golf courses
    Playground
    Garages
    Laundry facilities
    Landscaping
    Community rooms
    Storage spaces
    Security
Services provided
    Door guard
    Utilities
    Main service
    Automatic garages
Lease terms
    Rents
    Options
    Deposits
    Terms
    Nonmonetary covenants

Rental increases
Location on floor plan
  Views
  Level in building
  Corner units
  Distance from amenities
  Distance from parking
Marketing strategy
  Newspaper
  Advertising
  Direct mail advertising
  Models
  Access to street driveways
Tenant programs
  Social functions
  Tours
  Overnight guest suite
  Fitness classes
Image/prestige
  Reputation of building
  Tenant types and mix

FINANCIAL FEASIBILITY ANALYSIS.   All of the previous material concerning the prediction and analysis of cash flow and residuals applies to an investment in an apartment. Investors purchasing smaller apartments usually do not go through the process of a full internal rate of return cash flow analysis but resort to many of the rules of thumb previously discussed including:

Gross income multipliers
Capitalized income value
Breakeven point
Debt service coverage
Cash on cash
Tax saving plus cash flow
Equity buildup, tax savings plus cash flow
Broker's net before interest depreciation and taxes (B.N.B.I.D.T.)

Return on average investment
Margin
Accounting return

In addition to an analysis of the operating costs previously discussed, analysis of apartment cash flows should also include consideration of costs, which may be unique to the locality in which the unit is located. Such costs include:

Cost of compliance with local health, zoning, building, environmental, and business codes
   Trash disposal restrictions
   Elevator maintenance requirements
   Pool health standards
   Occupancy certificates
   Business licenses and taxes
Costs associated with differing legal rights and remedies
   Liability insurance cost differences due to local propensity to favor plaintiffs in lawsuits
   In-house management requirements due to local landlord-tenant laws
   Unlawful detainer cost differences due to local landlord-tenant laws

Finally, knowledgeable apartment investors usually make some provision for a reserve for replacement of such items as:

Refrigerators
Stoves
Sinks
Cabinets
Hot water heaters
Boilers
Furnaces
Roofs
Gutters and downspouts
Incinerators
Electric fixtures
Ventilating fans

Elevator equipment
Air-conditioning equipment
Carpeting
Furniture
Elevator cable
Faucets

ANALYSIS OF PHYSICAL CONDITION OF APARTMENT BUILDINGS. All investments in apartments should be made only after careful analysis of the structure and components, including each and every apartment being purchased and the costs necessary to repair defects. In addition, many investors have made large amounts of money buying properties needing relatively minor renovation and reselling such units based on the higher rents justified by appropriate improvements and repairs. Most of the factors described previously in the analysis of single-family home structures apply in the case of apartment investments. However, additional attention should be directed to the following areas:

Basement
    Is floor level, cracked?
    Is there evidence of settlement?
    Is basement dry?
    Is there adequate electrical service?
    Are walls in good condition?
    Is there evidence of dry rot?
    Is basement vented?
    Is there adequate light?
Plumbing
    Is there individual metering of water supplied to apartment units?
    Are there individual apartment units for each apartment unit?
    Is water system adequate to handle peak demand periods?
    Has there been a regular water heater replacement?
Electrical system
    Is there individual metering to each apartment?
    Is there sufficient common area lighting?
    Will minor changes involve major rewiring to comply with building codes?

Heating

    Is each unit heated on a separate system?

    Is the building adequately insulated?

    Are alternative energy sources/systems available?

Exterior building components

    Walls

        Is insulation between units adequate?

        Is there a regular program of repainting and redecorating?

        Is landlord responsible for cleaning, repairs, and renovating upon termination of tenancy?

    Paint

        Is matching paint on walls within older units obtainable?

    Windows

        Are windows easily replaced and common size?

        Are windows accessible for cleaning, and repairs?

    Roof

        Is the roof insulated against heat loss?

    Landscaping

        Is landscaping well maintained?

        Is landscaping appealing to tenants?

        Are there any dangerous conditions?

    Parking

        Is there adequate parking?

        Is parking area secure?

    Trash areas

        Is trash area accessible?

        Is trash area out of sight?

    Pool/tennis court/exercise room

        Are amenities well maintained?

        Are amenities safe?

    Driveways

        Are driveways in good repair?

        Does traffic flow present liability exposure?

Interior building components

    Flooring/walls

        Is noise insulation adequate?

        Is carpeting quality adequate?

Has there been a regular program for carpet replacement?
Are walls and floors in acceptable condition?
Individual units
Is size of units adequate?
Is size of various rooms within units adequate?
Is mix of units appropriate?
Do units contain clean, adequate, serviceable appliances?
Is layout of unit attractive?
Are draperies, carpets, and furnishings clean and acceptable?
Are units maintained?
Is there excessive deferred maintenance cleaning?
Are plumbing fixtures adequate and serviceable?
Is access to units adequate?
Are units free from disturbances?
Do units have adequate windows and patios?
Are kitchen fixtures adequate and serviceable?
Is heating adequate?
Is air conditioning adequate?
Are there an adequate number of electric sockets?
Is there adequate storage within each unit?
Is traffic flow within each unit acceptable?
Laundry facilities
Are laundry facilities attractive and adequate?
Are laundry facilities accessible and safe?

ANALYSIS OF LEASES AND RENTAL HISTORY. Any purchase of residential apartment units should be preceded by a careful study of leases, rent records, receipts, tenant files, complaint files, and tax returns. A thorough review of such data may reveal information concerning:

Side agreements with tenants
Liabilities to return security deposits
Expiration dates
Rental increase potential
Rent concessions
Rerental difficulties, expenses, and delays
Tenant complaints

Tenant organizations
Rent delinquencies
Late rent payment history
Rent collection problems
Incomparable unit mix
High tenant turnover

Apartment Leasing

DRAFTING APARTMENT LEASES.   Apartment leases tend to be form documents prepared by landlords and, on their face, are usually landlord-oriented. However, there are numerous landlord-tenant statutes that affect the rights of residential landlords and tenants, and the pricing of residential apartment units should reflect the restrictions of such laws. The following is a partial list of specific types of restrictions typically applicable to residential landlords:

Antidiscrimination statutes
    Race
    Color
    Religion
    National origin
    Age
    Sex
    Children
Statutes restricting rental charges
    Local rent control laws
    Federal Price Commission restrictions
    Presidential guidelines
Statutes relating to tenantable premises
    Windows
    Doors
    Plumbing
    Hot and cold water
    Heating
    Electrical
    Pets

Tenant's repair rights
Statutes relating to handling of security deposits
    Amount limits
    Use limits
    Accounting requirements
    Time periods for return
    Ownership upon transfer of landlord's interest
Statutes limiting remedies in the event of default
    Reentry
    Lockouts
    Abandoned property
    Notice requirements
    Curtailing utility services
    Tenant's right to set-off
    Retaliatory eviction
Statutes restricting late charges
Statutes requiring on-premises management
Statutes limiting tenant's ability to contract away rights
Statutes expanding landlord's tort liabilities
    Tenant
    Tenant's invitees
    Common areas
    Entry by outside parties
Statutes prescribing eviction procedures
    Notices
    Time limits
    Waivers
    Tenant's right to raise defenses
Statutes affecting landlord's right in the event of tenant's bankruptcy
    Damage limits
    Restrictions on right to terminate lease

The effect of the restrictions is to substantially reduce the number of items over which landlords and tenants can bargain.

SELECTING APARTMENT TENANTS.   The success of any investment in residential rental property depends on the quality of tenants occupying the apartments. Wise landlords carefully screen tenants in terms of their ability to pay rent, care for their apartment, and compatibility with other tenants. Helpful information includes the following:

Information from employers
Information from prior landlords
Information from banks
Information from personal references
Information from creditors
Information from prior neighbors

Knowledgeable landlords usually obtain such information from tenants on rental applications and verify such information prior to entering into any rental agreements. In addition, many landlords first enter into short-term rental agreements for a "trial run" prior to executing a long-term lease.

Tenant selection should be done in compliance with applicable Federal and state antidiscrimination laws which may prohibit discrimination on the basis of such categories as:

Race
Religion
Color
National origin
Age
Sex
Number of children

In addition, acts such as the Federal Fair Credit Reporting Act, or similar state acts may limit the landlord's ability to obtain and use credit information. Finally, various Federal and state privacy acts may limit the scope of a landlord's inquiry without express permission from the prospective tenant.

Tax Factors Pertaining to Apartment Ownership

All of the previous discussion relating to the taxation of yearly cash flow and residuals applies to the ownership of apartments. In addition, there are certain tax rules that are unique or at least highly significant to apartment ownership.

ACCELERATED DEPRECIATION. Applicable Treasury regulations permit the owners of apartments to use accelerated depreciation methods. The permitted methods are 200% declining balance for new residential real estate, 125% declining balance for used residential real estate acquired after July 24, 1969, and 150% declining balance for used residential real estate acquired before July 25, 1969.

FIRST-YEAR SPECIAL DEPRECIATION ALLOWANCE. Additional first-year special depreciation may be allowed for certain tangible personal property, including furniture.

COMMISSIONS, EXPENSES, AND FEES PAID BY LANDLORDS. Commissions, legal fees, title expense, and so on paid by the landlord normally must be prorated over the life of the lease.

ADVANCE RENTAL DEPOSITS. Advance cash payments of the rent for the last month(s) are normally taxable to the landlord in the year of receipt.

SECURITY DEPOSITS. If the amount received by the landlord is a true security deposit, it is not income to the landlord until the landlord gets an unrestricted right to the money (i.e., when he applies the deposit to the last year's rent). The difference between an advance rental deposit and a security deposit depends on numerous factors including: whether the funds are deposited with an escrow, whether the landlord must pay interest on the deposit, whether the landlord's use of the funds is effectively restricted, and whether the deposit is to be returned upon destruction of the premises.

PAYMENTS TO LANDLORD TO CANCEL A LEASE. Payments made to a landlord to permit the cancellation of a lease are taxable to the landlord in the year of receipt, or accrual, as ordinary income.

TENANT'S IMPROVEMENTS. Unless the tenant's improvements are made in lieu of rent, the landlord does not realize income either when the improvements are made or when he acquires them upon termination of the lease. The increase in value is only taxable when (and if) realized upon a sale of the apartment.

OFFICE BUILDINGS

Advantages and Disadvantages of Office Building Investment

Office buildings include many sizes and types: from massive "skyscrapers" to garden office complexes in the suburbs; from multipurpose downtown buildings to specialized professional buildings. The major advantages of office building investments over other real estate investments include:

Higher potential returns if right location selected
Economies to scale in larger buildings
Relatively efficient use of land
Multitenant buildings can provide cash flow diversification
Key tenants can provide cash flow stability
Rent escalators provide additional inflation protection
Sale-leaseback financing available
Tenant mobility lower than in residential units

Office building investment is a more sophisticated game than residential property investing, and while the returns can be high, the risks are numerous. Among such risks are the following:

Larger investment required
Higher ratio of current costs to revenues
Higher land costs
Supply of competitive space is highly cyclical
Tenants are more sophisticated in lease negotiations
Build-to-suit and tenant work is expected
Management costs may be higher
Tenants expect substantial services

Office Building Feasibility Analysis

QUALITATIVE ANALYSIS OF THE DEMAND FOR OFFICE SPACE. While one would expect the office tenant to be a price-sensitive, economic-oriented consumer, the demand for office space is subject to certain noneconomic variables including:

Office space users are sensitive to locational prestige
    Corporate headquarters
    Advertising exposure
    Financial districts
Office space users are sensitive to amenities
    Parking

Security
In-building shops
Restaurants
Concourses
Conference facilities
Private clubs
Air conditioning
Variable lights
Office space users are sensitive to services
Janitorial
Elevators
Security

QUANTITATIVE ASPECTS OF OFFICE BUILDING SUPPLY ANALYSIS. The potential supply of office space is made up of the following elements:

Existing square footage to be placed on the market
Tenants going out of business
Tenants moving to other areas
Tenants constricting operations
New construction to be available during measurement period
Construction in process
Completion times
Space available from rehabilitation
Space available from conversions
Existing square footage to be taken off the market
New tenants from other areas
New local business start-ups
Expansion of operations by existing tenants
Space demolished
Space converted to other use
Consolidation of outlying operations by existing tenants
Existing vacant space

QUALITATIVE ASPECTS OF OFFICE BUILDING SUPPLY ANALYSIS. While the analysis of existing and future office space is ultimately a counting process, the commodity "office space" actually consists of many gradients including:

Owner-user space versus competitive
Urban versus suburban
Single-purpose versus multipurpose
High-rise versus office park
Prestige location versus fringe location
Office use versus mixed use

In addition to the above "quasi-physical" differences, the same physical space may vary in numerous other respects such as:

Services provided
    Security
    Heating
    Electricity
    Air conditioning
Lease terms
    Rental increases
    Renewal options
    Tenant work
    Landlord's obligations to provide services
    Expenses passed on to tenants
    Landlord's ability to control tenant's use of premises
    Building rules
    Landlord's default rights

QUANTITATIVE ASPECTS OF OFFICE BUILDING DEMAND ANALYSIS. Analysis of the demand for office space is basically a process of predicting the number of persons employed in office-using industries (finance, insurance, and real estate versus mining, farming, and lumber) and the amount of office space such persons will be using. Measuring such variables involves the following considerations:

Factors influencing employment in office-space-using industries include:
    Increases in total employment
        National economic variables
            Gross national product
        Local economic variables

Influx of new industries

Expansion of existing industries

Shifts in employment structure

Service-oriented economy

Two-bread-earner families

Government employment increase

Multishift office doubling up

Factors influencing the space needs of office employees include:

Trends toward increased space utilization by employees

Increased space demands of new office machines (computers, duplicators)

Better communications systems eliminating the necessity for travel and increasing the need for fixed office space (telex, visual phones)

FINANCIAL FEASIBILITY ANALYSIS.   Once the real estate investor has an estimate of future rental revenues based on an analysis of the demand for office building space, financial feasibility analysis consists of applying cash flow and residual analysis techniques similar to those previously discussed.

Operating Expenses.   Generation of operating expense data is facilitated by *The Office Building Experience Exchange Report,* published by the Building Owners and Managers Association International, which publishes data on the following types of operating expenses:

Cleaning

Lighting

Heating

Air conditioning and ventilating

Plumbing systems

Elevator

General expenses

Energy

Tenant alterations

Repairs and maintenance

Fire insurance

Other insurance

Property taxes

Personal property taxes

Expenses Unique to Office Buildings. While all investments in real estate share certain common expenses, such as property taxes, water, and electricity, office building ownership also involves expenses uniquely associated with the business of providing office space to business tenants such as:

Cleaning and janitorial
Parking attendants
Elevator attendants
On-site engineers to handle facilities and equipment breakdowns
Security personnel

Ratios. Alternative investments are frequently compared in terms of the following ratios:

OPERATING RATIO:

$$\frac{\text{operating costs,}\ \text{taxes, insurance}}{\text{gross income}}$$

MANAGEMENT RATIO:

$$\frac{\text{operating costs}}{\text{gross income}}$$

LOAN TO VALUE RATIO:

$$\frac{\text{loan}}{\text{value}}$$

BREAKEVEN RATIO:

$$\frac{\text{debt service and}\ \text{expenses}}{\text{gross income}}$$

DEBT SERVICE COVERAGE RATIO:

$$\frac{\text{net income}}{\text{debt service}}$$

GROSS INCOME MULTIPLIER:

$$\frac{\text{value}}{\text{gross income}}$$

Investors and lenders also evaluate investments in terms of their respective capitalization rates (1/multiplier) and vacancy factors.

ANALYSIS OF THE PHYSICAL CONDITION OF OFFICE BUILDINGS. Office building investments should not be made without a careful analysis of the physical conditions of the buildings located on the site. Such an analysis should be done by a qualified contractor or engineer where the size of the proposed investment justifies the expenses incidental to having such professionals and evaluating the data that they may collect. The following is a partial list of the building areas and components which should be investigated:

Basement
    Are floors level?
    Is there evidence of subsistence?
    Is there adequate ventilation and drainage?
    Are structural supports in good condition?
    Is there adequate electrical service?
Building structure construction
    Is there evidence of cracking?
    Is the building still plumb?
    Is there evidence of material failure?
    Is facade obsolete or unattractive?
    Are there adequate fire walls?
    Are there adequate fire sprinkler systems?
Exterior surfaces
    Are walls in good condition?
    Are walls, windows, sash watertight?
    Are sidewalks in good condition?
    Are entrance walks and steps in good condition?
    Is there adequate drainage away from building area?
Interior lobby
    Is lobby attractive?
    Is lobby properly maintained?
    Is lobby adequate for tenant traffic?
    Is lobby adequately secure?
Building interior surface
    Are walls in good condition?
    Is there adequate insulation between walls?

Is floor covering or carpeting quality adequate?
Are floors and ceilings in good condition?
Heating, air conditioning
Is heating system in good condition?
Is heating system sufficient to heat building?
Is heating fuel storage adequate?
Is air-conditioning system in good condition?
Is air-conditioning system adequate?
Electrical
Is system adequate for present and failure needs?
Are fixtures in good condition?
Are fixtures attractive?
Are fixtures located conveniently?
Are number and type of fixtures adequate?
Plumbing
Is there evidence of age deterioration?
Is system in good condition?
Are washrooms adequately equipped?
Are washrooms in good repair?
Are fixtures in good condition?
Are fixtures adequate?
Elevators
Are elevator machinery and lifting components in good condition?
Are elevator cabs in good condition and attractive?
Is elevator signal system in good condition?
Is elevator service adequate?

ANALYSIS OF OFFICE LEASES AND RENTAL HISTORY.   The purchase of an office building should not be made without a careful analysis of leases, rental records, receipts, tenant files, complaint files, and tax returns. A thorough review of such data may reveal information concerning:

Side agreements with tenants
Liabilities to return security deposits
Lease expiration dates
Cost of living rental increase potential
Rent concessions

Expense increase pass-through potential

Tax increase pass-through potential

High turnover rate

Leasing difficulties

Single-tenant buildings

Collection difficulties

Uncooperative, demanding tenants

Incompatible tenant mix

Excessive utility use

Landlord repair obligations

Landlord service obligations

ANALYSIS OF EMPLOYEE AND SERVICE CONTRACTS PERTAINING TO OFFICE BUILDINGS. The ownership of office buildings involves a considerable number of relationships with employees and suppliers of goods and services. Many times such relationships are set down on contracts to which a prospective purchaser may be bound. Purchases of office buildings should be made only after careful review of such contracts to determine the answers to such questions as:

Are services and materials contracts binding on successor owners?

Are employees represented by unions with which a prospective purchaser will be required to deal?

Are the terms and conditions of such contracts acceptable to the prospective owner?

Will the owner be required to make unacceptable contributions to governmental and private pension plans, disability plans, or other benefits plans?

Drafting Office Leases

Office leases usually start as preprinted, form documents. Where there is a shortage of space and heavy demand by small business, such leases are often executed as drafted. However, it is not unusual for larger tenants to obtain substantial concessions, and leases within the same building often vary greatly from tenant to tenant. Among the more important terms and conditions negotiated by office building owners and tenants are included:

Parties

    Who has authority to lease?

    Is the lessee validly organized and empowered to contract?

Base rent

    When is rent due?

    Are setoffs for landlord's defaults (cleaning, etc.) permitted?

Rental increases

    Is method adequately understood?

        Fixed predetermined increase

        Cost of living increase

    Is base year for such increases adequately defined?

Use of premises

    Is tenant's use of the premises restricted?

    Are there building rules and regulations?

Sharing of expenses or increases and expenses

    Is method of sharing adequately described?

    Is base year for measuring increases adequately defined?

    May tenants challenge increases?

Assignability

    May landlords limit assignments and subletting?

    Under what circumstances can landlord limit assignments and subletting?

Services to be provided by landlord

    What types of services must landlord provide?

        Heat, air conditioning, and so on

    When must such services be provided?

        Business hours, weekends, and so on

    Is tenant's use of certain machines prohibited?

    Is landlord liable for failure to provide services?

Tenant work

    What improvements, alterations must landlord make for tenants?

    What costs must landlord/tenant bear?

Tenant's right to alter

    May tenant make alterations?

    Must landlord approve of the alterations?

    Who pays for alterations?

Must tenant restore premises at termination of tenancy?

Options

Does tenant have an option to extend term of lease?

Does tenant have an option for additional space?

Destruction of premises and eminent domain

Does landlord have to rebuild premises following fire?

Does lease terminate upon a condemnation?

Does tenant share in condemnation proceeds?

Many office buildings are owned subject to underlying ground leases, and leases in such buildings are often subject to those underlying leases. Wise investors should obtain and review copies of such underlying leases.

Tax Factors Unique to Office Building Ownership

Most of the previous material on apartment ownership tax factors is applicable to office building ownership, including:

First-year depreciation allowance to landlord for certain tangible personal property

Commissions, expenses, and fees paid by landlord

Landlord's treatment of advance rental deposits

Landlord's treatment of security deposits

Payments to landlords to cancel lease

Tenant's improvements

In addition, there are certain tax rules that apply more often to office building landlords than to residential landlords.

PAYMENT TO EXTEND A LEASE.   Payments made to a landlord to permit the extension of a lease are taxable to the landlord in the year of receipt as ordinary income.

PAYMENT TO CANCEL A LEASE.   Payments made to a landlord to permit the cancellation of a lease are taxable to the landlord in the year of receipt as ordinary income.

SALE/LEASEBACK TRANSACTIONS.   Office buildings are frequently the subject of "sale/leaseback" transactions wherein an existing owner sells the building and/or land and then leases back the space. Sale/leasebacks have the following potential advantages:

To seller (tenant)
Realization of appreciation in property value
Source of working capital
Deductibility of rent implies ability to depreciate land
Deductibility of rent allows the tenant to "expense" loan amortization payments
To purchaser (landlord)
Tax shelter (depreciation, interest, and operating expenses deductions)
Appreciation potential
Ease of financing owing to existence of key tenants

Sale/leaseback transactions are often disallowed by the Internal Revenue Service as either disguised loans, exchanges, or sale/salebacks. *Rev. Proc.* 75–21 contains guidelines for valid leases including:

Rental payments must not be specifically allocated to repayment of principal.

Title must not pass upon the payment of a certain amount of rent.

Rental payments must not be appreciably higher than current market rental.

Option exercise prices must be at or above market price at time of exercise.

Life of property must exceed lease term by at least ten years.

Residual at end of lease must exceed at least 10–15% of initial cost.

Landlord must have and maintain minimum, unconditional amount at risk equal to 20% (equity, residual).

Tenant cannot loan monies to landlord or guarantee landlord loans.

Transaction must have bona fide profit motive besides tax shelter aspects.

TAX CREDITS FOR HISTORIC STRUCTURES. The Tax Reform Act of 1979 created certain tax incentives to stimulate the preservation and rehabilitation of historic commercial and income-producing structures. If the owner so elects, the rehabilitation costs incurred in "certified rehabilitation" of "certified historic structures" may be amortized over a 60-month period. A "certified historic structure" is one that is either:

Listed in the National Register of Historic Places

Located in an historic district that is listed in the National Register of Historic Places and certified by the Secretary of the Interior as being of historic significance to the district

Located in an historic district that is designed under a statute (including an ordinance) of a state or local government, but only if the state or local statute authorizing establishment of the district is certified by the Secretary of the Interior as containing criteria that substantially achieve the purpose of preserving and rehabilitating historic buildings

Tax Factors Unique to Office Space Tenants

Since office space tenants are usually in a trade or business, certain deductions are available to them that are not available to residential tenants.

AMORTIZATION OF TENANT IMPROVEMENT COSTS. The costs incurred by a tenant in the making of permanent improvements are normally a capital investment and not deductible as an expense. Such costs must be amortized over the life of the lease or depreciated over the life of the improvements if such life is less than the term of the lease. On the other hand, where the tenant is permitted to make certain improvements and to reduce the rent by express agreement with the landlord, such costs are deductible. Repairs and replacements are currently deductible.

PAYMENTS TO CANCEL LEASE. Payments to a tenant to permit cancellation of a lease are normally subject to capital gains treatment. Payment made to a landlord for cancellation of a lease are deductible by the tenant as a current business expense. On the other hand, payments made to a tenant by a landlord constitute the cost of a property right, not a currently deductible loss or expense, and must be amortized by the landlord.

ADVANCE RENT DEPOSITS, SECURITY DEPOSITS. Tenants may deduct such payments only in the year in which they forfeit the deposit for failure to comply with the condition for which it was deposited or in the year to which the advance payment is applied.

INVESTMENT TAX CREDIT. Tenants may qualify for an investment tax credit on certain depreciable personal property purchased for use in their business.

RETAIL SITES

Types of Retail Sites

Investing in retail sites can take numerous forms including the following:

Strip stores	Buildings along downtown highways
Neighborhood shopping centers	Major tenant is a supermarket or large drugstore
Special retail centers	Architecturally stylized retail plaza
Community shopping centers	Major tenant is a junior department store—may include banks, professional offices
Regional shopping centers	One or two major department stores—includes general merchandise, apparel, and service establishments

While strip stores and neighborhood shopping centers are frequently owned by individual investors without any particular expertise, investment in larger shopping centers is usually undertaken by experienced, knowledgeable, and financially able investment groups, and involves complicated analysis, planning, financing, leasing, and management problems.

Advantages and Disadvantages of Investments in Retail Sites

The major advantages of ownership of property leased to retail establishments include:

Cash flow potential due to overage arrangements
Ease of financing if key tenants available
Increased tax shelter if land leased
Monopoly opportunities if neighboring land unavailable
Competition to acquire small centers lower than for similar size apartments, office buildings

Investment in retail sites involves certain risks common to all real estate investments as well as certain potential problems unique to reliance on retail tenants for cash flow, including:

High risk of new centers
Rentals tied to consumer spending patterns
Inefficient land use
Scale of investment high
High management and service requirements
Shorter loan amortization periods
High risk of obsolescence
Closer and more complex relationship with tenants
Owner shares risks of tenant failure

Feasibility Analysis for Investments in Retail Sites

PERCEPTIONS OF CUSTOMERS OF STORES IS AN ADDED VARIABLE. Feasibility analysis for investments in retail sites starts with the same principles of demand, supply, and cash flow analysis as all other forms of investment. However, investment in retail sites must also consider additional factors related to the behavior, needs, and perceptions of the customers of stores in such retail sites, including:

Tenant mix
Style
Promotional programs
Location of competitive centers
Attitudes of residents and customers toward center
Image of center
Prestige of center

ANALYSIS OF TRADING AREA AND SALES POTENTIAL. Investments in retail sites should not be made without first determining if there is an existing, clearly defined, and substantial trade area from which potential tenants can draw customers. Ideally, tenants in potential retail sites are able (or will be able) to draw customers free from the competition of other centers.

Trade Area Delineation. Determining the trade area for a particular center and measuring whether such a trade area will support a retail site involves a consideration of such factors as:

Travel distances
Travel times
Consumer perception of travel distance and time

Highway patterns

Relationship to other retail centers

Use of adjoining and neighboring land

Supply of space in neighboring centers

Consumer retail expenditure patterns

Attitudes of consumers to other retail centers

Appropriateness of potential tenant mix to community socioeconomic character

Determining the trade areas is often done by professional research companies.

Sales Potential.   Once the trading area is defined, measuring sales potential is a conceptually simple process of determining:

The number of household *a*

The median income in such households *b*

The percentage of such household's annual income spent on items to be sold (or selling) in the stores to comprise (or comprising) the shopping center *c*

Multiplying the items together ($a \times b \times c$)

Need for Retail Space.   Measuring the need for space in the retail site is a conceptually simple process of multiplying:

$$\text{potential sales in retail site stores} \times \begin{array}{l}\text{average square foot} \\ \text{per dollar sales of} \\ \text{store types making} \\ \text{up retail site}\end{array}$$

Threshold Analysis.   Another approach to analyzing space needs is called "threshold analysis" and consists of multiplying (*a*) the minimum number of persons in a trading area necessary to support the types of stores in the proposed (or existing) retail site, by (*b*) the population in the trading area, and measuring the amount so obtained against the number of existing stores of the same type within the area.

SITE ANALYSIS.   Investments in retail sites require careful consideration of numerous variables related to the land, buildings, and their location, including:

Physical characteristics of the land
    Soil, drainage, slope, vegetation
Basic services available to the land
    Water, sewers, roads, telephone, gas, electricity, refuse removal
Location
    Intersections of major highways
    Nearest pattern of primary traffic arteries in relation to site
    Pattern of secondary traffic arteries in relation to site
    Visual exposure from major highways
    Travel times from competition
    Frontage along major arteries
    Distance to customers
    Distance from competition
Size and shape
    Parking, contiguousness of site
Access
    Major traffic arteries
    Traffic signals
    Major traffic intersections
    Public transportation systems
    Traffic patterns or flow that does not generate shoppers
Restrictions on use of site
    Easements
    Zoning
    Building codes
Governmental regulation of site
    Planning boards
    Zoning boards
    Pollution control boards
    Highway departments
    Health, fire, and safety departments
Layout
    Pedestrian traffic circulation
    Dead spots that cause shoppers to lose interest
Adjoining land uses
    Zoning

Competitive centers
Adjoining area growth potential
Condition of structures
Obsolescence
Deferred maintenance
Heating, air conditioning
Covered malls
Aesthetics
Uncontrolled signs, trash
Separate from customer flow
Loading facilities
Rental history
Frequent shifts of occupants
Shifts of tenant types
Retail to nonretail or service
Vacancy rate

ANALYSIS OF COMPETITION.   The following is a partial list of the factors and data to be gathered for an analysis of existing competitive facilities:

Types of stores
Nature of major anchor tenants
Size of stores
Width/depth
Size of store fronts
Variety of stores
Breadth of selection
Compatibility of groupings
Merchandising ability of tenant stores
Adequacy of service
Price competitiveness
Management abilities
Physical aspects of center
Quality of construction
Malls
Open or closed
Mall embellishments

Widths
Air conditioning/heating
Service facilities
　Loading areas
Lighting
Security
Parking facilities
　Drainage
　Access
Accessibility from highway
Traffic flow within center
Travel time to/from population centers
Cleanliness and maintenance of center
　Necessary renovations
Style obsolescence
Use of peripheral land
　Free standing stores

TENANT MIX.　The tenant mix in a proposed or existing retail site affects potential return in numerous ways including:

Drawing power of the center
　One-stop center versus specialty center
Image of the center
　Surplus stores versus Saks Fifth Avenue, for example
Traffic flow
　Banks and professional service establishments versus eating and recreational establishments
Complementary demands on facilities and parking
　Banks versus bars, theaters
Effectiveness of joint promotional activities
　Auto dealer versus apparel
Overage potential
　Department stores versus ice cream stores
Stability of income
　Banks versus camera stores
Maintenance requirements

Service stations versus banks
Necessity for lease restrictions on goods offered for sale
Drug stores versus variety stores
Compatibility or drawing power
Shoe, clothing, and sporting goods stores versus appliance, radio, television, and musical instrument stores
Parking and access needs
Supermarkets and drug stores versus apparel and bookstores
Compatibility of customer class
Post offices, auto supply versus china, jewelry, and silver stores
Size of items
Furniture stores versus drug stores

TENANT LOCATION.   Not only is the proper tenant mix important, but also the location of tenants within the center is important. Factors to consider include:

Grouping of tenants with similar lines
Grouping stores versus variety, drug
Hardware, appliance versus food
Location of tenants in relation to parking
Personal service, drug, variety versus furniture, appliances, musical instruments
Location of tenants in relation to customer shopping behavior
Personal service, drug, variety versus furniture, appliances, musical instruments
Location of tenants in relation to traffic flow
Locating key tenants apart
Exposure of other tenants to traffic flow

LEASE TERMS.   Analysis of an investment in real estate used for retail sites must consider subtle differences in lease terms including:

Rent obligations
Fixed (minimum)
Overages
Term of lease
Landlord's obligations

Landlord work
Common areas maintenance
Maintenance of tenant's areas
Janitorial
Security
Promotion and advertising
Merchants Association
Tenant's rights
Renewal options
Options for additional space
Alterations
Remodeling
Management Associations
Restrictions on landlord
Leases to competing tenants
Restrictions on leasing other space owned by landlord
Hours of operation
Restrictions on tenants
Product lines
Operations in other centers
Expense sharing
Utilities
Taxes
Promotion
Operating expenses
Security deposits
Amount
Conditions under which landlord may use

OWNERSHIP INTEREST TO BE ACQUIRED.   Investment in retail sites may involve numerous parties, including:

Center developer
Land, mall, satellite buildings, parking
Financial institutions
Satellite buildings
Major department store
Department store buildings and land

MANAGEMENT, MAINTENANCE, AND OPERATIONS PROBLEMS.   While all
types of real estate involve management, maintenance, and operational
problems, retail sites present unique problems, including:

Sign control
Common area maintenance and security
Advertising and promotion
Parking regulation
Traffic control
Arrival and shipment of goods
Tenant's employee labor problems
Trespassers

INCOME AND EXPENSE ANALYSIS.   Retail sites involve numerous potential sources of income. The following is a list of some of the types of
income that a retail site owner may realize:

Minimum (base) rent
Cost of living increases
Overage rents
Mall rental charges
Common area rental charges
Heating/air-conditioning charges
Tax contributions
Common area maintenance charges
Expense reimbursement charges

Similarly, retail sites involve numerous expense categories including:

Building maintenance expenses
Mall maintenance expenses
Roof repair and maintenance expenses
Parking lot maintenance expenses
Painting and decorating expenses
Public area electricity charges
Public area water charges
Public area heating charges
Public area gas charges

Public area ventilation charges
Public area repair and maintenance expense
Fire sprinkler maintenance and repair
Escalator maintenance and repair
Elevator maintenance and repair
PA system maintenance and repair
Music system maintenance and repair
Service telephone maintenance and repair
Burglar and security system maintenance and repair
Landscaping maintenance and upkeep
Shopping center personnel payroll
Snow removal
Garbage removal
Janitorial
Fire insurance
Unemployment insurance
Boiler insurance
Workers compensation insurance
Plate glass insurance
Liability insurance
Legal
Accounting
Property taxes

FINANCIAL ANALYSIS. Analysis of cash flows from investments in retail sites is similar to the analysis of cash flows from other types of real estate investments and involves a consideration of such previously discussed ratios as:

Debt service coverage
Operating expense ratio
Vacancy and collection loss
Break-even ratio
Gross return on assets
Leasable area to total area
Loan to value
Capitalization rate

Loan per square feet
Property taxes per square foot
Minimum rent per square foot
Overage income to total gross income

Retail Site Lease Negotiations

SIZE OF TENANT MAY AFFECT LEASE NEGOTIATIONS. Negotiating leases for retail space with large, key tenants may differ significantly from negotiations with smaller satellite tenants. Key tenants are often able to win substantial concessions from landlords who need such tenants to obtain financing and to provide income stability. On the other hand, leases to smaller tenants tend to be more landlord-oriented.

CONSTRUCTION AND PERMANENT LENDER REQUIREMENTS. Lenders frequently require certain provisions in shopping center leases including:

Attornment clauses requiring the tenants to recognize the lenders' interest
Limits on tenant's rights to terminate lease
Limits on tenant's rights to prepay rent
Escalation clauses
Property and liability insurance
Limits on landlord's successor's obligations

RENT. There are numerous types of rental provisions available to retail landlords and tenants, including:

Fixed rent
Fixed rent with escalator clauses
    Taxes, operating expenses, interest
Stepped-up rent
    Rental increases at fixed intervals
Net leases
    Payment of all taxes, operating expenses
Percentage leases
    Percentage rental offset by minimum rental
    Minimum rental added to percentage rental
    Percentage rental no minimum

Percentage of appraisal

Rental increase based on percentage increase in property value

Fixed rent tied to consumer price index

Increases in rent corresponding to consumer price index increases

RESTRICTIVE COVENANTS. Tenants often want various rights with respect to other tenants (exclusives) and restrictions on landlord's uses of other property (radius clauses). Similarly, landlords often want to restrict tenants from opening other stores or establishments within certain distances from the retail center (trade area limitation). A sample follows of the types of radius clauses and exclusives tenants and landlords have negotiated:

Right to approve or disapprove of the entry of any other tenant

Right to limit discount selling or advertising

Right to limit the types of merchandise or services that any other tenant may offer for sale

Right to approve or disapprove the location of any other tenant

Right to prescribe the minimum hours of business operation of other tenants

Right to require balanced and diversified groups of retailers, merchandise, and services

Right to require that reasonable standards of appearance, signs, maintenance, and housekeeping be maintained

Right to terminate agreement to become tenant if developer does not obtain another major tenant acceptable to tenant's standards

Many of the exclusives, radius clauses, and trade area limitations landlords and tenants negotiate involve actual or potential violations of antitrust laws. Whether a particular clause violates antitrust laws depends on a variety of subtle criteria, and such clauses should not be negotiated without the advice of competent counsel. For example, in *Payless Drug Stores, Northwest, Inc. v. City Products Corp.,* [1975-2] Trade Cases ¶ 60,385 (D. Ore. 1975), a court held that a restrictive covenant (exclusive) that prohibited a landlord from leasing any property owned by the landlord located within 3,000 feet of the tenant's premises for a "variety store" violated Section 1 of the Sherman Antitrust Act, 15 U.S.C. § 1, because the dynamics of the market and the unavailability of alternate sites in the vicinity indicated that exclusion of another "variety store" would seriously restrain competition in the marketplace. On the other hand, in *Mendell v. Golden-Farley of Hopkinsville, Inc.*, [1978-1] Trade Cases ¶ 61,814 (Ky. 1978), a court held that a restrictive covenant (exclusive) that prohibited a landlord from leasing shopping center space to other stores selling "medium to better priced men's and boy's clothing" was not in violation of Kentucky's antitrust laws because it was narrowly drawn and would not seriously restrain competition in the marketplace.

COMMON AREA CHARGES. Retail sites involve numerous costs associated with common areas including:

Repairs
Parking line painting
Landscaping
Security protection
Bulb replacement
Cleanup
Snow removal
Garbage and refuse removal
Employees' wages and salaries including payroll taxes and workmen's compensation
Liability and property damage insurance
Real property taxes attributable to common areas
Legal expenses incurred in contesting real property tax assessments or in controlling picketing and labor disputes affecting common areas
Audit expense
Depreciation on machinery and equipment
Overhead and other costs of operating common areas

TENANT'S USE OF PREMISES—OBLIGATION TO CARRY ON BUSINESS. The lease should state the use that the tenant is to make of the premises and contain a covenant not to use the premises for any other purposes. Percentage lease provisions may imply an obligation to make reasonable efforts to carry on business and make profits upon which percentage rentals are based. Landlords occasionally require tenants to obtain insurance against business interruptions.

MERCHANT'S ASSOCIATION. Most leases provide for a Merchant's Association. Such clauses should cover such areas as the following:

Owner's role in the association
Assessments
   Amount
   Manner of levy
   Penalties for nonpayment
Voting
   Allocation of votes
   Cumulative voting
Activities of the association
   Promotional
Enforcement powers of the association

Tax Problems Unique to Investments in Retail Sites

DEPRECIATION OF LANDLORD'S IMPROVEMENTS. A capital improvement purchased or constructed by the landlord may normally be depreciated over its useful life. However, the amount of the landlord's depreciation will vary with the tenant's obligations to maintain the premises and to return the premises in the condition existing at commencement of the lease. "Ordinary wear and tear excepted," usually will not prevent the landlord from claiming a full depreciation deduction. However, if the tenant agrees to "maintain and restore the premises and, at the termination of the lease to return the premises in the same condition as that in which they were received," the landlord may be entitled only to a limited amount of depreciation based on obsolescence.

DEPRECIATION OF TENANT'S TRADE FIXTURES. A tenant will often install signs, light fixtures, display equipment, or other trade fixtures with useful lives that exceed the terms of the lease. As long as the trade fixtures are removable, the tenant must depreciate them over their respective lives despite the fact that the lease term is shorter than their useful lives.

TENANT IMPROVEMENTS. A tenant has the option of depreciating the cost of nonremovable improvements over their useful life or, if the lease term is shorter, amortizing the cost over the term of the lease.

PROPERTY TAX PAYMENTS BY TENANT. A tenant normally may deduct taxes paid under rent clauses providing for such payment. If the tenant pays real and personal property taxes assessed against the landlord's property, or reimburses the landlord for the amount of such taxes, the tenant's deduction usually will be in the form of additional rent. The landlord will be required to report as additional rental income the amount of such payment, and the landlord will be entitled to take an offsetting deduction for the taxes paid.

MAINTENANCE EXPENSES PAID BY TENANT. Tenants frequently perform ordinary operating maintenance on their premises. The tenant is entitled to deduct normal maintenance as a current business expense. However, where maintenance expenses result in a betterment of the premises or an alteration with a useful life beyond the current taxable year, the expense may have to be capitalized.

INDUSTRIAL REAL ESTATE

Advantages and Disadvantages of Industrial Real Estate Investments

Ownership of industrial real estate can be an excellent form of investment involving the following potential advantages:

Stability of revenue if the property is leased to prime tenant
Limited down-side risk if the property is leased to prime tenant
Minimal management responsibilities if the property is leased on triple-net basis
Potential monopoly pricing if neighboring land is unavailable
Potential tax shelter from efficient use of land
Reduced sensitivity to neighborhood economic decline
Reduced risk of landlord-tenant problems

Ownership of industrial real estate can take place on numerous scales from small industrial buildings to large industrial parks. Investments in industrial parks can provide the investor with certain additional advantages including increased stability of income due to diversification and increased ability to adjust cash flows as leases terminate.

Ownership of industrial real estate can also involve certain risks, including:

Need for large capital investment
Relative lack of liquidity due to infrequent trading

Higher exposure to governmental controls

Higher property tax rates

Changes in production technology may make investment obsolete

Appreciation potential less

Tenant sophistication in lease negotiations

Tenant price consciousness

Relative inability to adjust lease rents to inflation

Buildings are often single-user, custom construction

Where industrial real estate ownership takes the form of industrial parks, additional risks may be present, including:

Management problems in policing Covenants, Conditions and Restrictions (CC&R's), rules, and regulations

Higher scale of investment

Competition from development of adjoining acreage

Feasibility Analysis for Industrial Real Estate Investments

SUPPLY AND DEMAND ANALYSIS.   The demand for specific types of industrial space depends on trends in employment in industries likely to use such space and the space needs of the employees in such industries.

Employment Trends.   Trends in employment depend on the whole spectrum of variables previously discussed (economic, demographic, etc.). However, changes in such aggregate variables do not necessarily affect employment in all industries in the same way. For example, employment in the railroad industry is less sensitive to population changes than is employment in the automobile industry. Thus, an accurate estimate of the increase in employment in a particular area must first account for the specific types of industries in (or to be located in) the area and the effect of aggregate employment or economic changes on those specific industries.

Space Needs of Industrial Employees.   The space needs of employees varies considerably from industry to industry. For example, apparel manufacturers have very low square footage/employee ratios, while stone, clay, and glass products manufacturers have very high square footage/employee ratios. Thus, an accurate estimate of the demand for industrial space must take into account variations, within certain industries, of employee space needs.

Locational Preferences among Various Industries.   Industrial space users' locational decisions are in great part determined by their labor, material, and transportation needs. For example, certain industries are resource-oriented and need to locate near a specific natural resource (iron ore) or fuel (coal) used or needed in their production process. Similarly, other firms require specific labor skills (engineers) and need to locate in areas where such skills are plentiful. Other firms produce products that are expensive to transport to their markets or that require frequent servicing (computers) and need to locate close to their markets to minimize such transportation or servicing costs. Thus, any analysis of employment trends and space needs must also account for the locational preferences of certain industrial groups.

LOCATIONAL ANALYSIS. *Factors Important to All Industrial Users.* Whether a specific industrial use will find a particular locality attractive depends on numerous variables, including:

Basic materials, services
    Distance to raw materials
    Costs of construction of facilities
    Availability of storage facilities
    Availability of support services
        Subcontractors, attorneys, C.P.A.'s, technical services
Power and fuel
    Type
    Rate
    Capacity
    Record of interruptions
Transportation
    Raw materials transportation costs
    Water transportation
    Air service
    Highways
    Rail service
    Pipelines
Labor market
    Availability of skilled labor
        Age, sex
    Labor costs
        Minimum wage laws, overtime

Management-labor attitude, union dominance
Vocational training facilities, local training incentives
Labor laws, right-to-work, safety laws
Labor productivity
Controls, covenants limiting use
  Zoning
  Master plans
  Building codes
  Occupational safety laws
  Deed restrictions
  Environmental restrictions
  Traffic restrictions
  Activist groups
Community facilities
  Fire and police
  Medical facilities
  Recreational facilities
  Churches
  Educational facilities
  Shopping facilities
  Meeting facilities
Local governmental attitude
  No-growth policies
  Industrial promotion programs
  Revenue bond financing programs
  Direct loan programs
  Planning commission attitudes
  Policies with regard to zoning variances and zoning changes
Taxes
  Inventory tax exemptions
  Sales/use tax exemptions
  Material-in-process exemptions
  Personal income tax rate
  Property tax rate
  Franchise, corporate income tax rate
  Workmen's compensation tax rate

Gasoline taxes
Vehicle license tax
Local operating costs
Insurance costs
Business license fees

Factors Important to Specific Industrial Users.   Not all of the foregoing factors are equally important to all industrial users. For example, large, mature industrial firms may place more emphasis on the availability of local investment capital, labor, and transportation; smaller industrial firms may place more emphasis on land for expansion. Similarly, manufacturers may emphasize the availability of land for expansion and the costs of labor; service-oriented firms may emphasize commercial accessibility and the aesthetics of the site.

SITE AND BUILDING ANALYSIS. Factors Important to all Industrial Users. Whether a specific industrial user will be suitable for a particular site depends on numerous variables, including:

Site attributes
    Total area
    Soil bearing capacity
    Shape, topography, contours
    Frontage, depth
    Grading, drainage, floor risks
    Earthquake risk
    Advertising value of site
    Competing neighboring uses
    Easements, restrictions, zoning, setback requirements
    Building, fire, safety code requirements
    Access, highway, rail, water, airline
    Community services, garbage, electricity, water, gas, parking
Building attributes
    Floor space
        Amount
        Shape or conformation of usable space
        Floor load ratings
        Type of construction

Condition
  Deferred maintenance
  Slope, drainage
Roof
  Size
  Type of construction
  Ceiling heights
  Condition
  Deferred maintenance
  Ventilation facilities
Windows
  Number
  Location
  Type
  Size
  Condition
  Deferred maintenance
Columns
  Spacing
  Number
  Location
  Condition
Loading facilities
  Number of docks
  Size of docks
  Dimensions of doors
  Protection from weather
  Capacity
  Access to transportation routes
Office facilities
  Size
  Layout
  Location
  Lighting
  Partitions
  Air conditioning

Insulation
Elevators
   Type
   Size
   Capacity
   Location
   Condition
   Deferred maintenance
Cranes
   Type
   Number
   Size
   Location
   Condition
   Deferred maintenance
Lighting
   Type
   Number
   Size
   Location
   Condition
   Deferred maintenance
   Operating costs
Water
   Source of water service
   Size of main
   Size of meter
   Location
   Capacity
   House tanks
   Pressure
   Domestic hot water system
   Condition of fixture
   Deferred maintenance
Sewer
   Source of sewer service

Size of pipe
Restrictions on use
Location
Costs
Gas
Source of gas service
Size of main
Location
Limitations on use
Costs
Fire prevention system
Sprinklers
Fire extinguishers
Miscellaneous equipment, facilities
Type
Fences
Liquid storage facilities
ADT
Communications system
Muzak
Floor scales
Air and steam lines
Other
Condition
Capacity
Deferred maintenance

Factors Important to Specific Industrial Users. Not all of the foregoing factors are equally important to all industrial users, and different combinations of characteristics may be attractive to one type of user whereas other combinations may be more attractive to other users. For example:

Buildings with high walls and few windows make good warehouses.

Buildings with lower walls and many windows make good assembly or manufacturing uses.

Level floors are essential for most assembly or engineering operations.

However, sloping floors with drainage are essential for food processing uses, which require washing down floors.

Buildings with high, open ceiling space are easier to cool without air conditioning, but harder to heat.

Warehouse and distribution uses require minimal lighting. However, assembly and manufacturing uses require substantial lighting.

Warehouse and distribution uses normally require fewer toilet and washroom facilities than do manufacturing, office, and assembly operations.

Industrial Lease Negotiations

As with retail and office space leases, industrial space leases tend to be landlord-oriented where the tenant is weak and highly customized where the tenant is strong. Industrial leases differ from retail and office leases in many ways including the following:

More likely to be ground leases

More likely to be triple-net leases

More likely to involve substantial tenant work

More attention may be paid to ownership/disposition of improvements and reversionary interest in land at termination of lease

More likely to be for longer terms

Tax Factors Unique to Industrial Property

INVESTMENT TAX CREDIT. The investment tax credit is an incentive device intended to stimulate the purchase or modernization of certain types of productive assets. Real property, other than buildings and their structural components, is eligible if it is an integral part of the business process and is depreciable in nature. Elevators and escalators are eligible.

The maximum credit allowable in any year is limited to the sum of the tax liability for the taxable year or $25,000, whichever is less, plus, depending on the taxable year, up to 90% of the tax liability for the taxable year in excess of $25,000.

Qualified Investment. If new "qualified property" has an investment credit life of 7 years or more, its qualified investment is its basis. Otherwise, the qualified investment equals 66 2/3% of its basis if its life is 5 years or more but under 7 years, or 33 1/3% of its basis if its life is 3 years or more but under 5 years. The maximum basis available for used property is $100,000.

Qualified Property.   Generally the investment tax credit is not available for other than depreciable, tangible personal property. However, qualified property also includes, under certain circumstances: elevators and escalators; other tangible property consisting of inherently permanent structures (other than a building or its structural components) used in manufacturing, production, or in furnishing transportation, communication, or other public utility services, or related research or storage facilities; certain pollution control facilities; and rehabilitation expenditures (in tax years ending after October 31, 1978) for industrial or commercial buildings so used for 20 years or more.

Recapture of Investment Credit.   If before the end of the life period used to compute the credit, the property is disposed of or ceases to qualify for the credit, part or all of the credit will be recaptured.

Buildings and Their Structural Components.   Buildings and their structural components don't qualify for the investment tax credit. However, property used in connection with the furnishing of motel or hotel lodging may qualify for the credit. In addition, elements of a building may be eligible if they have a special purpose other than sheltering a normal work space or dwelling area.

Limitations on Noncorporate Lessors.   Noncorporate lessors, including Subchapter "S" corporations, can only claim the credit if the property subject to the lease has been manufactured or produced by the lessor; or if the term of the lease, including options to renew, is less than 50% of the property's useful life, and the lessor's expense deductions, other than those specifically allowable by the *Internal Revenue Code*, with respect to the property, exceed 15% of the first year's rental income.

LAND

Ways to Invest in Land

Investments in land usually take one of four primary forms: (1) pure land speculation, (2) purchase of land for development and resale, (3) investment in land for its current cash flow pending a change in use or demand, and (4) investments in rural recreation-oriented subdivisions produced by others. In the case of a purchase of land for speculation, the investor hopes to hold the land until a change in land use patterns or demand occurs. In the case of the land developer, the developer intends to perform certain entrepreneurial activities with respect to the land such as obtaining a zoning change, a subdivision permit, or grading the land and installing roads or sewers and selling the land at a profit. In the case of a purchase of land currently producing cash flows, the investor usually intends to receive current cash flows and tax shelter and future land value appreciation as local land use patterns and demands change.

Advantages and Disadvantages of Investments in Land

While all land investment forms involve similar advantages and disadvantages, there are some important differences between the various forms outlined in the following sections.

ADVANTAGES OF RAW LAND SPECULATION

High potential for appreciation
   Land use pattern shift may create rapid value increase
   Zoning changes may increase value of land due to new transportation routes
   Change in accessibility
Small capital may accomplish the control of large acreage
   Use of options may enable investor to tie up property
   Seller financing may permit low cash purchase
Carrying charges low compared to metropolitan property
   Taxes
   Maintenance
   Insurance
Capital gains treatment of sales proceeds may be available
   Dealer status problems may be avoided if appreciated acreage is sold in bulk
   Section 1237 of the *Internal Revenue Code* may provide a safe harbor for limited subdivision activities

DISADVANTAGES OF RAW LAND SPECULATION

High risk
   Profits only to come from uncertain future appreciation
Little tax shelter
   Land is not depreciable

Timing accurately is important

    Present value of future residual value declines as holding period increases

Financing opportunities are limited

    Lenders usually loan only on low loan-to-value (L/V) ratios

    Only limited funds may be available owing to government regulations imposed on lenders

Limited liquidity

    Market may be limited to other speculators

Little current cash flow

Interim uses may not be feasible

Appreciation potential may depend on unpredictable forces

    Subjective and chargeable policies of local planning authorities

    Uncertain and difficult to predict shifts in consumer tastes as to location preferences

    No-growth policies imposed by local authorities on electorates

    Coastal regulations

    Environmental control regulations

ADVANTAGES OF LAND DEVELOPMENT

High potential appreciation

    Zoning changes or the procuring of subdivision approval may produce incremental profits

Good vehicle for obtaining profits for entrepreneurial efforts

    Zoning changes, subdivision approvals

    Grading, improvements

    Creative marketing

Financial institutions may finance development activities by joint venturing

    Land warehousing

    Development joint ventures

DISADVANTAGES OF LAND DEVELOPMENT

Ordinary income tax treatment of proceeds unless requirements of Section 1237 of the *Internal Revenue Code* are met

Carrying costs high
  Interest
  Taxes
  Regulatory fees
  Engineering costs
Development activities are subject to extensive governmental regulation
  Zoning
  Subdivision map act requirements
  Environmental Impact Reports (E.I.R.) requirements
  No-growth
  Coastal regulation

ADVANTAGES OF INVESTMENTS IN INCOME-PRODUCING LAND

Predictable cash flow from interim use may help reduce risk
  Crops
  Golf course greens fees
  Parking fees
  Hunting fees
Tax shelter potential for certain interim uses
  Farm losses
  Depreciation of improvements
Appreciation potential
  Land use pattern shifts
  Increasing demands for land using activity
Capital gains treatment of sales proceeds
  Dealer status problems may be avoided if appreciated acreage is sold in bulk
  Section 1237 of the *Internal Revenue Code* may provide a safe harbor for limited subdivision activities

DISADVANTAGES OF INVESTMENTS IN INCOME-PRODUCING LAND

Local legislation may fix use permanently
  Coastal regulation acts
  Open space acts
  Farmland preservation policies of governmental agencies

Tax law revisions may change or alter treatment of cash flows and availability of tax shelter

Hobby loss limits imposed by Revenue Act of 1976

ADVANTAGES OF INVESTMENTS IN RURAL, RECREATIONAL-ORIENTED LAND DEVELOPMENTS PRODUCED BY OTHER SUBDIVIDERS

Potential modest annual growth in capital as area and amenities become more popular

Personal use satisfaction

Monopoly location as land use regulations change

DISADVANTAGES OF INVESTMENTS IN RURAL, RECREATIONAL-ORIENTED LAND DEVELOPMENTS PRODUCED BY OTHER SUBDIVIDERS

High risk

Developer may be unable to complete promised improvements

Financing for construction of improvements necessary to enjoy lot may be difficult to obtain

Governmental authority for necessary construction may be difficult to obtain

Limited growth potential

Subdivider's profits may have already taken short-term growth potential

Other developments in area may compete with resales

Subdivision restructions may limit resales

Potential for high-pressure sales tactics

Free vacations may be a means of delivering the prospective buyer to a battery of high-pressure salesmen in a distant place

Limited tax benefits, high carrying costs

Tax laws substantially restrict ability to obtain tax benefits from second home ownership

Property taxes, assessments continue whether or not land is used

Feasibility Analysis for Land Investments

MARKET ANALYSIS. Since a successful land investment depends on the land's ultimate use, analysis of the appreciation potential of land investments must predict not only those variables associated with real estate appreciation, generally, but also variables associated with specific types of real estate uses. A market analysis for land investment feasibility analysis thus involves prediction of the variables outlined in the preceding sections. The following list is a short summary of the major categories of variables to be analyzed.

Variables Affecting Real Estate Generally

Changes in population variables
    Household formation rate changes
    Age group distribution changes
    Other
Changes in aggregate economic variables
    Employment shifts
    Income shifts
    Business cycle stages
    Other
Changes in governmental policies
    Zoning changes
    Tax policy changes
    Environmental control policy changes
    Housing policy shifts
    Financing policy changes
    Other
Shifts in the local economic structure
    New influx of industry
    New influx of farming
    Other
Changes in the availability of land
    Land and bay fill
    New transportation routes
    Other
Changes in the supply of social services
    Schools
    Hospitals
    Cultural
    Other

Variables Affecting Specific Potential Uses

Single-family homes
 Commute times/distances
 Community facilities
 Other
Apartments
 Commute times/distance
 Community facilities
 Other
Office buildings
 New businesses
 Expansion of existing businesses
 Space needs
 Other
Retail
 Population
 Income
 Competition
 Other
Industrial
 Labor costs
 Governmental policies
 Accessibility
 Other

SITE ANALYSIS. Analysis of a proposed land investment site must take into account all of the potential uses for which the land may be used.

Residential
 Community services
 Community prestige
 Views
 Slope
 Other
Office
 Prestige

    Access
    Other
  Retail
    Access
    Competition
    Exposure
  Industrial
    Soil
    Drainage
    Access
    Resources
    Utilities
    Sewers
    Water
    Other

FINANCIAL FEASIBILITY ANALYSIS. Since land holding emphasizes the residual upon the sale of the land (raw or developed), financial feasibility analysis ultimately involves a measure of the cost of holding the land versus its projected appreciation. Analysis of the land holding costs should include a measure of the following:

Interest payments (land loans, construction loans)
Principal payments (land loans, construction loans)
Taxes (property, income)
Insurance (liability, worker's compensation)
Operating costs (harvesting costs, security personnel)
Development costs
    Fees, feasibility studies, plans, permits, labor, materials, selling costs

INTERIM USES FOR LAND. Often a land investor may be able to reduce the risks of holding land by producing cash flows through some interim use. Such uses include:

Farming or other agricultural use (timber, cattle, farming)
Golf or other recreational use (hunting, horses, skiing)
Temporary rental real estate uses (mobile homes, parking, fairs, rock festivals)

Tax Factors Unique to Land Investments

CLASSIFICATION AS A "DEALER."   Where the seller of land is held to be a "dealer," the proceeds received upon the sale of the land will not qualify for capital gains treatment. Among the factors to be considered in determining whether or not the land owner is a dealer are included:

The nature and purpose of the acquisition

The purpose for which the property was subsequently held

The duration of ownership

The purposes for which the property was held at the time of the sale

The activities of the taxpayer in selling the land

The extent of advertising and other promotional activities

The extent of other similar sales

The seller's main business or profession

SAFE HARBOR FOR SMALL SUBDIVISIONS.   When the owner has subdivided the land, additional difficulties are encountered in avoiding dealer status. Section 1237 of the *Internal Revenue Code* contains a means whereby certain "subdivision" sales may still qualify for capital gains treatment. The requirements of that section include:

The property must have been held for 5 years prior to the sale.

The owner cannot offer the lots for sale in the ordinary course of his trade or business.

The tract must not have been previously held by the taxpayer for sale to customers.

Substantial improvements cannot be made to the land prior to its sale.

ALLOCATION OF PURCHASE PRICE TO SUBDIVIDED LANDS.   In determining gain on the sale of parcels of land, the seller must equitably allocate the purchase price and capital improvement costs among the lots sold. Allocation of the purchase price must be made as of the purchase of the land and recorded in the taxpayer's books. Several methods have been used with IRS or court approval, including: the relative value method, the unit method, the selling price method, and the gross profit method. Where capital improvements clearly benefit only specific parcels, their cost is properly allocable to such parcels. However, where capital improvements benefit all parcels, such costs must be allocated under one of these methods.

ELECTION TO CAPITALIZE TAXES AND CARRYING COSTS.   Taxes, interest, and carrying charges are generally deductible. However, since raw land does not generally generate income in the development or holding period, a developer may find it advantageous to elect to capitalize such expenses. The owner of unimproved and unproductive raw land may elect to capitalize interest, taxes, and other carrying charges that are properly chargeable to the capital account of the land. Raw land that is rented or leased is not unproductive property, thus interest and taxes cannot be capitalized.

MANDATORY CAPITALIZATION OF CONSTRUCTION PERIOD INTEREST AND TAXES.   The 1976 Tax Reform Act added new rules requiring capitalization of construction period interest and taxes for individuals and Subchapter "S" corporations according to schedules varying with the year in which the construction period interest and taxes are paid or incurred.

TAXATION OF FARM LOSSES.   *Farmer Status.*   Farming is a land use that is treated specifically for Federal tax purposes. The opportunity to deduct in full the ordinary and necessary expenses of farming and to take advantage of a farmer's special elections depends upon the classification of the farming venture as a trade or business rather than as a hobby. The following are some of the tests to determine if a farming activity is engaged in for profit:

> Manner in which the taxpayer carries on the activity
>> Expertise of the taxpayer and his advisers
>> Time and effort expended by the taxpayer
> Expectation that assets used in the activity will appreciate in value
> Success of taxpayer in carrying on other similar and dissimilar activities
> Financial status of the taxpayer; and
> Elements of personal pleasure or recreation.

There is a presumption available where the farming activity produces a profit for 2 or more taxable years in a 5-year period.

Potential Tax Benefits of Farm Ownership.   If the investor is not disqualified by the foregoing "hobby" loss rules set forth, farming operations provide numerous potential tax benefits including:

> Depreciation deductions of orchards and vineyards
> Investment tax credit for certain farm assets

Deduction of real estate taxes

Deduction of certain land clearing costs

Deduction of certain soils and water conservation costs

Deduction of certain fertilizer and soil conditioning costs

Tax Reform Act of 1976. The 1976 Tax Reform Act imposed major changes in the taxation of certain farming operations including:

At-risk limits

Limitations on deductions for farming syndicates

Limits on accounting methods available in farming

INVESTMENTS IN REAL ESTATE SYNDICATES

What is a Real Estate Syndicate

A "syndicate" can be any number of forms of group investment such as a corporation, a real estate investment trust, a general partnership, or a limited partnership. However, when most people speak of syndicate they are referring to a limited partnership.

Limited partnerships are creatures of state statutes (uniform limited partnership acts). That is, upon compliance with state statutes concerning their formation by, for example, the recording of a limited partnership certificate with the County Recorder where the syndicate will be doing business, a legal entity springs into existence that, in many respects, will exist and be treated separately from its owners.

A limited partnership, as a legal entity, differs from a corporation or general partnership and real estate investment trusts in many respects.

GENERAL PARTNERSHIPS. General partners ordinarily share liability for the business obligations and losses equally, or according to their partnership agreement. General partners are liable to outsiders without limitation. All general partners have a right to participate in the management and control of the business, and, in the absence of an agreement otherwise, control is by numerical majority of all partners. A general partnership will be dissolved on a partner's death or withdrawal unless the partners have agreed that it shall not be dissolved, and the deceased or withdrawing partner's rights in partnership property or the loss of his services may make continuing the partnership's business impossible or difficult.

CORPORATIONS.   Shareholders do not ordinarily share liability for the business obligations and losses of corporate entities, and their only risk is loss of their capital investment. Management and control of corporations is highly structured and centralized. A corporation's existence is not affected by transfers of its stock among various owners or by the death of any shareholder.

REAL ESTATE INVESTMENT TRUSTS.   Beneficiaries do not ordinarily share liability for the business obligations and losses of real estate investment trusts (R.E.I.T.). Management and control must rest in specified trustees, and the existence of real estate investment trusts is not normally affected by death or withdrawal of a beneficiary.

LIMITED PARTNERSHIPS.   General partners of limited partnerships ordinarily share liability for the business obligations and losses. However, limited partners, except as may be provided in the limited partnership certificate, normally do not share liability for the business obligations and losses of limited partnerships, and their only risk is their capital investment. State statutes limit the amount of control limited partners may assert over the business affairs of limited partnerships, and management is normally centralized in the general partners. A limited partnership is not dissolved by death or withdrawal of a limited partner. However, the death or withdrawal of a general partner will normally cause the dissolution of a limited partnership unless the partnership continues according to rights contained in applicable, if any, state uniform limited partnership acts.

Limited partnerships and general partnerships normally enjoy "pass-through of profits." This is, when a dollar is earned by the partnership, it is taxed as if earned by the partners. However, in the case of corporations, other than "Subchapter S" corporations, a dollar earned by the corporation is subject to taxation at the corporate level and, again, as a dividend when distributed to the corporation's shareholders. Similarly, limited partnerships and general partnerships normally enjoy "pass-through" of loss. That is, when the partnership's business suffers a loss, such losses can normally be deducted, pro rata, by its partners. However, in the case of corporations other than Subchapter "S" corporations, a loss at the corporate level may not be deducted by the shareholders.

Types of Real Estate Syndicates

Since the nature of each real estate syndicate depends on the terms and conditions contained in its limited partnership certificate and limited partnership agreement, if any, no two real estate syndicates are alike. However, syndicates can be characterized according to certain broad classifications, as in the following sections.

NUMBER OF INVESTORS. Many syndicates are organized to be offered to large numbers of individuals. These so-called "public" syndicates are usually registered with governmental securities regulatory agencies and are often offered through large established securities brokerage houses. The requirements of the various securities regulatory agencies and legal counsel to underwriters offering these public programs usually result in a certain degree of similarity among most public programs, at least in terms of limited partnership participation rights and general partner's compensation.

SIZE AND TYPE OF PROPOSED INVESTMENTS. Syndicates have been formed to invest in real estate projects as small as a single residential home property for rehabilitation and resale. Other syndicates have been formed to purchase raw land for medium-term speculation and resale is subdivided lots. Still other syndicates have been formed to invest in high-rise suburban apartment complexes.

SPECIFIED PROPERTY VERSUS BLIND POOL. Many syndicates are offered with a specific real estate project in mind. Such syndicates are usually referred to as "specified property programs." Specified property programs have the advantage of providing the potential investor with certainty as to how partnership capital will be spent. However, it is often difficult for sponsors of such syndicates to tie up properties pending the formation of the syndicate without paying a premium to a seller. Blind pools, on the other hand, are syndicates that do not have a particular project in mind, but that will, according to the parameters of the syndicate's investment policy, seek out and acquire properties after the formation of the limited partnership. Blind pools may be able to purchase properties quickly at bargain prices because they do not have to spend any time obtaining capital. However, investors in such programs must rely on the general partners' skills and judgment in selecting suitable properties.

INCOME, RISK, ENTREPRENEURIAL, AND TAX-SHELTER OBJECTIVES. Many syndicates are organized to purchase cash flow producing properties with relatively stable incomes. Such syndicates are organized to provide unusually high tax-shelter or appreciation potential. Other syndicates are organized to take advantage of exotic tax-shelter producing laws (such as an investment credit for the renovation of an historical monument motel) but do not necessarily purport to provide immediate cash flow potential. Still other syndicates are organized to engage actively in development, subdivision, construction, or other entrepreneurial activities.

Advantages of Limited Partnership Investments

Investments in limited partnerships can provide investors with numerous advantages, including those in the following sections.

LIMITED LIABILITY.   Assuming the limited partnership is formed in compliance with local limited partnership acts, and that the limited partners do not otherwise lose their status as limited partners by being too active in the conduct of the affairs of the limited partnership, limited partners are normally not subject to any liabilities of the partnership and risk only their initial capital contribution or additional payments required as a consequence of any assessment rights.

LOW MINIMUM INVESTMENT.   While the typical direct real estate investment often requires substantial sums of money, many limited partnership syndicates are available at unit prices of only a few thousand dollars. The relatively low capital requirements to become a limited partner in such programs enable many investors who would not otherwise be able to invest in real estate to obtain the leverage, appreciation, tax-shelter, and equity build-up benefits available through real estate investments.

ECONOMIES TO SCALE.   The pooling of monies into syndicates permits individual investors with limited resources to buy larger size real estate projects and to reap certain economies to scale. For example, property acquisition analysis and appraisal involve substantial fees and costs. These, for a small project, can use up a large portion of capital available for investment. However, as the size of the project increases, such costs become relatively less significant. Similar economies to scale may be available in the case of property management services, legal services, and accounting charges.

DIVERSIFICATION POTENTIAL.   When an investor invests in a single real estate project, he is putting "all of his eggs" in one property type and economic locality "basket." However, many limited partnerships diversify their investments according to property types as well as locations. In addition, syndication provides investors with an ability to invest funds in different partnerships and thereby to increase the diversification of their assets among various investment strategies as well.

MANAGEMENT EXPERTISE.   Real estate limited partnerships organized by competent and skilled general partners provide an excellent means for individual investors to obtain the benefits of expertise in project screening, acquisition, negotiations, financing, leasing, management, development, accounting, law, rehabilitation, and marketing. Of course, individuals providing such expertise can be expected to charge for their services, either directly, or indirectly in the form of a portion of the profits from the syndicate, and the benefits of such expertise should be weighed against such costs.

Disadvantages of Limited Partnership Investments

Investments in limited partnerships are not without certain disadvantages. These follow in the next section.

GENERAL PARTNER'S INTEREST.   Sponsors of limited partnership syndicates normally share in ongoing cash distributions from rentals, the profits realized from the property following its sale, and may even take a portion of cash contributed upon the initial formation of the partnership as a sponsor's or acquisition fee. General partners may also reserve a right to property management fees, real estate commissions upon the acquisition or sale of partnership property, and may provide other services to the partnership. Sponsors may even sell projects to limited partnership syndicates in which they have an interest. Many of the regulators reviewing syndicates that apply for authority to offer partnership units to the public may impose substantial limitations on such compensation. In addition, the competitiveness of the limited partnership investment market imposes certain limits on the amount of such compensation. However, wise investors carefully evaluate the amount of such general partner compensation against the value of obtaining the particular skills and expertise of the general partner.

ILLIQUIDITY.   The requirements of tax laws and securities laws dictate that limited partnership units may not be freely transferable. Investments in limited partnerships should not be made by investors who cannot afford to have their capital tied up for long periods of time.

INABILITY TO PARTICIPATE IN MANAGEMENT DECISIONS.   State uniform limited partnership acts provide that if limited partners become too active in the affairs of the partnership, they lose their limited liability. As a consequence, most limited partnership agreements substantially limit the rights of limited partners to participate in the management of the limited partnership. The consequence of such limitations is that the limited partners must rely on the skills and judgment of the general partners, and wise investors carefully evaluate the management skills and abilities of the proposed general partners.

PARTNERS. Limited partnerships, by definition, involve the combination of one or more investors and may, therefore, involve numerous "group dynamics" that should be appreciated by investors. At best, limited partners will be paying for the cost of reports to, meetings of, and inquiries by other limited partners. At worst, a limited partner may accidentally join a syndicate with one or more particularly critical or litigious other limited partners who use up a general partner's time and energy on picayune matters not related to achieving profits from real estate investments. In either event, the investor in a limited partnership does not have the unfettered freedom of decision making characteristic of direct ownership of real property.

TAX RISKS. An investment in a limited partnership may significantly increase the probability that the investor will be audited. In addition, the status of a limited partnership for tax purposes depends on numerous subjective criteria, and there may be some risk that the entity could be considered an association taxable as a corporation. Similarly, there is usually some lack of certainty as to whether the IRS will disallow some or all of the expenses a limited partnership may claim or require an allocation of profits or losses other than as provided in the limited partnership agreement. Finally, tax laws and regulations and IRS interpretations of such laws and regulations are constantly changing, and such changes may even be applied retroactively to particular limited partnerships.

POTENTIAL FOR CONFLICTS OF INTEREST. Limited partnerships can present numerous opportunities for a sponsor to profit at the expense of limited partners. For example, the right of the general partner to a portion of the profits on the sale of partnership property may create an incentive for early sale of such property. Similarly, when a general partner provides services or sells property to the limited partnership, there may be an incentive to price the services or property at rates higher than those that would be arrived at by means of arm's length bargaining.

DIFFICULTY OF EVALUATION. While there is ample public information concerning the performance of many stocks, there is little data on the performance of even the largest public limited partnerships. In addition, each limited partnership has many provisions pertaining to such areas as limited partner's voting rights, transferability, and assessments that may not be subject to quantitative comparison at all. Also, most limited partnerships have widely different risks, property types, tax-shelter potentials, and general partner compensation arrangements. Such scarcity of data and difficulty in weighing and measuring the subtle differences between various limited partnerships makes evaluation of the attractiveness of such investments very difficult.

Who Should Invest in Limited Partnerships

Limited partnerships involve a considerable degree of illiquidity and substantial fees and compensation to general partners. Accordingly, such investments should not be undertaken unless

> The investor is one who needs the acquisition and management skills provided by the general partner.
> The investor can commit only a limited amount of capital to real estate investments.
> The investor is able to bear the risks of illiquidity, and a long-term holding period.

Where the proposed limited partnership investment is a highly tax-shelter oriented investment, the investor should carefully consider the feasibility of other alternatives, including:

> Income averaging
> Installment sales treatment of property sales
> Contributing to a pension and profit sharing plan
> Tax-free municipal bonds

Evaluating Limited Partnership Investments

SCREENING OUT TURKEYS.   *Carefully Evaluate Partnerships Investing in Long-Distance Properties.*   The inability or unfeasibility of visits to the site may permit a general partner to become complacent. In addition, foreign state laws or regulations may present problems with which local partnership counsel or managers are unable to cope.

Avoid Last Minute Deals.   Programs offered at the end of the year or during tax season may be capitalizing on the investor's emotional tax-avoidance feelings and not have sufficient other economic substance.

Avoid Partnerships with No Real Business Purpose. Many partnership investments are formed with high leveraging and high deductibility of expenses and are designed to take advantage of every possible tax credit and tax loophole. While such objectives may accompany otherwise economically sound investments, investors can become caught up in the tax-shelter aspects of such exotic partnerships and fail to investigate adequately the long-term economic substance of the investment.

Carefully Investigate the General Partner's Skills. Since substantial fees and compensation will be paid to a limited partnership's general partner, no investment should be made without carefully determining if such fees and compensation are justified.

EVALUATION OF GENERAL PARTNERS. The skills, capacities, and character of the proposed general partners are of primary importance to the investor in a limited partnership. The following list of areas should be investigated in analyzing a general partner:

Financial Resources. Can the general partner provide audited or otherwise verifiable statements?

Will the general partner have adequate financial capacities (liquid assets, net worth) to manage the syndicate in the best interest of all investors and not be motivated to embark on short-term distributions in which the general partner may share, at the expense of long-term goals?

Is the general partner faced with costly litigation involving other partnerships or past business activities?

Has the general partner overextended its financial resources by guarantees of other partnership's liabilities?

Does the general partner have sufficient other income to enable it to personally weather difficult times?

Experience and Abilities Pertaining to Real Estate. Does the general partner possess adequate educational background and training in real estate acquisition, leasing, development, tax law, marketing, and management?

Has the general partner had prior experience in other areas of real estate such as law, appraisal, finance, development, marketing, leasing, and management?

Does the general partner have access to professionals with experience and skills in those areas where his experience is not adequate?

Experience and Abilities Pertaining to Syndication. Has the general partner participated as a general partner in other similar limited partnerships?

What was the performance of the general partner's prior syndicates in terms of cash flows, tax shelter, and appreciation?

Can the general partner provide references from past investors?

Have any of the general partner's previous limited partnerships been audited by the IRS?

Is the general partner involved in any litigation over prior limited partnerships?

Does the general partner have access to competent securities and tax counsel?

Professional Reputation, Integrity, and Style.   Does the business style of the general partner or its affiliates fit with the proposed investor's style?

Do the general partner or its affiliates have a reputation in the financial community for fair dealing and financial prudence?

Have the general partner or its affiliates been involved in prior business bankruptcies or other insolvency proceedings?

Investment of General Partner.   Is the general partner committing its own funds to the proposed deal?

POTENTIAL FOR CONFLICTS OF INTEREST.   General partners of limited partnerships are frequently presented with numerous opportunities for profit at the expense of the limited partners. The fact that such opportunities occur and are taken advantage of by the general partner is not necessarily bad so long as the investor appreciates the nature and character of such conflicts and is willing to accept their existence in consideration of the general partner's services.

Purchase or Leases of Property from the General Partner.   Limited partnerships may purchase or lease real estate or other property from general partners. Such purchase presents a very great conflict of interest in that the general partner will have an incentive to sell or lease the property at a higher price than would have been arrived at by arm's length bargaining. Ideally such opportunities should not occur, or, if they do, the purchase price or lease rates should be at a value substantiated by outside appraisals.

Sale of Goods or Services to the Limited Partnership.   General partners are often entitled to property management fees or compensation for construction work they or their affiliates do for the partnership. In the event the general partner is compensated for such services and goods, fees, payments, and other consideration should be based on competitive rates, and the general partner should have some prior experience and abilities in the areas for which he is to be compensated.

Commissions upon the Acquisition, Leasing, or Sale of Partnership Property.
The share of profits upon the sale of partnership property may itself
create a potential for the general partner to profit at the expense of the
partnership by a sale at a point in time in its best interest rather than in
the best interest of the limited partners. In addition, the right to the commission may create an incentive not to drive the hardest bargain on behalf
of the partnership.

Participation in Other Real Estate Deals.   The general partner's activities in
other partnerships or in other real estate transactions on his own account
creates a potential conflict of interest in that partnership opportunities
(i.e., information pertaining to the local market or other available investments) may be kept for the general partner's own profit. In addition, the
general partner will be spending considerable amounts of his time and
effort analyzing and consummating such deals, which might have been
otherwise spent on the partnership's affairs. While the potential for such
conflicts of interest may be worth putting up with in order to obtain the
skills and experience of the general partner, investments in limited partnerships should not be made without assessing the costs and benefits of
such conflicts.

Availability of Professional Services and Skills.   A single general partner will
rarely be able to bring to the limited partnership all of the analytical,
negotiating, financing, management, development, leasing, and marketing
skills required to adequately engage in the business of real estate acquisition, development, leasing, and selling. One or more of such skills and
professional abilities is usually supplied by outside accountants, appraisers,
attorneys, and managers. Investments in limited partnerships should not be
made without carefully evaluating the skills of such outside professionals.

FEES AND COMPENSATION TO SYNDICATORS.   General partners do not,
generally, organize real estate syndicates for altruistic reasons and may
wish to take fees and compensation for their services in a variety of forms
and at various times throughout the life of the limited partnership.

Organizational Stage.   Potential forms of fees and compensation a sponsor
or a sponsor's affiliate may seek include:

> Reimbursement for partnership organizational expenses, consulting
> fees, and prepaid management fees in return for organizing the
> partnership
> Securities commissions for the sale of the limited partnership units
> Acquisition and finder's fees for location of suitable property for part-
> nership investment

Real estate commissions upon the purchase of partnership property

Mark-up profit on sales of property and services to the partnership

Loan fees or commissions in connection with partnership financing

Mark-up on seller's financing provided to partnership upon the purchase of property from the general partner

Operational Stage.   Potential forms of fees and compensation a sponsor, or a sponsor's affiliates, may seek include:

A portion of partnership capital

A portion of partnership profits or losses from rental cash flow

Property management fees

Partnership management fees

Reimbursement for expenses

A mark-up profit on sales of goods and services to the partnership

Commissions on leasing of partnership property

A developer's profit on development and rehabilitation work done for the partnership

Liquidation Stage.   Potential forms of fees and compensation a sponsor or a sponsor's affiliate may seek include:

Real estate commissions on sale of partnership property

A portion of partnership profits and losses from sale of partnership property

A portion of proceeds upon refinancing of partnership property

Real estate commissions and acquisition fees upon reinvestment of partnership funds

The evaluation of differing fee and compensation structures is difficult; among the criteria to consider are those of the following sections.

The Quality of the General Partner.   The success of a real estate syndicate depends on the skills and expertise of the general partner. Highly skilled general partners usually expect higher compensation for their services, and, if the general partner has a long history of outstanding performance, higher fees and compensation may be appropriate. On the other hand, many novice real estate agents organize syndicates, and higher fees and compensation to such unexperienced syndicators may not be justified.

The Nature of the Investment.   The amount of fees and compensation to be paid to the general partner, and the timing of such payments, should be proportional to the amount of time and effort the syndication must dedicate to the investment and the point in time when such efforts are expended. Some investments, such as a development project, by their very nature, require more managerial and supervisory time than others. In such a case, a substantially larger compensation to the general partner may be justified. Similarly, certain investments require a greater expenditure of time and effort by the general partner earlier in the deal than later on, after the property is purchased. In such cases, perhaps, a greater "front-end" compensation is appropriate.

The Sponsor's Needs and Initial Capacities. The ideal investment for the limited partners is generally one where the general partner shares in profits only in the form of a subordinated "back-end" interest, such as a right to a portion of cash realized from the sale of partnership property after the investors have been returned their capital plus a cumulative amount of earnings on such capital. Such an arrangement results in the maximum amount of capital being invested in the partnership business activities (no fees and compensation are paid out of partnership capital contributions) and also provides the maximum amount of incentive for superior investment management on the part of the general partner. However, such an arrangement can be undertaken by only a few financially able general partners. The investor who refuses to permit any "front-end" fees or interest in cash flows from operations to be paid to a general partner may arbitrarily rule out investments with equally competent general partners without the financial resources to take the gamble that a compensation arrangement based on only a "back-end" interest would require.

TAX ASPECTS.   No investment should be made without a thorough investigation into all of the applicable tax laws and regulations affecting taxation of revenues—deductibility of expenses. In the case of real estate limited partnerships, certain tax areas are especially critical and should be understood and evaluated prior to any investment. The following sections give some of the more important tax issues involved in limited partnerships.

Classification as a Partnership.   If a limited partnership is not treated for Federal income tax purposes as a partnership, but instead is treated as an association taxable as a corporation in any tax year, the limited partnership's taxable income or loss would be reflected on its "corporate" tax returns rather than being passed through to its partners. In such an instance, most distributions to partners would be taxable to them (at ordinary income rates to the extent of earnings and profits of the "corporation"), and no deductible expenses of the limited partnership would be available to partners in computing their taxable income. In addition, if a limited partnership operates for a period as a partnership, but is later deemed to be an association taxable as a corporation, that change in status could result in taxable income to the partners. Thus, classification of the partnership as an association taxable as a corporation could result in a substantial reduction in yield on his investment to the investor, and the investor should carefully investigate the likelihood that the IRS on audit would be successful in any claim that the limited partnership should be treated as an association taxable as a corporation.

Allocation of Profits and Losses. Limited partnership agreements typically allocate to the general partner a greater portion of profits and losses than would be allocated on the basis of capital contributions alone. According to applicable provisions of the *Internal Revenue Code*, a partner's distributive share of items of income, gain, loss, deduction, or credit will be determined in accordance with the limited partnership agreement only if such allocation under the agreement has substantial economic effect. If an allocation under the limited partnership agreement does not have substantial economic effect, a partner's distributive share of such income, gain, loss, deduction, or credit (or item thereof) would be determined in accordance with the partner's interest in the limited partnership (determined by taking into account all of the facts and circumstances).

If the IRS were to succeed in reallocating a greater portion of a partnership's net losses and taxable losses to the limited partners, such reallocation may occur in a year in which the limited partners would be unable to deduct such losses because the applicable statute of limitations for the year in which such losses could properly be deducted has run. In this event, a limited partner's tax base in his units would be reduced by the losses reallocated to him, although he will not have received a tax benefit from such losses, thereby increasing the recognized gain or decreasing the recognized loss on a sale of units or on liquidation of the partnership. If the IRS were to succeed in reallocating a portion of the general partner's distributive share of gain on the sale of the partnership property, the limited partners would recognize a greater share of the partnership gain, which would affect not only the amount of gain taxable to the limited partners, but also the tax basis of their units, thereby affecting the recognized gain or loss on a sale of units or on liquidation of the partnership. If the IRS were to succeed in reallocating all or a portion of the gross revenues of the partnership specifically allocated to the general partners, the limited partners would be allocated a greater share of the partnership's gross income, which would either decrease their distributive share of partnership losses or increase their distributive share of partnership income, and the limited partners might be required to pay additional tax.

Basis of Partnership Units. A limited partner's tax basis for partnership units includes not only the amount of money he contributed to the partnership, but also his share (proportionate to his share of partnership profits) of any nonrecourse liability (i.e., a partnership liability as to which no partner is personally liable), to the extent that such liability does not exceed the fair market value of the property subject to such liability, and provided that the partnership's principal activity continues to be investing in real property other than mineral property.

A limited partner's tax basis is increased by such partner's distributive share of any partnership taxable income. The basis of the limited partnership unit will also be increased by any contributions to partnership capital (including an increase in nonrecourse liabilities). The limited partners' basis will be decreased by distributions from the partnership (including the decreases in nonrecourse liabilities). Their basis will also be decreased by his distributive share of partnership losses. For Federal income tax purposes, an increase in nonrecourse liabilities is treated as a cash contribution, and a decrease in nonrecourse liabilities is treated as a cash distribution, even though a partner receives no cash. Furthermore, a reduction in the fair market value of the property owned by the partnership below any nonrecourse liability encumbering that property may be treated as a reduction of the nonrecourse liability to an amount equal to the reduction in the fair market value of such property.

To the extent that a limited partner's share of partnership losses exceeds the basis of his partnership units at the end of the partnership year in which such losses occur, such excess losses cannot be utilized in that year by such limited partner for any purpose. They are allowed as a deduction at the end of the first succeeding partnership taxable year, and subsequent partnership taxable years, to the extent that the partner's adjusted basis for his partnership units at the end of any such year exceeds zero (before reduction by such loss for such year).

If the tax basis of a limited partner should be reduced to zero, the amount of any cash distributions or reduction in his share of partnership nonrecourse liabilities for any year in excess of his share of income of the partnership for the year generally will be taxable to him in the manner gain is taxed upon the sale of partnership units.

Gains or Losses on the Sale of Partnership Property. When partnership property is sold (including a sale or disposition resulting from foreclosure), a partnership realizes gain or loss based on the difference between the amount realized (which includes the amount of indebtedness to which the property is subject) and the partnership's tax basis for the property. Any profit realized by the partnership on the sale of the partnership property will be ordinary income to the extent of accelerated depreciation previously allowed with respect to the property sold. The remaining gain, or any loss realized on the sale of partnership property held for more than 12 months and not held primarily for sale to customers or as capital assets, should constitute gain and loss described in Section 1231 of the *Internal Revenue Code* (i.e., generally, from sale or exchanges of real or depreciable property used in a trade or business). A limited partner's allocable share of gains and losses from Section 1231 assets would be combined with any other Section 1231 gains or losses incurred by him that year, and his net Section 1231 gains or losses would be taxed as capital gains or constitute ordinary losses as the case may be. Gains and losses on the sale of the partnership property held primarily for sale to customers will result in ordinary income or loss. Gains or losses from the sale of the partnership property held as capital assets will constitute capital gains or capital losses.

Other Tax Areas Important to Limited Partners.   In addition to the foregoing areas, investments in limited partnerships may involve various other tax issues and tax risks, including (*a*) the deductibility of prepaid interest; (*b*) the deductibility of payments to the general partner; (*c*) the validity of depreciation methods, depreciable lives, and salvage values used in calculating yearly depreciation deductions; (*d*) the taxation of proceeds received upon the sale of partnership property; (*e*) the deductibility of interest on funds borrowed to purchase partnership assets; (*f*) minimum tax rules; (*g*) the capitalization of organization and syndication fees; and (*h*) the treatment of proceeds upon dissolution and liquidation of the partnership.

PLAN OF BUSINESS.   As previously discussed, limited partnerships are formed with many different business objectives. No investment should be made without first making sure that the objectives of the partnership, the proposed use of proceeds and assessments, the partnership's property acquisition, leveraging policy, and all risks associated with achieving such objectives and policies are thoroughly investigated and understood.

Objectives of Program.   Many syndicates are formed to purchase cash flow producing properties with relatively stable incomes. Such syndicates are not organized to provide unusually high tax-shelter or appreciation potential and would be unsuitable to high-income participants needing higher "write offs" and desirous of higher risk/higher potential investments. On the other hand, other partnerships are formed to take advantage of every conceivable exotic tax-shelter-producing law and may not provide any immediate cash flow. Such investments would not be suitable unless such tax-shelter and income objectives were in line with the investor's objectives.

Use of Proceeds and Assessments.   No investment should be made without carefully analyzing and understanding the uses to which initial capital contributions and assessments, if any, are to be put. Investors should determine if the partnership's philosophy regarding the use of proceeds for such items as down payments and reserves matches their own investment philiosophies.

Acquisition and Leveraging Policy.   In the case of a blind pool limited partnership the general partners do not necessarily have property ready for acquisition by the partnership. Prospective investors should carefully determine if the types of property to be purchased fit their investment objectives and whether the methods to be used by the general partner to screen prospective acquisitions are adequate. Financing policies should be understood and analyzed to determine if the amount and types of mortgages to be incurred match the prospective limited partners' investment objectives. For example, financing in the form of hybrid devices such as interest only short-term loans or the retention of equity interests by lenders or sellers may not be suitable to investors seeking relatively constant cash flows. On the other hand, partnerships that are not highly leveraged and organized to maximize interest deductions in initial years may have little chance of meeting the tax-shelter needs of other investors.

Risks.   Prospective limited partners should clearly understand the numerous risks and obstacles associated with the proposed partnership investment. For example, partnerships organized to actively develop or redevelop property may not be successful in getting zoning changes, construction permits or financing. Similarly, partnerships organized to buy existing rental property with stable cash flows may be faced with adverse political changes such as rent control, or expense increases such as energy costs, or unforeseen economic changes such as the construction of more competitive neighboring projects.

ANALYSIS OF INVESTMENT REQUIREMENTS.   All investments in limited partnerships require limited partners to make an initial cash investment. However, some syndicates may require additional cash contributions in a variety of forms.

Cash Plus Notes.   Many syndicates are designed to permit the investor to pay his capital contribution in the form of cash and notes. The low initial cash required is attractive to certain investors who may be able to obtain large amounts of tax shelter with minimal initial cash outlay. However, the eventuality of the notes coming due should be clearly understood and appreciated.

Staged Capital Contributions. Other syndicates are organized to require capital contributions in stages. For example, many syndicates require capital contributions as various phases of a project's development are reached. Investors in such programs should carefully assess their ability to make such serial contributions as they become due. For example, the investor's earning capacity and cash resources may not remain at the same level as when the limited partnership unit was first purchased, and such required contributions could come at a time when tax shelter is not needed or cash is short.

Assessable Partnerships. Still other limited partnership agreements give the general partner the right to assess the limited partners should the need for additional cash arise. Investors in such programs should determine the circumstances under which assessments may be made, carefully analyze the penalties for a failure to make a required capital contribution, and make sure that their earning capacity and liquid cash resources will continue to be sufficient to enable them to make any such required contributions.

ANALYSIS OF OTHER POTENTIAL PARTICIPANTS. Limited partnership interests should not be purchased by investors who are not financially sophisticated and economically able to bear the risk of the loss of their investment. The level of financial sophistication and economic strength may vary with the type of program. For example, investments in conservative cash flow producing income property may be suitable for many investors whereas investments in unusually exotic tax shelter programs with hybrid financing may be suitable only for very wealthy and financially wary investors. While the suitability of prospective participants is often considered to be only the problem of sponsors of limited partnerships, prospective partners should also be concerned since bad matches of investor sophistication and financial capacities may produce dissent and litigation, which can take a general partner's time and energies away from the partnership's affairs.

LIMITED PARTNER'S RIGHTS AND DUTIES. Real estate syndicates are based ultimately on a limited partnership agreement containing the basic economic structure of the deal, as well as numerous other provisions that may not initially appear to be important, but that, in the event of a dispute as to the partnership's business operations or the performance of the general partner, may become very important.

Voting Rights of Limited Partners.   Limited partnership agreements usually provide limited partners with rights to approve or disapprove of certain actions, such as the sale of all of the partnership's property or the right to remove the general partner. Many investors feel such rights are very important and want as broad powers to control the general partners as local limited partnership statutes will permit. Others feel that such powers only restrict the general partner's ability to act quickly when unusual investment opportunities arise and can lead to nit-picking by limited partners.

Prospective limited partnership investors should carefully read limited partnership agreement provisions giving them the right to approve of partnership actions and remove the general partners and make sure such rights are consistent with their needs and investment philosophy.

Reports and Records.   Investments in limited partnerships are made, ultimately, for the purpose of producing cash flows, and investors should expect periodic information about the business activities that are generating such cash flows. Regulatory agencies may demand that numerous reports be provided to holders of limited partnership units including statements of income and cash flows, balance sheets, reports of investments made, reports of expenditures made, reports of property sales and leasing activities, summaries of reserves available, summaries of fees and compensation paid to the general partners, and comparisons of actual performance to projections provided investors. Such agencies may require also that all or some of such reports be prepared in accordance with generally accepted accounting principles and accompanied by an auditor's report containing a qualified opinion of an independent certified public accountant. The costs of providing investors with all of the reports required by regulatory agencies can be quite high and can result in an expenditure of the general partner's time, which might have otherwise been available for partnership business purposes. For this reason many good limited partnerships provide their investors with less extensive reports and records. A prospective investor should carefully evaluate the number, type, and frequency of reports to be provided by the general partners and make sure that the type of information the investor wants will be provided at a reasonable and appropriate cost.

Restrictions on Transfer of Limited Partnership Units.   Because of tax and securities laws the transfer of limited partnership units is usually restricted. Free transferability could result in the loss of numerous tax benefits associated with limited partnerships. Similarly, a failure to limit resales may result in the unavailability of an exemption from securities registration laws and thereby expose the general partners to litigation concerning compliance with such securities laws. On the other hand, limited partners may want to gift their limited partnership rights to trusts of family members as part of general estate planning activities or to pledge cash flows to come from the limited partnership as part of future borrowings. Many limited partnership agreements also limit such transfers. Thus, a prospective investor should make sure that any restrictions on their right to transfer their partnership units in consistent with their future financial plans.

STUDIES, DOCUMENTS, AND OPINIONS RELATING TO THE PROPOSED PARTNERSHIP BUSINESS. Offering circulars prepared in connection with many syndicates often contain the sponsor's summaries of relevant feasibility studies, appraisals, title reports, leases, management agreements, and tax opinions. Investors should carefully review such studies, documents, and opinions as part of their investment decision process. Where such studies, documents, and opinions have not been provided, investors should inquire as to whether such studies and opinions have been prepared. The following is a partial list of some of the studies and opinions that may provide the investor with additional information, and, perhaps, comfort the investor about the investment.

Locational analysis
    Studies concerning the area in which the investment is to be made
Appraisals
    Studies concerning the specific site at which funds are to be expended
Feasibility analysis
    Financial calculation of data concerning profitability of the proposed investment
Lease analysis
    Economic and legal review of leases pertaining to existing projects

In addition to these studies, investors should be provided with copies of documents and agreements concerning the investment, such as:

Title report
Managerial agreements
Construction contracts
Brokerage agreements

Finally, investors may want to review the legal and accounting structure of the partnership, such as:

Tax opinions

Securities law compliance opinions

Proposed partnership certificates

GUIDELINES PROMULGATED BY GOVERNMENTAL REGULATORY AGENCIES. Many regulatory agencies have enacted guidelines by which their personnel process real estate offerings seeking registrations or qualifications. Such guidelines can help investors analyze potential investments in all syndicates. Appendix H contains the "Midwest Securities Commissioners' Guidelines" which contain detailed rules concerning every aspect of real estate limited partnerships.

INVESTING IN MORTGAGES

Lenders and sellers who take notes from borrowers and buyers do not always sit by and collect the principal and interest payments on such notes. Frequently they will sell the notes to other investors who, if the price is right, are willing to pay cash to the seller or lender and either collect the note payments themselves or, in turn sell the notes to other investors. Such individuals are commonly referred to as mortgage investors.

Mathematics of Loan Discounting

The amount purchasers of notes, payable to lenders and sellers, are willing to pay depends on the yield the purchasers desire. If the investor wants a yield higher than the interest rate of the note he must pay the lender or seller less than the face value of the note (a discount). On the other hand, if the investor is satisfied with a yield less than the note's interest rate, the lender or seller may be able to sell the note at a premium.

The exact amount to be paid in order to achieve a particular yield can be found by taking the present value of the loan payments using as the present value factor (discount rate) the desired yield of the investor. For example, if an investor borrowed $1,000 at 5% interest per annum to be repaid in 5 years, he would be required to pay $231 per year in order to amortize the loan. If an investor purchased the borrower's promise to repay the loan (the Note) for $1,000 he would earn 5% per year on his investment. That is:

$$\$1,000 = \frac{\$231}{(1 + 0.05)^1} + \frac{\$231}{(1 + 0.05)^2} + \frac{\$231}{(1 + 0.05)^3} + \frac{\$231}{(1 + 0.05)^4} + \frac{\$231}{(1 + 0.05)^5}$$

On the other hand, if the investor wanted to earn 10% he should only pay $906.00. That is:

$$\$906 = \frac{\$231}{(1+0.10)^1} + \frac{\$231}{(1+0.10)^2} + \frac{\$231}{(1+0.10)^3} + \frac{\$231}{(1+0.10)^4} + \frac{\$231}{(1+0.10)^5}$$

Tables for Loan Discounting

The mathematical process of determining the amount to pay for a loan with equal payments is commonly referred to as "funding the present value of an ordinary annuity." Numerous tables exist that give such present values for a variety of loan terms and desired yields. Appendix H is an example of such a table. Using the Appendix, if an investor were considering the purchase of a note with equal monthly payments of principal and interest of $500 at a remaining loan of 23 years (276 months), then the amount the investor should pay if the investor wants a yield of 20% on his money is $29,687, that is, 59.373585 × $500.

Mortgage Investment Feasibility Analysis

Investments in mortgages require a combination of skills. Since the underlying collateral for the notes being purchased is real estate, prospective mortgage investors must be skilled at investment analysis. On the other hand, the primary right the prospective mortgage investor is acquiring is a series of cash flows coming from a borrower, and an ability to evaluate borrowers' credit characteristics is also important. In addition, the purchase of notes secured by real estate can also involve numerous and diverse legal rights and relationships with which the prospective investor should be familiar.

ANALYSIS OF UNDERLYING PROPERTY. While the property pledged as collateral for a mortgage is only available in the event of a default and, in theory, should not be a mortgage investor's primary consideration, most mortgage investors pay particular attention to the underlying collateral.

Type of Property. There is a belief in the mortgage banking community that owner-occupied single-family homes are excellent collateral. Supposedly borrowers will be more apt to curtail expenditures and "bite the bullet" in bad times to keep their homes than to keep investment or vacation properties. However, other types of collateral such as well located income property with good tenants and escalator clauses in leases may provide equally good collateral under certain circumstances and should not be arbitrarily ruled out.

Location of Property. The collateral must be able to maintain its resale value over the term of the note, and the location of the collateral must be carefully studied to determine if adverse economic changes or declines are foreseeable.

Type and Quality of Construction. The type and quality of construction affects the value of the collateral during the loan amortization period. The likelihood that the note holder will be forced to expend additional sums for repairs and renovations in order to sell the collateral if possession is acquired after a default should be evaluated prior to any mortgage purchase.

Conformity with Local Laws. A property that does not comply with local zoning laws, environmental laws, building codes, condominium acts, or health and safety laws may result in a borrower who is unable to perform under the terms and conditions of the note as well as a property that, upon acquisition following a default, is not able to be sold for sufficient funds to recoup the mortgage investor's money.

Leases Pertaining to the Property. Income property pledged as collateral for a loan may be subject to various leasehold rights. Such leases may contain terms and conditions adverse to mortgage investors such as the right to prepay substantial amounts of rent or the right to terminate the lease in the event of any financial difficulties on the part of the landlord (borrower.) On the other hand, leases of pledged property on attractive terms to prime tenants can help ensure the performance of the borrower's obligations and provide additional safety to the mortgage investor.

Appraisals. Prudent real estate lending is based on collateral with a market value acceptable to the lender that is substantiated by independent appraisal. While an individual mortgage investor may, personally feel that a formal appraisal is not necessary, the lack of such an independent appraisal may reduce the future marketability of the note.

ANALYSIS OF LOAN TERMS AND CONDITIONS. The amount, frequency, and duration of the cash flow to be received by the mortgage investor depends on the terms and conditions contained in the loan documents.

Prepayment Rights. Loan documents may permit prepayment of outstanding principal balances. Any such prepayment may put the mortgage investor in the possession of a lump sum cash payment at a time when reinvestment at a similar yield is difficult.

Further Encumbrances and Conveyances. Loan documents frequently restrict the borrower's ability to further pledge the collateral or to sell the collateral to other parties. The justification given by most lenders for restricting further encumbrances is that the borrower's ability to repay the loan may be impaired and subject them to the conflicting claims of other lenders. Similarly, lenders frequently argue that a restriction on the sale of underlying collateral is necessary to ensure that the property does not come into the possession of parties who are not able or willing to ensure that it is properly cared for and maintained. A lender's ability to prohibit such encumbrances and conveyances may be subject to certain limitations in some states.

Assurances that Property Taxes and Insurance Premiums Will Be Paid.   Loss of the underlying collateral as a result of the failure of the borrower to pay property taxes or as a result of fire or other natural disasters may result in the inability or unwillingness of the borrower to continue to make payments on account of the note. Loan documents, subject to the limits of certain state statutes, frequently require the borrower to impound funds to ensure that such taxes and insurance premiums are paid and give the lender the right to step in and make such payments for the account of the borrower.

Application of Proceeds in the Event of a Condemnation or Other Loss of the Collateral.   Where there is a condemnation or other loss of the lender's collateral, cash proceeds may be payable to the owner. Lenders normally prefer to have the option to have the proceeds from a condemnation or other loss of the collateral paid toward their loan rather than used to repair or replace the collateral. State laws may, under some circumstances, limit a lender's right to such an option.

ANALYSIS OF LOAN DOCUMENTS.   The making of a valid loan involves numerous legal documents as well as other backup reports.

Note.   Mortgage investments should be based on a valid and binding note with terms and conditions that are not ambiguous and that comply with the legal requirements of the state whose law would govern the enforceability of the note.

Security Agreement.   The deed of trust or mortgage given by the borrower should conform to the legal requirements of the state on which the property is located and should be duly recorded as required by local laws.

Title Reports, Abstracts, and Certificates.   Title reports, abstracts, or certificates should be obtained to ensure that the lender's security interest has priority as to any proceeds realized upon a foreclosure. Similarly, the title to the property should be examined to ensure that the property is not subject to any encumbrances or clouds that are not acceptable to the mortgage investor.

Consumer Law Compliance Documents. Numerous "consumer" laws, such as Truth-In-Lending, the Equal Credit Opportunity Act and the Real Estate Settlement Procedures Act, prescribe loan procedures and require certain disclosure documents. Mortgage investors may, under many circumstances, be subject to such laws and should ensure that applicable procedures have been taken to provide required disclosure documents to the borrowers.

ANALYSIS OF LOCAL MORTAGE LAW. There are as many varieties of statutes prescribing lender and borrower rights and remedies as there are states. For example, certain states require specific notices to borrowers in the event of a default, or they may give borrowers lengthy time periods within which to cure defaults. Other states may not require such notices or may give borrowers only minimal time periods within which to cure defaults. Other states may prohibit suits against borrowers, personally, if the loan involves certain types of property or if a contractual power of sale has been exercised. Other states may not provide for such protections. Mortgage investors should ensure that they are familiar with applicable local creditor and debtor laws and that any limitations on their foreclosure rights are acceptable.

BORROWER ANALYSIS. A mortgage investment should not be made without a careful analysis of the borrower who will be repaying the note.

Subjective Criteria. Analysis of individual borrowers is usually done in terms of such subjective criteria as the character and business reputation of the borrower, the borrower's motive for borrowing and owning the property pledged, the stability of the borrower's income, and the nature of other obligations for which the borrower is liable.

Objective Criteria. Mortgage investors may consider such objective ratios as the ratio of total obligations to net effective income and the ratio of housing expenses and other recurring charges to net effective income. Where the borrower is a corporation other ratios may be analyzed, such as the ratio of current assets to current debt and the ratio of total debt to tangible net worth.

ANALYSIS OF THE NOTE PURCHASE AGREEMENT. The agreement pursuant to which the mortgage investor purchases the note (and mortgage or deed of trust) from the lender may contain numerous provisions specifying and limited the parties' respective rights.

Warranties and Indemnification. Sophisticated mortgage investors are often able to obtain certain warranties from lenders such as those concerning the procedures followed in making the loan, the loan's compliance with applicable laws, and the quality or nature of the underlying collateral. Lenders may also be required to indemnify mortgage investors in the event there has been a failure to comply with applicable consumer laws (such as truth-in-lending) or other lender regulations.

Recourse Rights. Mortgage investors may also require lenders to agree to repurchase loans in the event of any default by the borrower or other circumstances, such as a failure to comply with applicable loan laws.

ANALYSIS OF LOAN PAYMENT HISTORY. The ideal loan purchase is one involving an established on-time payment record. Knowledgeable mortgage investors carefully review loan payment records to determine the frequency of late payments and the risks of future defaults requiring expensive legal action.

Appendix A   COMMUNITY ECONOMIC PROFILE

SANTA ROSA, SONOMA COUNTY, CALIFORNIA
prepared by the
SANTA ROSA CHAMBER OF COMMERCE
Based on the format established for statewide
use by the California Chamber of Commerce
July, 1979

1. Location

Santa Rosa, incorporated 1868, is located 446 miles north of Los Angeles and 52 miles north of San Francisco.

2. Economic Growth and Trends

	1950	1960	1970	1978–79
Population in the County	103,405	147,375	204,885	274,300**
Total Taxable Retail Sales—County	106,955	179,856	385,310	910,616**
Population in City Limits	17,955	31,027	50,006	75,200*
Total Taxable Retail Sales—City	—	76,651	152,660	378,665**
Occupied Dwellings—City	6,380	10,897	16,669	39,101***
School Enrollment, GR 1–6	2,074	3,614	7,154	6,736

Sources:
* State Department of Finance
** State Board of Equalization—Add: $,000
*** Housing Assistance Plan—6% Vacancy Factor

3. Climate   (50 year average)

	Average Temperature			Rain	Humidity			Elevation: 167'
Period	Min. °	Mean °	Max. °	Inches	4 a.m.	Noon	4 p.m.	Prevailing Winds:
Jan.	38.3	48.6	58.9	13.98	95	65	70	Direction:
Apr.	40.3	54.1	67.9	3.97	80	50	60	Mean Hrly Speed:
Jul.	50.3	67.7	85.0	.00	70	45	40	5.8 MPH
Oct.	40.4	58.9	77.4	2.00	69	44	40	Source:
Year	43.0	57.8	72.2	29.95	78.5	51	52.5	U.S. Weather Bureau

4. Transportation

Rail: Northwestern Pacific Railroad (Freight Only)
Truck: Numerous common carriers providing Interstate & Intrastate
Overnight delivery to: San Francisco, Los Angeles & Eureka, nationally via United Parcel

Air: West Air serves from Sonoma County Airport located 7 miles north of Santa Rosa.
Bus: Western Greyhound Lines, Golden Gate Transit and Santa Rosa Municipal Transit
Water: None. Closest facilities San Francisco or Oakland.
Highways: U.S. 101 and State Highway 12

5. Industrial Sites

There are 296 acres in the city limits zoned for light and heavy industry: about 100%
is vacant and available in parcels ranging in size from ½ to 30 acres. Included in this
acreage total are 4 industrial parks or districts. Typical sales prices during 1978 ranged
from $40,000 to $60,000 per acre. The terrain is level. Drainage is excellent. Subsoil is
sandy clay, and piling is not required except where unusually heavy floor loadings are
planned. Sizes of water mains range from 8 to 12 inches. Sizes of sewer lines range from
6 to 24 inches.
Description of sites on or off rail lines, zoned for industry, outside the city limits in other
tracts or districts: 1600 acres of land zoned for industry are located outside the city
limits but within the Santa Rosa General Plan area. About 10% is occupied.

Site data compiled in cooperation with: Sonoma County Economic Development Board

6. Water Supply

Name of Supplier: Sonoma County Water Agency
Maximum pumping capacity 40 million gal/day. Average consumption 12.6 mg/d
Cost per 1,000 gallons in quantities of 100,000 gal/month: 76¢ per 1000 gal
Cost per 1,000 gallons in quantities of 1,000,000 gal/month: 56¢ per 1000 gal
Water connection charges: Single family connection $600.00. Industrial by meter size.

7. Sewer Service

Name of Supplier: City of Santa Rosa
Capacity of sewer plant: 16.7 million gal/day. Peak flow: 28 million gal/day.
Sewer service charge: (yes-no) yes. On what basis rated? Water use, 2 lowest months
Type of treatment plant: Primary   Secondary   ×   Tertiary
Any facilities for non-recoverable industrial waste water: —No
Sewer connection charges: Single family connection $600.00

8. Storm Drains & Flood Control

Master plan of storm drains adopted? (yes-no) No. Charges assessed on following basis:

9. Street Improvements

Dedication requirements: Yes, one-half the width required to conform to the City Street
list or General Plan.
Improvement requirements: Yes, one-half standard street pavement (20 ft) or 24 ft of
pavement for initial street construction—also, curb, gutter, sidewalk, storm drains, street
lights, sewer, water, landscaping.

10. **Natural Gas**

Name of Supplier: Pacific Gas & Electric Company
For rates applicable to the city of Santa Rosa contact the District office located at 3965 Occidental Road, Santa Rosa, CA 95401.

11. **Electric Power**

Name of Supplier: Pacific Gas & Electric Company
For rates applicable to the city of Santa Rosa contact the District office located at 3965 Occidental Road, Santa Rosa, CA 95401.

12. **Telephone**

Name of Supplier: Pacific Telephone Company
For rates and type of service applicable to the city of Santa Rosa contact the Business office located at 1899 Mendocino Ave., Santa Rosa, CA 95401

13. **Governmental Facilities—Tax and Insurance Rates**

(a) Santa Rosa has the City Manager (Charter) type of government.
Assessed valuation 1978–1979: $392,928,281 County—$1,254,891,785
Ratio of assessed value to appraised value:
Appraised value is 25% of real cash value.

(b) Combined total industrial property tax rates 1978–1979 per $100 assessed value.
Code Area(s) 4006 TOTAL $4.3950
City tax rate: $0 County: $4.00 School: $.385 Other: $.01
Adjacent unincorporated area: Code Area—64007 TOTAL TAX RATE: $4.395
County—Outside: $4.00 School: $.385 Other: $.01

(c) Combined total commercial property tax rates 1978–1979 per $100 assessed value.
Code Area(s) 4009 TOTAL $4.44
City tax rate: $0 County: $4.00 School: $.43 Other: $.01
Adjacent unincorporated area: Code Area—148002 TOTAL TAX RATE: $4.45
County—Outside: $4.00 School: $.44 Other: $.01

(d) Retail Sales Tax: State 5% City/County 1% Total 6%
0% included in total for mass transit district funding.

(e) Police Department: 116 employees with 92 sworn officers; 1.2 per 1000 population.

(f) Fire Department: Six fire stations with 72 employees; 66 Firefighters, 15 Fire Captains, 1 Fire Marshall and 3 Battalion Chiefs. 1 fire employee per 1000 population.

(g) Fire Insurance Classification: Source of Rating: Insurance Services Office of Calif.
City Rating 3 to — Adjacent unincorporated area: **** to
**** Each Fire District has its own rating.
corporated areas: Construction of the Municipal Services Center, Construction of

(h) Major projects authorized for improvement of city services or to adjacent unincorporated areas: Construction of the Municipal Services Center, Construction of the New Emergency Services Center, Multiple street improvements, 2 new bridges (Alderbrook and Brookwood).

14. The Santa Rosa Labor Market Area February 1979

Area includes SONOMA COUNTY
Estimated area population 274,300. Estimated total employment 118,800

3400 Agriculture	16800 Retail Trade
N/A Agriculture Services	3200 Wholesale Trade
4500 Construction	5300 Finance/Real Estate/Insurance
13300 Manufacturing	16000 Services
4100 Transp/Comm/Utilities	19400 Government
	25800 Other

NOTES:
Above figures are for February 1979—latest figures available.
SOURCE: Coastal Area Labor Market Information Group, P.O. Box 7774, San Francisco 94120

15. Characteristics of the Labor Force

Extent of unionization Construction workers, metal trades, food checkers, and meat, shoe, cannery and public utility workers highly organized. Majority of transport, culinary and winery workers organized.
Wage rates, extent of unionization, fringe benefits, and related information for specific industries and job classifications may be obtained from the State Employment Development Department located at 606 Healdsburg Avenue, Santa Rosa, CA 95401 or at 800 Capitol Mall, Sacramento, CA 95814.

The Community Area referred to below includes the Santa Rosa area.

16. Manufacturing Employment

There are 235 manufacturing plants in the community area. Leading group classes of products are: Electronics, scientific instruments, fabricated metals, printing, leather. The largest manufacturing firms in the community area are: products, machinery & specialty wood products.

Name of Company	Employment	Products
Hewlett-Packard Company	2000	Microwave Instruments
Optical Coating Laboratories, Inc.	900	Optical goods
Santa Rosa Shoe Corporation	329	Shoes and boots
National Controls, Inc.	549	Automatic weighing devices
The Press Democrat	280	Newspapers
Ecodyne Cooling Products	180	Cooling Towers
Standard Structures, Inc.	375	Glue laminated beams
Bepex Corp., Rietz Division	149	Food processing equipment
Malm Fireplaces, Inc.	73	Free standing fireplaces
Optical Engineering, Inc.	223	Electro-optical components
C & D Batteries	100	Industrial batteries
Electroscale Corporation	140	Electronic weighing

Facilities include (if applicable): 3 machine shops, 1 grey iron foundries, 0 steel foundries, 1 non-ferrous metal foundries, and 3 public warehouses.
Major raw material resources include: Agriculture products and lumber

17. Non-Manufacturing Employment

Name of Company	Employment	Type of Business
County of Sonoma	2420	County government
Santa Rosa City Schools	1030	Education
Pacific Telephone Company	1239	Telephone Service
Santa Rosa Memorial Hospital	900	Medical service
City of Santa Rosa	525	Local government
Pacific Gas & Electric Co.	445	Electric and gas utility
J.C. Penney, The Emporium	283, 300	Department Store
Sears Roebuck & Co.	300	Department store

18. Community Facilities

Health: Santa Rosa has 4 general hospitals with 498 total bed capacity. 230 physicians/ surgeons, 77 dentists, 16 optometrists, 37 chiropractors, and other:

Education: 11 elementary schools, 5 junior high schools, 4 high schools, 1 junior colleges, 1 colleges or universities, and other: numerous private schools.

Cultural: 83 churches, 2 libraries, 2 newspapers, 7 radio stations, 5 TV channels received direct, 1 TV cable systems, 23 banks, 20 savings and loan, 26 parks, 18 playgrounds, 15 theaters. Other recreational facilities include: Annadel State Park and Spring Lake County Park.

19. Housing Availability, Prices and Rentals

Rentals for one and two bedroom apartments and duplexes range from $155 to $325 per month. Rentals for two and three bedroom houses range from $265 to $750 per month. Sales prices of existing homes were from $50,000 to $125,000 during 1978. There are many suburban residential areas within 8 miles of Santa Rosa offering homes priced from $50,000 to $125,000.
There are 0 hotels with 0 total rooms and 32 motels with 1250 total rooms in the community area. There are 35 mobile home parks in the community area.

20. Remarks

Santa Rosa is the County seat of Sonoma with a number of regional State and Federal offices, too. Its economic base is primarily marketing and merchandising and professional services oriented—medical in particular. In recent years, light industrial plants have been growing or have been added to the community. Sonoma County is still heavily agricultural and tourist-oriented.

Reviewed for statewide standardization by the California Chamber of Commerce, Department of Economic Development and Research, 455 Capitol Mall, Sacramento, California, 95814, on July 24, 1979.

For further information contact SANTA ROSA CHAMBER OF COMMERCE
637 FIRST STREET PHONE (707) 545–1414, SANTA ROSA, CALIFORNIA, 95404

Appendix B ECONOMIC ACTIVITY IN THE SAN FRANCISCO BAY AREA: CHARACTERISTICS OF THE ECONOMY

The San Francisco Bay Area, covering 7,000 square miles and consisting of nine counties bordering San Francisco Bay, can be analyzed and considered as a single social and economic unit. It is also necessary, however, to recognize that the Bay Area comprises a series of subregions encompassing a broad range of development patterns consisting of compactly structured central cities, sparsely populated woodlands and agricultural lands, suburban bedroom communities, and major complexes of economic activities.

During the last two decades, the Bay Area has developed a highly complex and diversified economy. Trade and shipping are almost as important now as when the area's economic activities focused solely on the use of the Bay Area and its tributaries. Financial institutions and administrative offices locating in San Francisco, the heart of the region's economy, have also helped make the Bay Area a dominant economic force. Today, as the leading West Coast center for finance, administration, and trade, the region's influence extends far beyond the immediate area, encompassing all of the western states. The San Francisco Bay Area, as an economic mechanism, also supplies an important economic link between the West and the major urban centers of the eastern United States, between the West and Hawaii and the South Pacific, and between the West and the Far East.

Wholesale and retail trade, government, services, and manufacturing are the Bay Area's largest sources of employment. Although the number of employees in each of these economic sectors has increased during the past decade, the increase has been most significant in the services sector. This sector is highly diversified and is related to industry and trade as well as to the needs of the resident and tourist population.

In regard to manufacturing, it is important to understand that, in contrast with the older metropolitan areas in the eastern United States, the Bay Area's manufacturing base is dominated by newly emergent research and development industries such as aerospace, electronics, and scientific instruments. The location of such industries in the Bay Area helps make it

Reprinted from *Economic Activity in the San Francisco Bay Area,* Technical Report P–368 1.1, Association of Bay Area Governments, Berkeley, California, August 1971, Chapter 1, pp. 7–28.

a major center for education and scientific research which, in turn, provides impetus for continued growth of highly skilled, high-wage industries and services.

Activities in which the region is relatively self-reliant are transportation, communication, utilities, and construction. There is little need to import these goods and services from outside the region.

AN OVERVIEW OF THE BAY AREA ECONOMIC STRUCTURE

Trade, government, manufacturing, and services are the Bay Area's main employment sectors.

Trade

This sector, accounting for 21 percent of nonagricultural employment in 1970 as indicated in Table 1.1, is as important locally as it is in California where 22 percent of employment is in trade, and in the nation where 21 percent is in trade. Because of its strategic location the Bay Area is a major wholesale trade center serving northern California and Nevada. The wholesale sector is more important locally than it is for California as a whole and the United States, as indicated by the comparative percent distribution in Table 1.1. While retail trade accounts for slightly more than 15 percent of nonagricultural employment, this sector accounts for a larger share of employment in the state and in the nation.

Government

This sector accounts for 21 percent of nonagricultural employment as compared to almost 20 percent in California and 17 percent in the United States. Almost 6 percent of the Bay Area's nonagricultural workers are employed by the Federal government as compared to 4.7 percent in California and 3.8 percent in the United States. Historically, the Bay Area has served as a major center for Federal government activities. San Francisco is a major regional administrative center for the Federal government, and there is substantial employment related to the military installations located in the Bay Area. State and local government employment is equally important locally and statewide where this sector accounts for 15.1 percent of employment, while nationally the percentage share is 13.3 percent.

TABLE. 1.1   Percent Distribution of Nonagricultural Employment in the San Francisco Bay Area, California, and the United States, 1970

Industry	Bay Area	California	United States
Mining	0.1%	0.5%	0.9%
Contract construction	5.0	4.5	5.1
Manufacturing	19.2	22.3	27.4
Nondurable goods	7.6	7.4	11.6
Durable goods	11.6	14.9	15.8
Transportation, communications, and utilities	9.1	6.8	6.5
Transportation	5.6	3.9	4.0
Communications, utilities, and sanitary services	3.5	2.9	2.5
Trade	21.0	22.3	21.1
Wholesale	5.9	5.7	5.5
Retail	15.1	16.6	15.6
Finance, insurance, and real estate	6.5	5.4	5.3
Finance	3.1	2.6	2.3
Insurance and real estate	3.4	2.8	3.0
Services	18.1	18.4	16.6
Government	21.0	19.8	17.1
Federal	5.9	4.7	3.8
State and local	15.1	15.1	13.3
Total	100.0%	100.0%	100.0%

Manufacturing

The next largest economic activity in the Bay Area, measured in terms of nonagricultural employment, is manufacturing. This sector accounts for 19.2 percent of all nonagricultural employment. However, the Bay Area has less of its employment in manufacturing than does California, where 22.3 percent is employed in manufacturing, and the United States, where 27.4 percent is employed in this sector. The Bay Area's manufacturing sector is dominated by new major research and development industries, such as aerospace, electronics, and scientific instruments, in contrast with older metropolitan areas throughout the United States.

Services

The services sector is highly diversified and is related not only to the demands of the residents and tourists but to industry and trade as well. Accounting for 18 percent of nonagricultural employment it compares with California, where 18.4 percent of employment is in services. This sector, however, is more important locally than nationally, where 16.6 percent of nonagricultural employment is in the services sector.

Because of the Bay Area's geography it has become a shipping and transportation center. As a result, the transportation, communications, and utilities sector has become the source of employment of 9.1 percent of nonagricultural workers. This sector is relatively more important in the Bay Area than in California and the United States, where 6.8 percent and 6.5 percent of employment is in this sector.

Finance, Insurance, and Real Estate

While the finance, insurance, and real estate sector employs only 6.5 percent of nonagricultural employment, this sector is also more important in the Bay Area than in California and the United States. The significance of this sector is reflected in the role the Bay Area has assumed as the leading West Coast center for finance and insurance headquarters and the administrative center for regional offices.

Contract construction and mining follow in order of importance in terms of employment. While construction accounts for 5 percent of nonagricultural employment in the Bay Area, it is a larger share than California's 4.5 percent btu almost the same as the national share.

Whereas California's distribution of nonagricultural employment is similar to that of the United States, with the largest concentrations in the manufacturing sector and the trade sector, the Bay Area's total nonagricultural employment is concentrated mainly in nonmanufacturing activities such as trade, services, and government.

The Bay Area has developed a highly complex and diversified economy and does not depend on one or two major industries for its economic livelihood. As an economic area, it forms a vast and wealthy market. Having a high degree of self-sufficiency, more than half of the Bay Area's work force (approximately 54 percent) is employed in population-serving activities while 46 percent is in basic activities serving outside markets.*

REGIONAL EMPLOYMENT TRENDS: 1960-1970

During the decade of the sixties nonagricultural employment in the San Francisco Bay Area increased by about 43 percent, exceeding the national

* Association of Bay Area Governments, *Regional Plan 1970–1990, San Francisco Bay Region,* Berkeley, July 1970.

TABLE 1.2   Growth in Nonagricultural Employment, 1960 and 1970 San Francisco Bay Area (in Thousands)

Industry	1960	1970	Change 1960–1970	
			Number	Percent
Mining	2.3	2.6	0.3	13.0%
Contract construction	82.0	88.7	6.7	8.2
Manufacturing	283.9	339.1	55.2	19.4
Nondurable goods	133.3	134.1	.8	.6
Durable goods	150.6	205.0	54.4	36.1
Transportation, communications, and utilities	118.6	160.4	41.8	35.2
Transportation	79.7	99.0	19.3	24.2
Communications, utilities, and sanitary services	38.9	61.4	22.5	57.8
Trade	261.7	370.3	108.6	41.5
Wholesale	82.1	104.7	22.6	27.5
Retail	179.6	265.6	86.0	47.9
Finance, insurance, and real estate	77.7	114.3	36.6	47.1
Finance	31.2	54.0	22.8	73.1
Real estate	46.5	60.3	13.8	29.7
Services	178.0	319.8	141.8	80.0
Government	233.5	370.1	136.6	58.5
Federal	84.8	104.0	19.2	22.6
State and local	148.7	266.1	117.4	79.0
Total	1,237.7	1,765.3	527.6	42.6%

July data. Source: California Department of Industrial Relations.

growth rate of 30 percent and growing at a slightly slower rate than California's 43.3 percent.

As a result of this growth the employment distribution in 1970 differed significantly from the 1960 distribution in some sectors, but in most the change was minor. The proportion of total employment decreased in all sectors during this 10-year period, except in the finance, insurance, and real estate sector and in the services and government sectors which showed large increases in employment during the last decade. The trade sector's proportion of total nonagricultural employment remained almost static during this 10-year period.

TABLE 1.3   Percent Distribution of Nonagricultural Employment, 1960 and 1970 San Francisco Bay Area

Industry	1960	1970	Distribution change 1960–1970
Mining	0.2%	0.1%	−0.1%
Contract construction	6.6	5.0	−1.6
Manufacturing	22.9	19.2	−3.7
Nondurable goods	10.8	7.6	−3.2
Durable goods	12.1	11.6	−0.5
Transportation, communications, and utilities	9.6	9.1	−0.5
Transportation	6.4	5.6	−0.8
Communications, utilities, and sanitary services	3.1	3.5	0.4
Trade	21.1	21.0	−0.1
Wholesale	6.6	5.9	−0.7
Retail	14.5	15.1	0.6
Finance, insurance and real estate	6.3	6.5	0.2
Finance	2.5	3.1	0.6
Insurance and real estate	3.8	3.4	−0.4
Services	14.4	18.1	3.7
Government	18.9	21.0	2.1
Federal	6.9	5.9	−1.0
State and local	12.0	15.1	3.1
Total	100.0%	100.0%	0.0%

Services experienced an impressive increase of 80 percent. At the same time it registered the largest numerical gain in employment, accounting for an increase of almost 142,000 employees.

The government sector maintained its dominating role as an employer in the Bay Area during the past ten years. While government employment increased by 59 percent, it accounted for an increase of 137,000 employees. However, the fastest growing portion of government was the state and local component. This subsector increased by 79 percent, and measured by number of workers gained, it was responsible for an increase of 117,000 employees.

Finance, insurance, and real estate employment increased by more than 47 percent, but only accounted for an increase of 37,000 employees. The finance subsector was the fastest growing portion of this sector. It increased by 73 percent and was responsible for almost two-thirds of the sector's increase in employment.

Trade, also a large employer in the Bay Area, showed the fourth largest sector gain. Growing by 42 percent, it was responsible for an increase of 109,000 employees. Most of the increase, however, was in retail employment, which registered a gain of 48 percent and a numerical increase in employment of 86,000 workers.

Although manufacturing employment grew by only 19.4 percent, this sector was responsible for increasing nonagricultural employment by more than 55,000 workers since 1960. Almost all of the increase took place in the durable goods subsector, reflecting the growth of research and devlopment in the Bay Area.

All other sectors showed employment gains between 1960 and 1970. However, with the exception of communications, utilities, and sanitary services, the percentage increases were below the total Bay Area rate of growth.

Tables 1.4 and 1.5 illustrate the change in employment distribution by industry in 1960 and 1970 for California and the United States.

TECHNIQUES FOR EVALUATING REGIONAL ECONOMIC GROWTH

An important consideration in evaluating the economy of a region is its overall performance in the recent past expressed in terms of employment trends, although these trends alone do not fully reflect or explain the reasons for regional economic growth. Nor do they identify broad sources of employment growth stimuli. Moreover, employment trends do not indicate whether a region has fallen behind or forged ahead in the neverending competition for new jobs and industry.

In order to understand the economic growth of the San Francisco Bay Area, it is important to look beyond the performance of employment trends to examine why employment changed as it did. Many complex techniques have been developed by regional economists and planners to analyze in detail the process of economic growth.

Differential Shift Technique

One technique to identify sources of employment change, termed the Differential Shift Technique, has been refined and developed more fully by the Regional Economics Division of the Office of Business Economics, U.S. Department of Commerce to be used as a tool for evaluating economic growth by areas.

TABLE 1.4   Percent Distribution of Nonagricultural Employment, 1960 and 1970, California

Industry	1960	1970	Distribution change 1960–1970
Mining	0.6%	0.5%	−0.1%
Contract construction	5.9	4.5	−1.4
Manufacturing	26.9	22.3	−4.6
Nondurable goods	8.8	7.4	−1.4
Durable goods	18.1	14.9	−3.2
Transportation, communications, and utilities	7.3	6.8	−0.5
Transportation	4.3	3.9	−0.4
Communications, utilities, and sanitary services	3.0	2.9	0.1
Trade	21.8	22.3	0.5
Wholesale	6.0	5.7	−0.3
Retail	15.8	16.6	0.8
Finance, insurance and real estate	5.1	5.4	0.3
Finance	2.2	2.6	0.4
Insurance and real estate	3.0	2.8	−0.2
Services	14.5	18.4	3.9
Government	17.9	19.8	1.9
Federal	5.2	4.7	−0.5
State and local	12.7	15.1	2.4
Total	100.0%	100.0%	0.0%

Inasmuch as increases in national economic activity have brought about dramatic employment changes, in interest in these changes with regard to geographic and industrial distribution has resulted. In an economy as large and diverse as that of the United States, with the variability in both geographic and industrial growth posing numerous questions, it is sometimes difficult to find answers in the total pattern of change. Moreover, because of the multiplicity of industries and geographic areas, an evaluation of the performance of each industrial-regional combination over a period of time presents a formidable task in the handling of data and information. However, once the data have been organized into an analytic structure, it is possible to identify the basic facts which relate to the differences in the rates of growth of employment among regions. Further, additional resources of insight and analysis may be used to yield

TABLE 1.5   Percent Distribution of Nonagricultural Employment, 1960 and 1970
United States

Industry	1960	1970	Distribution change 1960–1970
Mining	1.3%	0.9%	−0.4%
Contract construction	5.9	5.1	−0.8
Manufacturing	30.8	27.4	−3.4
Nondurable goods	13.5	11.6	−1.9
Durable goods	17.3	15.8	−1.5
Transportation, communications, and utilities	7.4	6.5	−0.9
Transportation	4.7	4.0	−0.7
Communications, utilities, and sanitary services	2.7	2.5	−0.2
Trade	20.9	21.1	0.2
Wholesale	5.5	5.5	0.0
Retail	15.3	15.6	0.3
Finance, insurance, and real estate	5.0	5.3	0.3
Finance	2.0	2.3	0.3
Insurance and real estate	3.0	3.0	0.0
Services	13.9	16.6	2.7
Government	14.8	17.1	2.3
Federal	4.1	3.8	−0.3
State and local	10.7	13.3	2.6
Total	100.0%	100.0%	0.0%

meaningful generalizations concerning a particular industrial or regional situation.

The differential shift technique considers the growth rate of the nation as a whole, measured by total employment and employment within the various industry sectors, as the standard for determining growth of smaller divisions of the nation. Essentially, the technique is built on the assumption that employment growth due to national growth factors in a region would occur at the same rate as that in the nation as a whole. Therefore, if a local area exceeds this growth rate, it is an indication that national growth factors have had a positive or favorable impact on the region. If the local area experiences a slower growth rate than that of the nation, indications are that the national growth factors have had a negative or unfavorable impact on the economy of the region.

The differential shift technique is also built on the assumption that such favorable or unfavorable impacts depend on two basic factors regarding the growth situation. One is industrial mix and the other is regional share. Industrial mix indicates whether a region has a rapid-growth or a slow-growth distribution of industries. For example, the growth rate of each industry nationally must be compared with the overall national growth rate for all industries combined. The rate of growth of a particular national industry is characterized as rapid-growth if it exceeds the growth rate of all national industries, and slow-growth if it falls short of the growth rate of all national industries combined over the same time period. Thus, industries growing more rapidly than the growth rate of all industries nationally make a favorable or positive impact on the industrial mix or composition of a region in which these industries exist. Industries growing more slowly than all industries nationally make an unfavorable or negative impact. The change related to industrial mix of each industry in a region, then, is actually the difference between that industry's national growth rate and the growth rate of all industries combined nationally, applied to the region's base year employment. The algebraic sum of the industrial mix component for all industries in a region is that region's total change relative to industrial mix. The impact is favorable if the sum is positive and unfavorable if the sum is negative. Thus, if a region has in its industry mix a number of nationwide rapid-growth industries, its industry mix growth component will be positive. If the region has a number of slow-growth industries on a nationwide basis, it will show a negative industry mix component.

The regional share component indicates whether a region has an increasing or decreasing share in this industrial mix or distribution of industries. It is calculated by comparing growth rates in each industry of a region with the growth rate in each industry at the national level, with the difference applied to the region's base year employment. The result shows the change in employment in each industry in the region, which would have taken place if the regional industry had grown or declined at the same rate that it grew or declined nationally. If an industry grew faster in the region than in the nation as a whole, or declined more slowly, its regional share component is positive. If it grew more slowly or declined more rapidly in the region than in the nation, its regional share component is negative. The total regional share component for a region is the algebraic sum of the changes in relative regional share for each industry. Its (positive or negative) sign indicates whether the region as a whole performed better or worse than could be expected on the basis of the industry mix of its employment-base year.

Since both the industrial mix and regional share factors are working simultaneously, they may be mutually reinforcing or they may work in opposite directions. It is possible for a region to be growing more rapidly in most or even all industries than the nation does, and yet to have a declining share of national employment because of an unfavorable industrial mix. It is equally possible for a region to have more than its share of fast-growing industries, yet at the same time experience a relative overall decline because its major industries are losing ground to their counterparts in other parts of the country.

The data presented in this analysis do not pretend to show what an area's industrial mix or regional share should be. For example, many areas have had low growth rates in total employment because their economy is dominated by agriculture. The decline in agricultural employment, however, is the result of a broad interindustrial technological revolution. Likewise, technological advances have held down the rate of employment growth in other industries. Thus, it is not being implied here that high rates of employment growth can be considered as desirable development objectives without regard to other economic considerations.

Therefore, an important weakness of the differential shift analysis is the fact that the technique does not include changes in other major variables such as regional realignments in population, total income payments, value added by manufacture, private investment expenditures, and public expenditures for infrastructure which may significantly influence or modify a region's industrial mix and regional share components.* Also, other considerations, such as supply of specific skills, local amenities, and locational advantages, to name a few, must be taken into account when evaluating the economic activities of a region. To the extent feasible, some of these variables and considerations are evaluated in this section and in other parts of this study.

Although employment growth cannot be accepted as the equivalent of general economic growth, the differential shift technique does provide to those concerned with the economy of the Bay Area a factual basis for comparing its past performance with that of the nation and other regions. Moreover, the analysis will be helpful in developing effective plans for future economic development.

Table 1.6 illustrates the results of the differential shift technique as applied to Bay Area nonagricultural employment data for 1960 and 1970.

The standard of reference used was the growth rate of the United States, measured in terms of total nonagricultural employment and em-

---

* Walter Isard, *Methods of Regional Analysis: An Introduction to Regional Science* (John Wiley and Massachusetts Institute of Technology, New York, 1960), p 259.

ployment in each industry.* By definition, then, any industry or area which exceeded the national rate of growth between 1960 and 1970 experienced relatively rapid growth, and any industry or area which did not meet this growth rate experienced relatively slower growth. While total national nonagricultural employment increased by almost 30 percent during the ten-year period, the Bay Area experienced a higher growth rate of more than 42 percent during the same period, exceeding the national rate by almost 13 percent. Thus, the overall performance of all industry sectors in the Bay Area far exceeded the national growth during this period. As a result, each industry sector in the Bay Area, growing at a higher rate than the total national rate of growth, has a positive net relative change component. Those having a lower rate of growth than the national rate have a negative change component.

Data in Table 1.6 clearly illustrate the dominant influence of national growth factors in the Bay Area economy. Also highlighted in the table is the dominance of nationwide rapid-growth industries such as services, state and local government, finance, and retail trade in the Bay Area's industrial mix. In several cases the Bay Area has an unfavorable industrial mix, in terms of employment growth trends within a given industry sector. This unfavorable impact is more severe in manufacturing and in the transportation, communications, and utilities sectors which are slow-growth national industries and relatively large employment sectors in the Bay Area economy. Despite these cases of unfavorable industrial mix where growth rates within these sectors have lagged behind the national growth rate, the overall industrial mix for the San Francisco Bay Area is favorable.

In terms of regional functions, it is apparent that the Bay Area's favorable industrial mix has been accompanied by an even larger favorable change in the regional share component. The advantageous competitive position of the Bay Area indicates that its employment in specific industries or sectors, with the exception of construction, nondurable manufacturing, and wholesale trade, grew more raipdly than national employment in the same industries or sectors. Illustrated in the table is the relative importance of services, state and local government, retail trade, transportation, communications, and utilities, and durable goods manufacturing (research and development) sectors of the Bay Area economy.

---

* The differential shift technique permits the use of any appropriate area as a standard of reference. Thus, in addition to the Nation, such areas as a region, state, transportation corridor, or a river basin provide useful alternatives or supplementary measures of comparison. Thus, the standard area need not coincide with the analytical universe.

TABLE 1.6 Components of Employment Change, 1960–1970 San Francisco Bay Area (Nonagricultural Employment in Thousands)

Industry	Changes related to			Total change	Net relative change
	National growth	Industrial mix	Regional share		
Mining	0.7	− 0.9	0.5	0.3	− 0.4
Contract construction	24.5	−14.8	− 3.0	6.7	− 17.8
Manufacturing	84.9	−41.4	11.6	55.1	− 29.8
Nondurable goods	39.9	−24.8	− 14.3	0.8	+ 39.1
Durable goods	45.0	−16.6	25.9	54.3	9.3
Transportation, communications, and utilities	35.4	−20.0	26.4	41.8	6.4
Transportation	23.8	−15.3	10.8	19.3	− 4.5
Communications, utilities, and sanitary services	11.6	− 4.7	15.6	22.5	10.9
Trade	78.2	3.9	26.4	108.5	30.3
Wholesale	24.5	− 0.2	− 1.8	22.5	− 2.0
Retail	53.7	4.1	28.2	86.0	32.3
Finance, insurance, and real estate	23.2	6.1	7.3	36.6	13.4
Finance	9.3	7.4	6.1	22.8	13.5
Insurance and real estate	13.9	− 1.3	1.2	13.8	− 0.1
Services	52.2	44.8	44.9	141.9	89.7
Government	69.9	39.4	27.4	136.7	66.8
Federal	25.4	− 8.0	1.8	19.2	− 6.2
State and local	44.5	47.4	25.6	117.5	73.0
Total	369.0	17.1	141.5	527.6	158.6

Source: Derived from Table 1.2 and Table A–2.

With regard to net relative change, in Table 1.6, this component also resulted in a large favorable change. It shows that the realized employment change in the 1960's was 158.6 thousand employees in excess of what would have occurred at the overall national rate for all industries combined.

A summary of Table 1.6 reveals that the Bay Area economy has been largely dependent on national factors in the past. Moreover, even though the area has a favorable industrial mix, the growth rates of some industry groups have fallen below the national growth rate. Further, the table shows that the Bay Area serves as a regional center in government, services, trade, and manufacturing.

Industry Orientation and Employment Change

The reason for favorable components of employment change in the Bay Area also vary from industry to industry. In some industries the change is caused by favorable factors at a finer level of industry detail than are considered in this study, since uniform detailed data for Bay Area employment are not readily available for the 1960–1970 decade. However, while the reasons for change are many, some general evaluations regarding broad industry orientation and functional relationships at the national, regional, and local level are explained below.

When industries are market oriented, they tend to locate in regions with rapid population growth and expanding markets. Recently issued 1970 Census population data have ranked California as the most populous state in the nation.* Also, figures from the same census show that Bay Area population increased 25 percent over the 1960 Census count. Not only is the San Francisco Bay Area one of the fastest growing economic units in the country, but also one of the largest, with three metropolitan areas and one labor market area located within its boundaries. Thus, as the Bay Area continues to increase its share of the nation's population it also expands its markets and increases its attractions for market oriented industries.

Other industries, such as those involved in scientific research and development, are attracted to regions with a skilled labor force and therefore toward those places which tend to attract people with above-average incomes and education. Areas such as the West Coast, California, and especially the Bay Area offer attractive physical and cultural amenities. Because of these features, a number of new industries, dominated by re-

* U.S. Bureau of the Census, *1970 Census of Population,* United States, PC(P3)–1.

search and development industries such as aerospace, electronics, and scientific instruments, have located in the area during the last decade or so. As a result, the Bay Area is one of the leading regions in the country producing aerospace electronics equipment for the federal government, while its importance as a center for research and development has grown steadily. Conversely, it has also become a major center for education and scientific research which will continue to attract high-wage industries requiring a highly skilled labor force. However, some of these industries are beginning to feel the impact of federal government cutbacks in defense spending. As a result, part of the Bay Area economy is experiencing stagnation.

Employment in noncommodity industries is generally determined by the distribution and growth of population. As pointed out earlier, California and the Bay Area have undergone phenomenal population growth. Thus, as the Bay Area grows in population, it will continue to generate its share of employment in industry sectors such as trade, finance, insurance and real estate, and transportation, communications, and utilities. Further, the growth of the highly diversified services sector in the Bay Area is functionally related to the growth of industry and trade as well as the affluence of the area's growing resident and tourist population.

Although the continuing dispersion of both manufacturing and noncommodity industries is leading to a more uniform distribution of such industries in both metropolitan and nonmetropolitan areas in the nation, the advantages of locating in metropolitan areas appears to be growing for at least one major activity. That activity includes administrative and auxiliary employment, encompassing central offices and research and development functions. For a number of reasons central or headquarters offices have always located in metropolitan areas. The development of advanced data-handling and communications techniques have been responsible for these offices moving from areas located outside metropolitan areas to the central city of a region's metropolitan area. Also, the opportunities for personal contact, facilities for rapid external communication, and the ample supply of clerical labor required by a large central office facility represent needs which are sometimes difficult to satisfy outside metropolitan areas. Moreover, while industrial research and development facilities tend to locate near the central headquarters of their firms, metropolitan areas tend to make available the amenities required by their highly skilled personnel.

Thus, the Bay Area's rapid growth reflects essentially a massive migration of people into the area from other parts of California and the nation. Also, its role as one of the largest and fastest growing economic units in the nation, with three metropolitan areas located within this megalopolis, has helped to make the Bay Area the West Coast center for administrative offices and auxiliary employment.

In adidtion to the national, regional, and local relationships examined in this study, there are further insights underlying economic growth with regard to these relationships. Certain recent events of national and international significance have been responsible for major economic growth stimulus in the Bay Area. For example, the Korean war and America's involvement in Vietnam have generated an increase in the Bay Area's military and commercial shipping activities. Also, the continued interest in space exploration is another major factor that has generated an increase in the area's research and development activity.

Because of the Bay Area's strategic coastal and bay location in northern California, and the existence of excellent harbors, its diversified industries have trade ties with other areas of the West, the major urban centers of the eastern United States, Hawaii and the South Pacific, and the Far East. Regionally, the San Francisco Bay Area comprises an expansive, diversified, and wealthy market, commanding attention from industries and investors from the nation and from many parts of the world. Thus, the diversity in the area's economic structure, in addition to its other assets, will provide the stimulus for steady growth in the Bay Area in future years.

Determinants of Bay Area Growth Potential

In order to understand the growth potentials of the San Francisco Bay Area, it is necessary to evaluate the economy in terms of the determinants of regional growth. In a previous section, to identify some broad sources of employment growth stimuli, the differential shift technique was applied to Bay Area employment data. Another theory which is effective for explaining or describing regional economic growth is the economic base theory, or, as it is sometimes referred to, the export base theory. Generally an economic base study, in which this theory is applied, identifies a region's key sources of employment and income and provides an understanding of the source and level of income in that region.*

The economic base theory may be characterized briefly by pointing out that it divides a region's total economic activity into two segments. One segment designates certain industries within the economic structure as ex-

---

* For a comprehensive treatment of the classical economic base concept see Charles Tiebout, *The Community Economic Base Study,* Supplementary Paper No. 16 (Committee for Economic Development, New York, 1962).

port or basic industries, serving markets outside the region, and consequently generating income for the region from sources located beyond its boundaries. The other segment, referred to as nonexporting or nonbasic, is comprised of industries whose goods and services are sold within the region. Thus, while the nonbasic or local consuming industry sector is involved in the selling of goods and services to the local market within the region, it generates no income from outside the region.

Implicit in the basic and nonbasic division of the economy is a cause and effect relationship. For example, the export industry sector is considered to be the principle force stimulating growth in the regional economy. Thus, if basic employment increases or decreases, changes in nonbasic employment will presumably move in the same direction. Assuming that over a long period the proportion of basic and nonbasic jobs will remain about the same, an increase in the number of basic jobs will eventually generate an increase in the number of nonbasic jobs. This method of analysis recognizes, however, that some firms within the industry groups sell their products to both export and local markets, and part of the employment in these firms and industries is basic and some is nonbasic. Consequently, employment in each industry group is assigned to a basic or nonbasic category, or divided between the two categories. Employment in each category is then summed to arrive at total basic and total nonbasic employment.

To measure quantitatively the basic or nonbasic components of a region's economy and to forecast increases in total employment, a fairly simple type of regional multiplier analysis is associated with economic base studies. It is based on the ratio of total employment in a region's basic activities to total employment in its nonbasic activities.* From the data necessary to compute this ratio, a regional multiplier can be calculated. It is equal to total employment in both basic and nonbasic activities divided by total basic employment.†

In an economic base study it is possible to make extensive use of the employment multiplier concept for forecasting purposes, although forecasting is not necessarily part of a base study‡ After the economic forces which have contributed to the region's structure have been evaluated and understood, it is possible to project how these and other economic forces will affect the region in the future. Thus, after evaluating the future

---

* The ratio between the increase in employment in a region's basic activities and the increase in its non-basic activities can also be used.

† For a complete statement on regional multiplier analysis as applied to economic base studies, see Walter Isard, *op. cit.,* pp. 190–213.

‡ Forecasting methods are examined in detail in chapters 6 and 7, Charles Tiebout, *op. cit.,* pp. 57–82.

prospects for growth in the basic activities, the employment level in basic industries can be forecast for some time period. By applying the employment multiplier to the basic employment forecasts, future levels of total employment and the associated nonbasic employment change can then be forecast. Hence, these forecasts can be used effectively to project changes in population, income, land use, and the tax base. Also, projections of trends in these areas can be used in the planning process to meet an expansive range of a region's public and private needs, such as in planning and zoning, capital improvements programs, taxes and expenditures, housing, transportation, and utility services.

Whether the basic/nonbasic ratio and the associated multiplier are used to simply describe a region's economy, or are adopted for forecasting purposes, some analysts have been cautious about using the economic base study and the multiplier concept and have preferred other methods of analysis when evaluating the economy of a region.* While it is not the purpose of this section of the study to take issue with statements for or against the economic base theory, it is in the interest of this study to identify basic and nonbasic industries in the Bay Area in order to broadly explain or describe regional economic growth. Hence, the summary of the economic base theory has been included here to point out one way to identify a region's key industries. Nevertheless, it is well beyond the scope of this study to actually undertake an economic base study, simply because the most accurate method of determining basic and nonbasic employment is by conducting an intensive survey of the region's economic base, through the use of personal interviews and mail questionnaires.

BATSC Basic and Population-Serving Employment

Because of the reasons mentioned above it was necessary to rely on data generated by the Bay Area Transportation Study Commission (BATSC) modeling system for a division of employment similar to the traditional economic base theory classification of basic and nonbasic employment.†

* For an extensive presentation of statements in support of the economic base theory as well as statements opposed to the economic base theory, see Ralph W. Pfouts, *The Techniques of Urban Economic Analysis* (Charles Davis Publishing Company, Trenton, 1960), and Hans Blumenfeld, *The Modern Metropolis: Its Origins, Growth, Characteristics, and Planning* (M.I.T. Press, Cambridge, 1967), Chapter 33.

† The BATSC publications containing the forecasts and entire modeling process are: *EMPRO: BATSC Employment Projections, 1965–1990*, Technical Report 218 (Bay Area Transportation Study Commission, Berkeley, September, 1968).

William Goldner, *Projective Land Use Model* (PLUM), Technical Report 219 (Bay Area Transportation Study Commission, Berkeley, September, 1968).

While an overview of all the models and their forecasting process is not entirely relevant to the overall objectives of this study, a relatively concise summary appears in Chapter 5 of the *Bay Area Transportation Report*.

However, because the models divide employment into basic and population-serving categories, which have an apparent similarity to the economic base concept of basic and nonbasic employment categories, it is appropriate to clarify the distinctions in classification. It should be pointed out, though, that Bay Area basic employment by industry group and total population-serving employment data included in this study were derived from *BEMOD*.*

This model divides all urban activity into a basic sector, a household sector, and a population-serving sector which locate successively and for the most part in response to locational decisions of previously located groups.† The basic sector, producing goods and services mainly for export out of the region or for intermediate use by other firms within the region, is composed of economic activities which depend primarily on interregional transportation facilities, unique site characteristics, inter-industry linkages, and natural resource advantages of a region. The decisions regarding the location of these basic industries are influenced by these characteristics and are assumed to have a high priority in the sequence of development and in the competition for urban land.

Basic activities, then, influence the location of household sectors which include the region's labor force and dependent population, dwelling units, and residential land. Finally, the population-serving sector, characterized for the most part by retail trade, personal and business services, and local government, is comprised of that sector of the economy which is dependent upon the location of the nighttime residential population from which most of the demand for consumer goods and services originates and the daytime location of workers who also generate some demand for these goods and services.

While there is a similarity between the sequence in the urban development process discussed above, and the economic base theory which regards the basic sector as the main generator of regional growth upon

---

Joseph Nathanson, *Basic Employment Allocation Model* (BEMOD), Technical Report 222 (Bay Area Transportation Study Commission, Berkeley, Draft).

"Controlled Trends" Zonal Forecasts 1965–1980–1990, Technical Report 226 (Bay Area Transportation Study Commission, Berkeley, May, 1969).

Bay Area Transportation Report (Bay Area Transportation Study Commission, Berkeley, May, 1969).

* Nathanson, *op. cit.*

† Based on the work of Ira S. Lowry, *A Model of Metropolis* (Rand Corporation, Memorandum RM–4035, Santa Monica, August, 1964).

TABLE 1.7   Classification of Standard Industrial Classification (SIC) Divisions and Major Groups, by Locational Orientation and Economic Base Orientation

	Locational orientation	
	Basic	Population-serving
Economic base orientation	Locate with respect to interregional transportation routes, resources and unique site features, interindustry linkages, agglomeration economies	Locate with respect to residential population and purchasing power, daytime population concentrations
Exports		
Generate income from sources outside metropolitan region	Agriculture (01, 07–09) Mining (10, 13, 14) Manufacturing (19–39) Transportation (40, 42, 44–46) Services (82)[1] Government (91, 92)[2] Finance (62, 63, 67) Banking (60)[3]	Retail trade (52)[5] Services (70)[5]
Local consumption		
Generate income from local population, firms	Manufacturing (part)[4] Wholesale trade (50) Retail trade (52) Services (73, 84, 89)	Construction (15–17)[6] Retail trade (53–59) Transportation, communications, utilities (41, 47, 48, 49) Finance (60, 61, 64–66) Services (70, 72, 75, 76, 78, 79, 80, 81, 82, 86, 88) Government, local (93–96)[7]

[1] Includes major private universities.

[2] Includes military bases, regional offices of federal departments, state universities and hospitals.

[3] Includes bank headquarters in central business districts.

[4] Predominantly nondurable manufacturing for local consumption (food products, apparel, printing and publishing).

[5] Portions of sales in these industries generated by tourism. Also includes amusement and recreation services, personal and miscellaneous services.

[6] Construction activity, while designated as population serving, may be distributed in part with respect to future basic locators.

[7] Should include branch post offices, state employment security offices, as well as local government and schools.

Sources: Nathanson, *op. cit.,* p. 16.

which nonbasic activities are dependent, it should be pointed out that the term basic as used in the BATSC modeling system is not used in the same sense as it is in the strict economic meaning. In the traditional economic base concept, industries which are termed basic generate income from sources outside the region, and nonbasic industries simply transfer income between residents of the region. In the BATSC modeling system basic and population-serving employment refer to the locational characteristics of industries. Thus, the point of interest in *BEMOD* is in the relationships of activity in space rather than in the dynamics of regional growth.

Nevertheless, while the economic base theory focuses attention on the distinction between export activities and local consumption, it does have a bearing on the urban development concept used in *BEMOD*. The major similarity connecting these concepts is revealed by the observation that the locational decision of firms serving local consumption requirements are in response to the spatial distribution of population. In contrast, basic activities concerned with outside economic forces place a higher priority on access to other firms and those facilities that accommodate interregional communications.

To further clarify the economic base distinction between basic and nonbasic industries and the basic and population-serving distinction used in the BATSC modeling system, Table 1.7 presents a four-way classification of industries classified in the Standard Industrial Classification (SIC) System.*

A review of Table 1.7 reveals that the ambiguities inherent in the industry-by-industry approach are obvious, and it points out some of the limitations in using SIC categories with regard to locational phenomena. For example, State and Federal government activities, including many major employers with large scale site requirements such as a university or a military base, have been classified as basic in the BATSC modeling system. With regard to the economic base concept, this classification is also used since these establishments generate income from sources outside the region. However, they should be distinguished, in terms of location, from such activities as branch post offices and department of motor vehicle offices, which provide services that are primarily dependent on the needs of the local population. Thus, all State and Federal employment is classified as basic, and all employees of cities, counties and special districts as population-serving. They were classified as such for practical considera-

* The four-way classification system was copied from Nathanson, *op. cit.*, p. 16. It was developed in Goldner, *op. cit.*, p. 30. The industry groups distributed in this table are specified in BATSC, *"Controlled Trends" Zonal Forecasts, op. cit.*, p. 7.

tions, since the processing time required to identify basic and population-serving activities below the two-digit SIC level was prohibitive.*

With regard to population-serving activities, similar classification problems were encountered. For example, if all retail trade and personal services employment is classified as population-serving, some service establishments such as hotels and motels and some trade establishments such as retail stores and eating and drinking establishments are, in fact, export activities since they depend primarily on tourism rather than on the spending habits of the local population.

Further, while branch banks are population-serving establishments, their central headquarters are closely related to national and international capital markets. Thus, while the service functions of these large population-serving establishments locate near local users, their headquarters offices tend to locate in response to other considerations and frequently in central business districts which then become centers of concentration for activities that are not population-serving. Consequently, and as indicated in this table, some industry groups should be classified partly as basic (or export) and partly as population-serving (or local consumption).

In view of the above ambiguities basic employment in the Bay Area was estimated for 1965, 1980, and 1990 and classified into twelve industry groups in *BEMOD*.† On the basis of data generated in *BEMOD,* it was possible to aggregate Bay Area basic employment into nine major industry groups, as shown in Table 1.8. Total population-serving employment was also estimated in *BEMOD* and has been included in this table.

As indicated therein, employment in the Bay Area is expected to increase to more than three million workers by 1990. At that time, population-serving activities, or those economic activities which depend upon the spatial distribution of resident population and the day-time location of workers, are expected to account for almost 55 percent of total employment. These activities include population-serving components or services, trade, and government, in addition to construction, and some elements of manufacturing, transportation, communications, and utilities, and finance, insurance, and real estate. They tend to grow and locate in direct relation to the location of households.

While basic industries include those activities which depend on interregional transportation facilities, special site requirements, or interindustry linkages, their locational decisions are generally based on a site's desirability for access to transportation and materials, and its ability to fulfill

---

* Nathanson, *op. cit.,* p. 17.
† The allocation process for basic employment is explained in *BEMOD* and summarized in the *Bay Area Transportation Report.*

TABLE 1.8 Estimated Basic and Population-Serving Employment for the San Francisco Bay Area: 1965, 1980, and 1990

Basic employment	Employment			Percent distribution		
	1965	1980	1990	1965	1980	1990
Agriculture	44,600	19,500	15,200	2.7%	0.8%	0.5%
Mining	2,600	2,600	3,100	0.1	0.1	0.1
Manufacturing	319,100	426,000	516,300	19.2	16.8	16.6
Transportation	65,200	79,600	88,500	3.9	3.1	2.8
Trade	96,000	135,300	156,700	5.8	5.3	5.0
Finance, insurance, real estate	34,300	48,200	57,700	2.1	1.9	1.9
Services	93,500	193,400	256,000	5.6	7.6	8.2
Government	140,200	239,700	317,100	8.4	9.4	10.2
Total basic employment	795,900	1,144,300	1,410,600	47.8	45.0	45.3
Total population-serving employment	868,500	1,401,300	1,703,700	52.2	55.0	54.7
Total employment	1,664,000	2,545,600	3,114,300	100.0%	100.0%	100.0%

Source: Joseph Nathanson, *Basic Employment Model*, (BEMOD), Technical Report 222 (Bay Area Transportation Study Commission, Berkeley. Draft).

special industrial needs. Since these industries serve as major attractions to population and to service employment, they significantly influence the region's development patterns. Employment in the Bay Area's basic industries is expected to comprise more than 45 percent of all employment in the Bay Area in 1990. While manufacturing activities provide the most jobs in the basic sector, and they are expected to increase to 516,000, this sector's share to total employment is expected to drop to 16.6 percent by 1990.

The data in this table illustrate present and future patterns of the industrial composition of the Bay Area. In addition to the fact that locational decisions of basic industries influence the region's developmental patterns, the area's economic growth measured in terms of employment increases will continue to be generated by a combination of internal and external forces. As national and international markets expand, existing and new employment opportunities will increase to meet the needs for goods and services. While employment and a desirable living environment act as attractions to the Bay Area, the resulting population increase will generate new demands for household goods and services. At the same time, an increasingly skilled labor force acts as an additional stimulus to industry. Thus, to the extent that the region maintains a healthy physical environment, a well educated and productive labor force, and continues to be a favorable location for investment, all indications are that its economy will continue to grow at a fast pace.

Appendix C CASE G FROM "A GUIDE TO THE USE OF FEDERAL AND STATE STATISTICAL DATA"

Sample local area economic analysis

U.S. Department of Commerce Domestic and International Business Administration, August 1979, pp. 72, 73.

CASE G

FREEMAN'S SUPERMARKET, INCORPORATED

Objective:

To select a county in the Syracuse, New York, Standard Metropolitan Statistical Area to locate new supermarkets. The area is composed of Madison, Onondaga and Oswego counties.

Kind of Business:

A firm operating a local chain of supermarkets.

Problem:

The company wished to explore the possibility of expanding their operations into the Syracuse metropolitan area. It had experienced rapid growth in the area it already operated in and felt that its territory was saturated with supermarkets. In selecting a new area within the SMSA, the firm wanted to choose the county that had experienced the greatest economic growth rate and appeared to have future development characteristics.

Source of Data:

(1) *Census of Housing; 1960 and 1970—Detailed Housing Characteristics.*

(2) *Census of Population; 1960 and 1970—General Population Characteristics.*

(3) *Census of Population; 1960 and 1970—General Social and Economic Characteristics.*

(4) *Census of Business; Retail Trade—1963 and 1972.*

Assumption:

The company's marketing department held preliminary discussions with the firm's top management to determine which economic growth factors would most affect grocery store sales. Based upon their combined experience, it was concluded that the most important growth market indicators are

population, income, housing, car ownership, and grocery store sales. The *Census of Business, Retail Sales* gives sales of establishments both with and without payroll. The marketing department chose those with payroll, because they represented an overwhelming majority of sales in the metropolitan area.

Procedure:

(Calculations are shown in Table G-1)

(1) Oswego County showed the greatest growth in population and in number of families (columns 1 and 2) in 1970 above 1960 than either Madison or Onondaga Counties.

(2) When examining median family income (column 3) Oswego County grew 3.3 percentage points more rapidly than its closest rival.

(3) Oswego County also had the greatest percent increase in housing units (column 4) and continued to maintain the largest share of units occupied by owners (column 5). While med an rent in Oswego and Onondago counties increased by the same percentage (Column 6), it was felt that Oswego had a better growth potential due to its land development possibilities.

(4) Column 7 shows that Oswego County had the greatest decline in number of housing units without automobiles, which is also an indication of economic growth.

(5) Only in grocery store sales did Oswego County display the slowest growth rate. Based on percentage increase (column 8), it grew about 23 percentage points less than Madison County.

Conclusion:

With the exception of grocery store sales the market factors analyzed clearly reveal that Oswego Coun y had the greatest growth and should continue to offer future development potential. Selection of an exact site for each supermarket within the county will be determined by an analysis of data in *Census Tract Reports*, and in *Major Retail Center Reports* (both published by the Bureau of the Census), the usual onsite survey, and other sources and methods to be determined by management.

Table G–1—Market Factors for Evaluating Location Factors of a Food Store in Syracuse, New York, Standard Metropolitan Statistical Area

County	Population [1] (number)	Families [1] (number)	Family median income [2] (dollars)	Occupied housing units [3] (number)	Percent owner occupied [3]	Median rent [3] (dollars)	Housing units without automobiles [3] (number)	Grocery store sales [4] ($1,000)
	(1)	(2)	(3)	(4)	(5)	(6)	(7)	(8)
Madison								
1960	54,635	13,282	5,451	15,236	74.4	70	11.5	
1970	62,864	14,660	7,123	17,741	74.6	108	11.3	
Percent change	15.1	10.4	30.7	16.4	0.2	54.3	1.7	
1963								17,694
1972								30,661
Percent change								73.2
Onondaga								
1960	423,028	106,065	6,691	124,090	64.5	81	18.4	
1970	472,746	114,707	8,208	145,322	62.6	121	16.7	
Percent change	11.8	8.1	22.7	17.1	2.9	49.3	9.2	
1963								137,345
1972								226,750
Percent change								65.1
Oswego								
1960	86,118	21,063	5,580	24,323	76.0	69	17.9	
1970	100,897	24,057	7,479	29,179	76.1	103	12.6	
Percent change	17.2	14.2	34.0	20.0	0.1	49.3	29.6	
1963								28,548
1972								42,985
Percent change								50.6

[1] Census of Population, 1960 and 1970 General Population Characteristics, U.S. Department of Commerce.
[2] Census of Population, 1960 and 1970 General and Social Economic Characteristics, U.S. Department of Commerce.
[3] Census of Housing, 1960 and 1970 Detailed Housing Characteristics, U.S. Department of Commerce.
[4] Census of Business, Retail Trade 1963 and Census of Retail Trade 1972, U.S. Department of Commerce.

Appendix D   GUIDE 60

60. Preparation of Registration Statements Relating to Interests in Real Estate Limited Partnerships.

References to the General Partner and its affiliates are intended to include references to the General Partner(s), promoters of the partnerships, and all persons that directly or indirectly, through one or more intermediaries, control or are controlled by or are under common control with, such General Partner(s) or promoters.

It is suggested that where appropriate, the information in the prospectus be presented in the same order as the following comments. Where the registrant believes that specific comments are not relevant or are otherwise inappropriate, the registrant should bring this to the staff's attention in letter indicating the reasons therefor.

1.   COVER PAGE

A. The disclosure on the cover page should be as succinct and brief as possible.

B. The cover page should set forth, in addition to basic information about the offering (see Guide 5), the termination date of the offering, any minimum required purchase and any arrangements to place the funds received in an escrow, trust or similar arrangement.

C. The cover page should contain a tabular presentation of the total maximum and minimum interests to be offered:

	Price to Public	Selling Commissions	Proceeds to the Partnership
Per Limited Partnership Interest			
Total Minimum			
Total Maximum			

D. The cover page should also contain, as noted in Guide 5(g), a brief identification of the material risks involved in the purchase of the securities with cross-reference to further discussion in the prospectus. The most significant risk factors should be identified where applicable, for example:

   (i) *Tax Aspects*
     For example:
      There are material income tax risks associated with the offering.

   (ii) *Use of Proceeds*
     For example:
      The proceeds of the offering are insufficient to meet the requirements for funds as set forth in the partnership's investment objectives.

(iii) *Conflicts of Interests*

For example:

The operation of the partnership involved transactions between the partnership and the General Partner or its affiliates which may involve conflicts of interest.

2. SUITABILITY STANDARDS

Standards, if any, to be utilized by the registrant ("suitability standard") in determining the acceptance of subscription agreements should be described immediately following the cover page. Suitability standards should include those established by the registrant, if any, or by any self-regulatory organization or state agency having jurisdiction over the offering of the securities. Registrant should disclose the method(s) it intends to employ to assure adherence to the suitability standards by persons selling the interests and should briefly discuss the factors pertaining to the need for such standards such as lack of liquidity (resale or assignment of securities), importance of the investor's Federal income tax bracket in terms of the tax-benefits to be derived, the long term nature of the investment and possible adverse tax consequences of premature sale of the interests. If suitability standards apply to resale of the interests, this should be discussed.

3. SUMMARY OF THE PARTNERSHIP AND USE OF PROCEEDS

A two-part, concise outline summary relating to the partnership and a tabular summary of use of proceeds should follow the Suitability section of the prospectus. These summaries may replace the Introductory Statement and Use Proceeds Sections required by the relevant Form if such sections would merely repeat the information in the summaries.

A. *Summary of the Partnership.* The following information should be disclosed in outline form with appropriate cross-references, where applicable:

(i) Name, address and telephone number of the General Partner and names of persons making investment decisions for the partnership;

(ii) The intended termination date of the partnership;

(iii) State, if true, that the General Partner and its affiliates will receive substantial fees and profits in connection with the offering;

(iv) If current distributions are an investment objective, state the estimated maximum time from the closing date that the investor might have to wait to receive such distributions;

(v) Describe briefly the properties to be purchased. If a material portion of the minimum net proceeds of the offering (allowing for reserves) is not committed to specific properties, so indicate;

(vi) Describe the depreciation method to be used;

(vii) State the maximum leverage expected to be used by the partnership as a whole and on individual properties, where it may differ;

(viii) Include a cross-reference to the Glossary.

B. *Use of Proceeds.* The use of proceeds tabular summary will vary according to the partnership but should include, where appropriate, estimates of the public offering expenses (both organizational and sales), the amount available for investment, non-recurring initial investment fees, prepaid items and financing fees, cash down payments, reserves, and acquisition fees, including those paid by the seller. Estimated amounts to be paid to the General Partner and its affiliates should be identified. The summary should include both dollar amounts and percentages of the maximum and minimum proceeds of the offering. Inclusion of percentages of the estimated maximum and minimum total assets is optional. An example of a summary of Use of Proceeds is attached, but the summary will vary according to the circumstances.

4. COMPENSATION AND FEES TO THE GENERAL PARTNER AND AFFILIATES

A. This section should include a summary tabular presentation, itemizing by category and specifying dollar amounts where possible, of all compensation, fees, profits, and other benefits (including reimbursement of out-of-pocket expenses) which the General Partner and its affiliates may earn or receive in connection with the offering or operation of the partnership. If more detailed information is required it should be located in the Summary of Partnership Agreement section with cross-reference to that Summary. The presentation should identify the person, including affiliations with the General Partner, who will receive such compensation, fees, profits, or benefits and the services to be performed by such person.

The summary should be organized so as to indicate clearly whether the compensation relates to the offering and organizational stage, the developmental or acquisition stage, the operational stage or the termination and liquidation stage of the partnership. Separate sub-captions are recommended.

The type of compensation, fees, profits or other benefits that should be disclosed includes, but is not limited to, the following: disbursements incident to the purchase and sale of the limited partnership interests, including sales commissions, reimbursements for expenses, and real estate commissions; finder's fees; fees for property acquisitions, marketing or leasing up of properties, financing or refinancing, management of properties, insurance and miscellaneous services; commissions and other fees to be paid upon sale of the partnership's properties; participation by the General Partner in cash flow or profits and losses or capital gains and losses arising out of the operation, refinancing or sale of properties; fees or builder's profits; overhead absorption and/or land write-ups; and all profits on the purchase of investments for the partnership from the General Partner or its affiliates. If the partnership agreement limits the losses the General Partner and its affiliates can sustain, this should be discussed.

B.   Maximum aggregate dollar front-end fees to be paid during the first fiscal year of operations should be disclosed based upon the assumption that the partnership's maximum leverage is utilized.

C.   Where compensation arrangements are based upon a formula or percentage, the terms of such arrangements should be disclosed and illustrated. The assumptions underlying the dollar figures should be disclosed and the calculations underlying the figures should be submitted to the staff supplementary with the initial filing. Compensation based upon a given return (percentage of contributed investor capital) to investors should disclose whether such return is cumulative or non-cumulative.

D.   Where the General Partner or an affiliate receives a disproportionate interest in the partnership in relation to its own contribution, registrant's attention is directed to Guide 6. A bar chart comparison of the various interests and contributors should be provided.

5.   CONFLICTS OF INTEREST

A.   This section should include a summary of each type of transaction which may result in a conflict between the interests of the public investors and those of the General Partner and its affiliates, and of the proposed method of dealing with such conflict. The types of conflicts of interest which should be disclosed and discussed, if apppropriate, include, but are not limited to:

(i) The General Partner is a general partner or an affiliate of a general partner in other investment entities (public and/or private) engaged in making similar investments or otherwise makes or arranges for similar investments.

(ii) The General Partner has the authority to invest the partnership's funds in other partnerships in which the General Partner or an affiliate is the general partner or has an interest.

(iii) Properties in which the General Partner or its affiliates have an interest are bought from or partnership properties are sold to the General Partner or its affiliates or entities in which they have an interest. Where appraisals are used in connection with any such transaction, it should be made clear that appraisals are only estimates of value and should not be relied on as measures of realizable value. If the appraiser is named as an expert, a consent to the use of his name should be furnished. If specific appraised values are included in the registration statement, the appraiser should be named as an expert, his consent furnished and the appraisals filed as exhibits to the registration statement. If a statement that the purchase price of the property does not exceed its appraised value is included and the appraiser is not named and specific values are not cited, there need not be furnished a consent to use the appraiser's name. In that event, a copy of the appraisal should be submitted supplementally with the registration statement. If any relationship exists between the appraiser and the General Partner or its affiliates this should be stated. If the General Partner intends to buy any properties in which the general partner or any of its affiliates have a material interest, such properties should be appropriately described in the prospectus along with the investment objectives [of the partnership (see paragraph 10, Investment Objectives] and Policies). If it is disclosed in the prospectus that the partnership may purchase properties in which the General Partner or its affiliates have a material interest, but no properties are described, and such properties are thereafter purchased for the partnership, the General Partner will have the heavy burden of demonstrating that it did not intend to purchase such property at the time the registration statement became effective.

(iv) The General Partner or its affiliates own or have an interest in properties adjacent to those to be purchased and developed by the partnership.

(v) Affiliates of the General Partner who act as underwriters, real estate brokers or managers for the partnership, act in such capacities for other partnerships or entities.

(vi) An affiliate of the General Partner places mortgages for the partnership or otherwise acts as a finance broker or as insurance agent or broker receiving commissions for such services.

(vii) An affiliate of the General Partner acts (a) as an underwriter for the offering, or (b) as a principal underwriter for the offering thereby creating conflicts in performance of the underwriter's due diligence inquiries under the Securities Act.

(viii) The compensation plan for the General Partner may create a conflict between the interests of the General Partner and those of the partnership.

B.   An organization chart should be included in this section showing the relationship between the various organizations managed or controlled by the General Partner or its affiliates that will do business with the partnership where the relationships are so complex that a graphic display would assist investors in understanding such relationships.

6. FIDUCIARY RESPONSIBILITY OF THE GENERAL PARTNER

A. A discussion of the fiduciary obligation owed by the General Partner to the Limited Partners should be set forth. The following disclosure is suggested with appropriate modification for the laws of the state of organization:

A General Partner is accountable to a limited partnership as a fiduciary and consequently must exercise good faith and integrity in handling partnership affairs. This is a rapidly developing and changing area of the law and Limited Partners who have questions concerning the duties of the General Partner should consult with their counsel.

B. Where the limited partnership agreement contains an exculpatory provision and/or the right to indemnification, the following disclosure is suggested, as modified to reflect the substance of such provisions:

Exculpation

(i) The General Partner may not be liable to the Partnership or Limited Partners for errors in judgment or other acts or omissions not amounting to willful misconduct or gross negligence, since provision has been made in the Agreement of Limited Partnership for exculpation of the General Partner. Therefore, purchasers of the interests have a more limited right of action than they would have absent the limitation in the Partnership Agreement.

Indemnification

(ii) The Partnership Agreement provides for indemnification of the General Partner by the Partnership for liabilities he incurs in dealings with third parties on behalf of the partnership. To the extent that the indemnification provisions purport to include indemnification for liabilities arising under the Securities Act of 1933, in the opinion of the Securities and Exchange Commission, such indemnification is contrary to public policy and therefore unenforceable.

Registrant's attention is also directed to Note A of Rule 460 under the Act relating to disclosure of indemnification agreements.

7. RISK FACTORS

A. This section should include a carefully organized series of short, concise subcaptioned paragraphs, with cross-references to fuller discussion where appropriate, summarizing the principal risk factors applicable to the offering and to the partnership's particular plan of operations. See Guide 6 of the Guides. The risk factors section should be brief.

B. This subsection should summarize each material risk of adverse tax consequences with appropriate cross-references to fuller discussions in the Federal tax section. For example:

(i) Where no Internal Revenue Service (IRS) ruling as to partnership tax status has been applied for or obtained, the risk that the IRS may on audit determine that for tax purposes the partnership is an association taxable as a corporation, in which case, investors would be deprived of the tax benefits associated with the offering. As part of this disclosure, it should be stated that a material risk of IRS classification as a corporate association may exist even though registrant relies on an opinion of counsel as to partnership tax status as such opinion is not binding on the IRS. It may also be stated that IRS classification of the partnership as a corporate association would deprive investors of the tax benefits of the offering only if the IRS determination is upheld in court or otherwise becomes final. Any such additional disclosure should explain that contesting an IRS determination may impose representation expenses on investors. (See Federal tax section.)

(ii) Where the IRS has advised registrant that it proposes not to rule, or to rule adversely, on any tax issue as to which a ruling was applied for, the risk that investors may lose some or all tax benefits associated with the offering. (See Federal tax section.)

(iii) The risk that after some years of partnership operations an investor's tax liabilities may exceed his cash distributions in corresponding years and that to the extent of such excess the payment of such taxes will be out-of-pocket expenses.

(iv) Upon a sale or other disposition (*e.g.*, by gift) of a partnership interest or, upon a sale (including a foreclosure sale) or other disposition of partnership property, the risk that an investor's tax liabilities may exceed the cash he receives and that to the extent of such excess the payment of such taxes will be out-of-pocket expenses. The disclosure should indicate to what extent the gain may be taxed as ordinary income, to what extent as capital gain. (See Federal tax section.)

(v) The risk that an audit of the partnership's information return may result in an audit of an investor's own tax return. (See Federal tax section.)

C. Risk factors relating to the specific partnership might include, where applicable:

(i) Management's lack of relevant experience, or management's lack of success with similar partnerships or other real estate investments;

(ii) Where the proceeds of the offering will be insufficient to meet the requirements of the partnership's investment objectives, a discussion of the additional sources of capital for the partnership and of the risk of not being able to satisfy the partnership's objectives as a result of not obtaining additional necessary funds;

(iii) Where the partnership has high risk investment objectives, including high leveraging, these should be explained;

(iv) The risk that no public market for interests is likely to develop and that holders of interests may not be able to liquidate their investment quickly;

(v) Risks associated with contemplated rent stabilization programs, fuel or energy requirements or regulations, and construction in areas that are subject to environmental or other federal, state or local regulations, actual or pending;

(vi) Where a material portion of the minimum net proceeds of the offering is not committed to specific properties, disclosure of the particular risk associated with an investment in such an offering. Such disclosure should include the increased uncertainty and risk to investors since they are unable to evaluate the manner in which the proceeds are to be invested and the economic merit of the particular real estate projects prior to investment. Also it should be disclosed that there may be a substantial period of time before the proceeds of the offering are invested and therefore a delay to investors in receiving a return on their investment.

D.   Risk factors relating to real estate limited partnership offerings in general should be briefly discussed after those relating to the specific partnership. Such risks might include, where applicable: the risks associated with the ownership of real estate, including uncertainty of cash flow to meet fixed and maturing obligations, adverse local market conditions, risks of "leveraging," and uninsured losses.

8.   PRIOR PERFORMANCE OF THE GENERAL PARTNER AND AFFILIATES

A.   Tabular presentations providing a reasonable summary of the experience of the General Partner and its affiliates during the last five years in the investment of investor funds in real estate, including both registered and exempted offerings. Such presentations should generally follow the format in Table II. Where the investment objectives of any such prior programs were different from those of the partnership being registered, this should be disclosed. Where the General Partner and its affiliates' experience is such that a lengthy and costly presentation would be necessary, the staff should be consulted as to appropriate modifications. In addition, in some cases, depending on the circumstances, more information may be called for in this area.

B.   The information required by Item 16(e) of Form S-1 as it applies to the General Partner (its officers and directors, if a corporation) or any of its affiliates who may be doing business with the partnership should be included.

C. The amount of, and reason for, any contingent liabilities of the General Partner with regard to prior programs now in existence should be disclosed. If this information appears in the financial statements it may be incorporated hereunder by reference.

9. MANAGEMENT

A. If a material portion of the maximum net proceeds (allowing for reserves) is not committed to specific properties, disclosure should be made of the identity of the individuals who will make the investment decisions, with appropriate background information, including that required by Item 16(o) of Form S-1.

B. Any substantial reliance on a nonaffiliate in running the operations of the partnership should be disclosed and any relevant prior experience should be discussed. If material amounts of compensation or fees are to be paid to nonaffiliates, a separate heading should be provided entitled, "Fees and Compensation Arrangements with Nonaffiliates" and a tabular presentation describing such fees should be provided.

C. If there is provision in the partnership agreement or otherwise for a change in the management of the partnership, a description of how such change could be accomplished should be included.

10. INVESTMENT OBJECTIVES AND POLICIES

A. Disclosure should be made of the nature of the property intended to be purchased (e.g., commercial, residential) and the criterial (e.g., method of depreciation, location) to be utilized in evaluating proposed investments.

B. If there is provision in the partnership agreement or otherwise for change in the investment objectives of the partnership, a description of how such change could be made should be included.

C. Generally, where the net proceeds of the offering will be invested in non-specified properties or in properties that do not have any significant operating histories, it is not appropriate to make any statement setting forth a rate of return on the investment.

11. DESCRIPTION OF REAL ESTATE INVESTMENTS

A. Risks associated with specified properties, such as competitive factors, environmental regulation, rent control regulation, fuel or energy requirements and regulation should be noted.

B. If a material portion of the minimum net proceeds (allowing for reasonable reserves) is not committed to specific properties, the issuer should clearly so indicate in the prospectus.

Where a reasonable probability exists that a property will be acquired and the funds to be expended represent a material portion of the net proceeds of the minimum offering, the issuer should describe such property in the registration statement at the time of filing. Where after the registration statement has been filed but prior to its effectiveness a reasonable probability arises that a property will be acquired, a description of such property should be included in a pre-effective amendment to the registration statement. Where a reasonable probability that a property will be acquired arises after the effectiveness of the registration statement and during the distribution period, a 424(c) supplement or post-effective amendment, as appropriate, should be promptly filed. (See Undertaking D.)* Whether adequate disclosure of properties to be acquired has been timely made can only be determined by an examination of the facts in each case. This may vary due to different business practices particular to each issuer. Thus, as in all other situations, the burden of making adequate and timely disclosure rests solely with the issuer.

12. FEDERAL TAXES

A. *General Instructions.* This section should summarize under a series of appropriate headings all material Federal income tax aspects of the offering. State tax aspects need usually be summarized only to the extent required by Subsection L, below. Proper citations should be used whenever reference is made to sections of the Internal Revenue Code (the "Code"), the Treasury regulations, decided cases or other sources. An opinion of counsel as to all material tax aspects of the offering should be filed as an exhibit. Such opinion should cite relevant authority for any conclusions expressed. The tax sections of the prospectus should summarize or restate the tax information contained in the opinion.

The function of the tax opinion is to inform investors of the tax consequences they can reasonably expect from an investment in the partnership. If, with respect to an intended tax benefit, counsel are unable to express an opinion that such benefit will be available because of uncertainty in the law or for other reasons, the opinion should so state and also disclose that there is or may be a material tax risk the particular benefit will be disallowed on audit. The tax effect of such disallowance should be explained. Each material risk of disallowance of an intended tax benefit should be disclosed in the tax opinion and under the appropriate heading in the prospectus.

Tax counsel should be aware that their opinion speaks as of the effective date of the registration statement. Such opinion should be updated for any material changes or events occurring subsequent to

---

*It has come to the staff's attention that on a number of occasions issuers have identified properties to be purchased and have delayed proceeding with the purchase in order to avoid the necessary disclosure. In the staff's opinion, such practice is not consistent with the obligation of the issuer to disclose material facts relating to the offering.

filing and prior to the effective date. Ruling requests (including amendments) and rulings should also be filed as exhibits with the original filing, or by amendment as soon thereafter as available.

B. *Partnership Status.* This subsection should state whether an IRS ruling has been requested as to the entity's classification as a partnership for Federal income tax purposes. The contents of any ruling, including any conditions therein, should be summarized. Where a ruling or opinion of counsel as to partnership status is conditioned on the maintenance of certain net worth or other standards, there should be disclosure as to how these standards will be maintained in the future. If no IRS ruling as to partnership tax status has been requested or obtained, counsel's opinion as to partnership tax status should be summarized and the risk of IRS classification of the entity as a corporate association, referred to in the Risk Factors section, should be discussed.

C. *Taxation of Limited Partners.* Insofar as necessary to an understanding of the intended tax benefits and any material risks of their disallowance, this subsection should summarize basic rules of partnership taxation, e.g., that a partnership is not a taxable entity, that a partner will be required to report on his Federal tax return his distributive share of partnership income, gain, loss, deductions or credits, whether or not any actual distribution is made to such partner during his taxable year. The tax treatment of cash distributions to partners should also be explained.

If the partnership agreement provides special allocations among partners of distributive shares of income, gain, loss, deductions or credits, this subsection should set forth an opinion of counsel to the effect that the principal purpose of the allocations is not tax avoidance or evasion under Code Sec. 704(b)(2), and/or a risk disclosure to the effect that the IRS may on audit disallow any special allocation which it determines to have tax avoidance or evasion as its principal purpose. The tax consequences to partners of disallowance of a special allocation should be explained. Where applicable, the tax consequences of retroactive allocations to new partners should be discussed.

D. *Basis.* This subsection should explain that a partner may deduct his share of partnership losses only to the extent of the adjusted basis of his interest in the partnership. Inclusion of a partner's share of the partnership's nonrecourse debt in the adjusted basis of his partnership interest should be explained. If there is a question as to whether the partnership's nonrecourse debt will enter into bases of the limited partners' interests, that should be disclosed.

Where appropriate, there should be an explanation of the consequences to a limited partner of a reduction in his share of the partnership's nonrecourse debt as may result, for example, from a change in his profit sharing ratio.

E. *Depreciation and Recapture.* This subsection should explain the method or methods of depreciation to be used by the partnership on its depreciable property as well as the basis for determining useful lives of such property. Any material risk that the IRS may challenge useful lives chosen by the partnership should be disclosed together with an explanation of the possible tax consequences of applying longer useful lives to partnership property. If methods of depreciation available only to a "first-user" are to be utilized, the basis of such "first-user" status should be explained. Depreciation recapture may be explained here with appropriate cross-reference to subsections on Sale or Other Disposition of Partnership Property and Sale or Other Disposition of a Partnership interest.

F. *Deductibility of Prepaid and Other Expenses.* As to prepaid interest, possible nondeductibility in the year of payment should be discussed. It should be explained that if a partnership takes a large deduction for prepaid interest in its first year of operation, having little or no income in such year, the IRS may determine that the prepayment created a material distortion of income at the partnership level and require that it be allocated over the term of the loan.

As to other material partnership expenses (e.g., interim commitment fees, management fees, permanent mortgage fees, etc.) it should be stated which are deductible, which are nondeductible and as to which deductibility is uncertain. Where applicable, the possible nondeductibility of guaranteed payments under Code Sec. 707(c) should be discussed.

G. *Tax Liabilities in Later Years.* This subsection should discuss the Risk Factors disclosure that after some years of partnership operations an investor's tax liabilities may exceed cash distributions in corresponding years. The tax problems that will arise after partnership property reaches the point when the partnership's nondeductible mortgage amortization payments exceed its depreciation deductions (the crossover point) should be explained.

It should also be explained that where partnership losses offset an investor's earned income taxable at a 50 percent rate, partnership income in later years may be taxed to the investor at a higher rate.

H. *Sale or Other Disposition of a Partnership Interest.* This subsection should begin with a restatement of the Risk Factors disclosure that an investor may be unable to sell his partnership interest as there may be no market for it. The subsection should then discuss the Risk Factors disclosure that taxes payable on a sale of a partnership interest may exceed cash received. The discussion should explain the tax effect on a partner of being relieved from his share of the partnership's nonrecourse liabilities. The discussion should also state to what extent the gain recognized will be taxed as ordinary income, to what extent as capital gain.

Whether or not the partnership plans to make the Sec. 754 election should be disclosed together with an explanation of the possible tax consequences on a transferee Limited Partner should the election not be made.

This subsection should also explain that a gift of an interest in a partnership holding leveraged property may result in Federal income tax (as well as Federal gift tax) liability to the donor. It should be explained that the IRS is likely to consider that a partner who gives away his partnership interest is relieved of his share of the partnership's nonrecourse liabilities and that he may realize a taxable gain on the gift to the extent that his share of such liabilities exceeds his adjusted basis in his partnership interest. It should be stated to what extent the gain will be taxed as ordinary income, to what extent as capital gain.

I. *Sale or Other Disposition of Partnership Property.* This subsection may use cross-reference to, or be combined with, subsection H in order to avoid repetition.

The subsection should discuss the Risk Factors disclosure that upon a sale (including a foreclosure sale) or other disposition of partnership property an investor's tax liability may exceed cash he would receive. The discussion should explain that the amount received by the partnership on sale (including a foreclosure sale) or other disposition of property will include any nonrecourse indebtedness to which the property was subject. It should be stated to what extent the gain will be taxed as ordinary income, to what extent as capital gain.

If appropriate, the tax treatment of dealer property should be explained. Should the sale of condominium units by the partnership be contemplated, it should be pointed out such units may be treated as dealer property.

J. *Section 183.* The possible impact of this Code section on investors lacking a profit objective in investing in any tax shelter program which is expected to generate annual net losses for tax purposes for a period of years should be discussed. The discussion should note that the section may apply to the Limited Partners of a partnership notwithstanding any profit objective the partnership itself may be deemed to have.

K. *Liquidation or Termination of the Partnership.* The tax consequences to a Limited Partner of partnership liquidation or termination should be explained.

L. *State, Local and Foreign Taxes.* It should be disclosed whether partners will be required to file tax returns and/or be subject to tax in any state or states other than their state of residence, or any foreign countries. Where applicable, state and foreign tax rates should be noted.

M. *Tax Returns and Tax Information.* It should be disclosed what kind of tax information will be supplied to Limited Partners and when, and whether the same kind of information will also be supplied to assignees who are not substitute limited partners.

It should be explained that the information return filed by the partnership may be audited and that such audit may result in adjustments or proposed adjustments. Any adjustment of the partnership information return would normally result in adjustments or proposed adjustments of a partner's own return. Any audit of a partner's return could result in adjustments of nonpartnership as well as partnership income and losses.

N. *Other Headings.* Where applicable the tax section should also discuss the limitation on deductions of investment interest, the minimum tax on tax preference income, the impact of tax preference items on the maximum tax on earned income, and any other tax information deemed material in the particular offering.

13. GLOSSARY

If terms are used in the prospectus that are technical in nature or are susceptible to varying methods of computation, e.g., acquisition fees, book value, capital contribution, cash flow, cash available for distribution, construction fees, cost of property, development fee, net worth, organization and offering expenses, profit, partnership management fee and property management fee, definitions should be provided. For purposes of uniformity, it is suggested that these definitions conform to those that appear in the Rules for the Offer and Sale of Real Estate Programs of the Midwest Securities Commissioners' Association, or that any variations, and the economic effect thereof, be disclosed.

14. SUMMARY OF PARTNERSHIP AGREEMENT

A brief summary of the material provisions of the Limited Partnership Agreement should be included.

15. REPORTS TO LIMITED PARTNERS

The registrant should identify all reports and other documents that will be furnished to Limited Partners as required by the partnership's Limited Partnership Agreement and the undertakings to the registration statement. In particular, registrant should disclose: (1) whether the financial information contained in such reports will be prepared on an accrual basis in accordance with generally accepted accounting principles, with a reconciliation with respect to information furnished to limited partners for income tax purposes; (2) whether independent certified public accountants will audit the financial statements to be included in the annual report; (3) whether the annual report will be provided to limited partners within 90 days following the close of the partnership's fiscal year; (4) that a detailed statement of any transactions with the General Partner or its affiliates, and of fees, commissions, compensation and other benefits paid, or accrued to the General Partner or its affiliates for the fiscal year completed, showing the amount paid or accrued to each recipient and the services performed, will be furnished to each limited partner at least on an annual basis pursuant to the registrant's undertaking; (5) that the information specified by Form 10-Q (if such report is required to be filed with the Commission) will be furnished to limited partners within 45 days after the close of each quarterly fiscal period pursuant to the registrant's undertaking; and (6) if the registrant has applied for, but not received an IRS ruling as to the tax status at the time of effectiveness of the registration statement, that the registrant will promptly notify each limited partner, in writing, pursuant to its undertaking of the receipt of the ruling or of an adverse ruling or refusal to rule by the IRS.

16. THE OFFERING—DESCRIPTION OF THE UNITS

In addition to the disclosure required by the relevant items of Form S-1 or S-11, disclosure should be made of all restrictions on transfer of the interests, including those in the Partnership Agreement, those imposed by state suitability standards or blue sky laws, and those resulting from the tax laws.

17. REDEMPTION, REPURCHASE AND RIGHT OF PRESENTMENT AGREEMENTS

There should be a discussion of any provisions in the partnership agreement that allow the General Partner or its affiliates to redeem or repurchase the offered security or that allow the investor to seek redemption or repurchase. The conditions or formulae used, *e.g.*, purchase price less capital returns, should also be disclosed. Registrant should be careful to appropriately describe the investor's right—whether it be redemption, repurchase, or merely a right of presentment. The discussion should include the following factors:

(1) That appraisals are simply estimates of value and may not necessarily correspond to realizable value;

(2) The order in which redemption requests will be honored (post mark or other objective standard);

(3) Whether the General Partner and its affiliates will defer their redemption requests until requests for redemption by the Limited Partner public investors have been met;

(4) The source and amount of funds (together with any legal or practical limitations) available for this purpose;

(5) The circumstances under which a later request will be honored, while an earlier request is still pending;

(6) Tax consequences related to redemption;

(7) The period of time during which a redemption request may be pending prior to its being granted or rejected;

(8) Whether there is to be allocation of funds among partners requesting redemption in circumstances where redemption requests exceed funds available for this purpose. If so, state and briefly describe the allocation process;

(9) Whether Limited Partners must hold an interest in the partnership for a specified period prior to making a redemption request; and

(10) A detailed statement of the procedure that must be followed in order to redeem or seek repurchase of the interest, including the forms that must be presented, and whether signature guarantees will be required.

18. CAPITALIZATION

Disclosure should be made in accordance with Form S-1 or S-11, as appropriate.

19. PLAN OF DISTRIBUTION

A. If there is an understanding or arrangement, whether written or oral, between the registrant and any broker or dealer, relating to the distribution of the interests, which is intended to be finalized after effectiveness of the registration statement, such understanding or arrangement should be disclosed.

B. If, after the registration statement becomes effective, the registrant enters into any selling arrangement which calls for the payment of more than the usual and customary compensation, a sticker supplement (Rule 424(c)) describing such arrangement should be filed.

C. If the registrant intends to pay referral or similar fees to any professional or other persons in connection with the distribution of the interests, this fact should be disclosed.

D. If the General Partner or its affiliates intend to purchase interests, and such interests will be included in satisfying the minimum offering requirements, it should be disclosed whether such interests are intended to be resold, and if so, the period of time these interests will be held prior to being resold. Depending on the circumstances, such interests may be considered to be unsold allotments under Section 4(3) of the Act. (See Securities Act Release 4150.)

20. SUMMARY OF PROMOTIONAL AND SALES MATERIAL

A. The sales material should present a balance discussion of both risk and reward. The contents of the sales material or sales meetings or seminars should be consistent with the representations in the prospectus.

B. A section which identifies all written sales material proposed to be transmitted to prospective investors orally or in writing should be included. The sales material should be appropriately identified by title and character and should be separately categorized either as the registrant's material or that of another person. If material provided by the latter is to be used, state the name of the author and publication and the date of prior publication, if any, identify· any persons who are quoted without being identified, and, except in the case of a public official document or statement, state whether or not the consent of the author and publication have been obtained for the use of the material as sales material. Sales materials include memoranda, summary descriptions, graphics, supplemental exhibits, media advertising, charts and pictures relating to the offering of the security and proposed to be transmitted to prospective investors.

C. If any other material is to be used subsequent to the effective date, a "sticker" supplement (424(c) prospectus) should be filed to describe any such sales material.

D. Any sales material that is intended to be furnished to investors orally or in writing, other than that which is used for internal purposes of the registrant, and including all material described in paragraph B above, should be submitted to the staff supplementally, prior to its use. For purposes of this paragraph only, sales material includes all marketing memoranda that are sent by the General Partner or its affiliates to broker/dealers or other sales personnel and may include material labeled "for broker dealer use only." Staff comments, if any, will be promptly communicated to the registrant. Registrant should check with the staff before using sale material that has been submitted to the staff.

E. Wherever public sales meetings or seminars are to be employed to discuss the offering, individually or in conjunction with other tax sheltered offerings, the staff should be provided, as supplemental information, copies of any written scripts or outlines which are prepared for use in such meetings a reasonable time prior to their use.

F. Reference in sales material or at such sales meetings or seminars to Federal income tax treatment of the partnership and its investors should refer to either a ruling of the IRS or an opinion of counsel. Counsel should be named, his acknowledgement furnished supplementally with respect to such use, and any qualification contained in counsel's opinion should be referred to in such material by cross-referencing to the prospectus. Where the program has not sought a ruling as to the tax status (partnership) from the IRS and is relying on an opinion of counsel, it should be indicated that an opinion of counsel is not binding on the IRS.

21. UNDERTAKINGS

A. The following undertaking should be included in the registration statement if the securities to be registered are to be offered in a continuous offering over an extended period of time:

The registrant undertakes (a) to file any prospectuses required by Section 10(a)(3) as post-effective amendments to the registration statement, (b) that for the purpose of determining any liability under the Act each such post-effective amendment may be deemed to be a new registration statement relating to the securities offered therein and the offering of such securities at that time may be deemed to be the initial bona fide offering thereof, (c) that all post-effective amendments will comply with the applicable forms, rules and regulations of the Commission in effect at the time such post-effective amendments are filed, and (d) to remove from registration by means of a post-effective amendment any of the securities being registered which remain at the termination of the offering.

B.   The following undertaking should be included in every registration statement:

The registrant undertakes to send to each limited partner at least on an annual basis a detailed statement of any transactions with the General Partner or its affiliates, and of fees, commissions, compensation and other benefits paid, or accrued to the General Partner or its affiliates for the fiscal year completed, showing the amount paid or accrued to each recipient and the services performed.

C.   The following undertaking should be included in every registration statement:

The registrant undertakes to provide to the limited partners the financial statements required by Form 10-K for the first full fiscal year of operations of the partnership.

D.   The following undertaking relating to investment of the proceeds of an offering in which a material portion of the maximum net proceeds (allowing for reasonable reserves) is not committed (i.e., subject to a binding purchase agreement) to specific properties should be included in the registration statements:

The registrant undertakes to file a current report on Form 8-K to reflect each commitment (i.e., the signing of a binding purchase agreement) made after [the effective date of the offering involving the use of 10% or more (on a cumulative basis) of the net proceeds of the offering and to provide the information contained in such report to the Limited Partners at least once each quarter after] the distribution period of the offering has expired. The report to Limited Partners will contain the financial statements required by Item 6(b) of Form S-11, or, at the discretion of the registrant, a summary of the full financial statements with a statement that the full financial statements will be sent upon request.

The registrant undertakes to file a sticker supplement pursuant to Rule 424(c) under the Act during the distribution period describing each property not identified in the prospectus at such time as there arises a reasonable probability that such property will be acquired and to consolidate all such stickers into a post-effective amendment filed at least once every three months, with the information contained in such amendment provided simultaneously to the existing Limited Partners. Audited financial statements for properties acquired during the distribution period need only be filed with the post-effective amendment. Such sticker supplement should also disclose all compensation and fees received by the General Partner(s) or its affiliates in connection with any such acquisition.

NOTE: Offers and sales of the interests may continue after the filing of a post-effective amendment containing information previously disclosed in sticker supplements to the prospectus, as long as the information disclosed in a current sticker supplement accompanying the prospectus is as complete as the information contained in the post-effective amendment.

E. If the registrant has applied for a ruling from the IRS as to tax status, and has not received it at the time of effectiveness:

The registrant undertakes to promptly notify each limited partner, in writing, of the receipt of the ruling or of an adverse ruling or refusal to rule by the IRS, and undertakes to file with the Commission a Form 8-K describing such event.

TABLE I
EXAMPLE OF SUMMARY OF THE USE OF PROCEEDS SECTION
Estimated Application of Proceeds of This Offering

	Minimum Dollar Amount	Percent	Maximum Dollar Amount	Percent
Gross Offering Proceeds	$	100.00%	$	100.00%
Public Offering Expenses:				
Underwriting Discount and Commissions Paid to Affiliate				
Organizational Expenses(1) .				
Amount Available for Investment	$	%	$	%
Prepaid Terms and Fees Related to Purchase of Property(2)				
Cash Down Payment (Equity) Acquisition Fees (Real Estate Commissions)(3)				
Working Capital Reserve				
Proceeds Invested				
Public Offering Expenses				
Total Application of Proceeds .	$	%	$	100.00%

The Corporate General Partner and its affiliates may receive a maximum of $ (%) if the minimum dollar amount is sold and $ (%) if the maximum dollar amount is sold from the sellers of the properties as Real Estate Commissions on purchases of properties. Real estate commissions are normally paid by the seller of a property rather than the buyer. However, the price of a property will generally be adjusted upward to take into account this obligation of the seller so that in effect the Partnership, as purchaser, will bear all or a portion of the commission in the purchase price of the property. The partnership also expects to pay commissions in connection with the sale of properties which will reduce the net proceeds to the Partnership of any such sales.

(1) Includes a $ non-recurring organization fee to be received by the Corporate General Partner and legal, accounting, printing and other expenses of this offering. To the extent, if any, that expenses of the offering exceed $ per interest, the excess will be paid by

(2) Includes prepaid interest, points, loan commitment fees and legal and other costs of acquisition. The percentage of such items to be capitalized is . . . . %.

(3) "Real Estate Commission" is defined as the total of all fees and commissions paid by any person to any person, including the Corporate General Partner or affiliates in connection with the selection, purchase, construction or development of any property by the Partnership, whether designated as real estate commission, acquisition fees, finders fees, selection fees, development fees, construction fees, non-recurring management fees, consulting fees or any other similar fees or commissions howsoever designated and howsoever treated for tax or accounting purposes. (See "Compensation to Management." Page . . .)

TABLE II

(To be used for each prior partnership)

		Name of Partnership		
	Year	Year	Year	Year
SUMMARY OF OPERATIONS— GAAP Basis*				
1. Gross Revenues . . . . $				
1(a) Gain (Loss) on Sale of Property . . . . $				
2. Less:[1] Operating Expense. . $ Interest Expense . . . $ Depreciation . . . . . . $				
3. NET INCOME (LOSS)— GAAP BASIS . . . . $——				
Computation to Tax Basis				
4. Less:[2] . . . . $				
5. Plus:[2] . . . . $				
6. TAXABLE INCOME (LOSS) . . . . $——				

TABLE II—(Continued)

	Year	Name of Partnership		
		Year	Year	Year

Computation of Cash Generated

7. *Plus:* Capitalization of
   Loan Fees .... $
   Depreciation ....

8. *Less:* Mortgage Reduction . $——

9. CASH GENERATED
   (DEFICIENCY)[3][7] .... $

10. Cash Distributions to
    Partners[4] .... $

11. CASH GENERATED
    (DEFICIENCY) AFTER
    DISTRIBUTION (BE-
    FORE SPECIAL ITEMS) $

12. Special Items[5] .... $

13. Cash Generated
    (Deficiency) After
    Special Items .... $——

*Tax and Distribution Data per
$1,000 Investment*

Federal Income Tax Deductions[6]

Ordinary Income (Loss) ...... $
Capital Gain (Loss) .... $

Cash Distributions to Partners[4]

Investment Income .... $
Return of Capital .... $

---

*Generally Accepted Accounting Principles.

[1]Should include all operating and other appropriate deductions from revenues necessary to arrive at a calculation of net income on a GAAP basis.

[2]Lines 4 and 5 should include any differences between GAAP (line 3) and Taxable Income (Loss). Detail major items and aggregate all others.

[3]Explain any cash deficiency (line 9). If distributions are made to partners in excess of the amount of cash generated (line 9), appropriate disclosure should be made of the sources and amount of the funds used in making the distribution shown in line 10.

[4]See Guide 25 of Release 33-4936.

[5]All sources and uses of cash from refinancings, purchase and sales of properties, loans and other similar items not directly associated with partnership operations, which result in a material cash effect, should be individually disclosed in line 13 for those periods in which such transactions occur.

[6]Any expense items challenged by IRS should be indicated in a footnote.

[7]In any interim period (fiscal quarter), subsequent to that shown above, where a deficit cash flow occurs, such deficit should be reflected in a note with the corresponding interim period of the preceding fiscal year.

Instruction: The foregoing tabulation should include: (a) Summary Income and Expense Data prepared on the basis of Generally Accepted Accounting Principles (GAAP), (b) adjustments necessary to GAAP Net Income (Loss) to compute Taxable Income (Loss), (c) adjustments necessary to Taxable Income to compute Cash Generated (Deficiency), and (d) Tax Deductions and cash distribution data both on an income and cash basis (see Guide 25, Release 33-4936).

Appendix E CALIFORNIA SAVING & LOAN ASSOCIATIONS LOAN GUIDELINES

GUIDE TO LOAN LIMITATIONS
FOR CALIFORNIA STATE-LICENSED ASSOCIATIONS

(Not an Official Interpretation or Complete Listing of Law and Regulations)

Please See Financial Code Section References in Parentheses
Together With Information in This Chart and Additional Comments

TYPE OF LOAN	MAXIMUM TERM	MAXIMUM % TO VALUE	PRINCIPAL PAYMENT MUST START WITHIN	PRINCIPAL PAYMENT MADE
Certificate loans with shares or investment certificates pledged as collateral (7157 as amended by 235.29**)	No limitation (7157)	90% of value (7157)	No requirement (7157)	By maturity
To invest in money market certificate of $10,000 or more (235.29**)	No limitation (235.29**)	50% of money market certificate and no further loan shall be made on security of that MMC (235.29**)	No requirement (235.29**)	By maturity
Collateral loans with existing loans as collateral (7158)	No limitation but not exceeding term of collateral (7158)	90% of unpaid principal of notes evidencing loans pledged as collateral (7158)	No requirement (7158)	By maturity
Collateral loans with bonds, treasury certificates, notes and other securities as collateral (7159)	No limitation (7159)	Lesser of 90% of unpaid principal or 90% of market value (7159)	No requirement—principal payments must be paid to maintain balance at not more than 90% of market value (7159)	By maturity
Nonresidential improved real property (7150) (See Subchapter 14**)	*30 years (7150)	70% of appraised value or 75% of appraised value subject to Commissioner's regulations (7152(a))	36 months construction 3 months all others (7151)	Monthly (5074)
Commercial improved real property (7152(b)) (See Subchapter 14**) Limitations of Sections 7172 and 7174 apply (232.2**) (See Comments, Item 11(a))	31 years (7152(b))	90% of appraised value subject to Commissioner's regulations, if association takes as additional security assignment of long-term lease (7152(b))	36 months construction 3 months all others (7151)	Monthly (5074)
80% loans, improved real property, one or more residential units (7153)	*30 years (term of variable interest rate loan may be extended to maximum of 40 years on mutual agreement between lender and borrower) (7150)	80% of appraised value (7153)	36 months construction 6 months if 1-to-4 residential as trade-in or exchange 3 months all others (7151)	Monthly (5074)
Planned development loans, improved real property, residential, condominium, co-op and cluster-type units, one-family occupancy. Such loans in project limited to 1% of association's assets unless binding contracts have been entered into for bona fide sale of not less than a majority of residential units in project or loan is approved by Commissioner (7153.1)	*30 years (term of variable interest rate loan may be extended to maximum of 40 years on mutual agreement between lender and borrower) (7150)	80% of appraised value (7153.1)	36 months construction 6 months if 1-to-4 residential as trade-in or exchange 3 months all others (7151)	Monthly (5074)
90% loans, improved real property, 1-to-4 family residential structures with at least one unit to be occupied by borrower, no other liens permitted, condominium, co-op and cluster-type units included. Such loans limited to 50% of association's total assets (7153.2 as amended by 235.27**)	*30 years (term of variable interest rate loan may be extended to maximum of 40 years on mutual agreement between lender and borrower) (7150)	Lesser of (1) for 1-family structures, $93,750, and for 2-to-4 family structures, greater of $60,000 per dwelling unit or amount allowable under Section 207(c)(3) of National Housing Act, as amended, or (2) 90% of appraised value or purchase price (7153.2 as amended by 235.27**) (See Comments, Item 11(b))	36 months construction 6 months if 1-to-4 residential as trade-in or exchange 3 months all others (7151)	Monthly plus impounds for taxes in advance until unpaid loan balance reduced to 80% of lesser of appraised value or purchase price (7153.2)

* From due date of first principal installment
** S&L Commissioner's Regulations

TYPE OF LOAN	MAXIMUM TERM	MAXIMUM % TO VALUE	PRINCIPAL PAYMENT MUST START WITHIN	PRINCIPAL PAYMENT MADE
95% loans, improved real property, 1-or-2 family residential structures with at least one unit to be occupied by borrower, no other liens permitted, condominium, co-op and cluster-type units included. Such loans limited to 25% of association's assets without prior approval of Commissioner. Aggregate principal amount of 95% and 90% loans in excess of 80% limited to 50% of association's assets (7153.8 and 7153.2 as amended by 235.27** and 235.28**)	*30 years (term of variable interest rate loan may be extended to maximum of 40 years on mutual agreement between lender and borrower) (7150)	Lesser of (1) for 1-family structures, $75,000, and for 2-family structures, amount allowable under Section 207 (c)(3) of National Housing Act, as amended, or (2) 95% of appraised value or purchase price (7153.8 as amended by 235.28**) (See Comments, Items 11(b) and (c))	36 months construction 6 months if 1-to-4 residential as trade-in or exchange 3 months all others (7151)	Monthly plus impounds for taxes in advance until unpaid loan balance reduced to 80% of lesser of appraised value or purchase price (7153.2)
Housing for elderly (over 55), improved real property, rest homes and nursing homes included. Such loans limited to 5% of association's total assets (7153.3)	*30 years (term of variable interest rate loan may be extended to maximum of 40 years on mutual agreement between lender and borrower) (7150)	90% of appraised value (7153.3)	36 months construction 6 months if 1-to-4 residential as trade-in or exchange 3 months all others (7151)	Monthly (5074)
Cooperative housing development (real property comprising group of single-family dwellings owned by nonprofit cooperative housing organization) if units equal to 90% of value or purchase price of development, whichever is greater, are presold to bona fide purchasers and development maintains resources at least equal to those required for comparable developments insured by FHA (235.26** which repeals 7153.4)	*30 years (term of variable interest rate loan may be extended to maximum of 40 years on mutual agreement between lender and borrower) (7150)	Maximum loan amount for development shall be sum of applicable maximum loan amounts for each unit (includes 80%, 90% and 95% loans having first security interest in stock or membership certificate issued to tenant stockholder or resident member by nonprofit cooperative housing organization and assignment of borrower's interest in proprietary lease or occupancy agreement issued by organization) (235.26**)	36 months construction 6 months if 1-to-4 residential as trade-in or exchange 3 months all others (7151)	Monthly (5074)
Urban renewal area, (as defined in Section 110(a) of Housing Act of 1949), improved real property. Such loans limited to 5% of association's total assets (7153.5)	*30 years (7153.5)	80% of appraised value (7153.5)	6 months (7153.5)	Substantially equal payments at least semiannually to retire loan including interest by maturity—periodic payments of principal to be made in direct reduction of outstanding obligations (7153.5)
Low-rent housing under leased housing program, improved real property, one or more units. Such loans limited to 10% of association's assets (7153.6-234.2**) (See Subchapter 16**)	Under U.S. Housing Act of 1937, as amended Section 23 Loans Maturity date shall not exceed by more than 10 years termination date of Local Housing Authority lease including borrower's options, but maximum term shall not exceed 30 years (234.2**) Section 10 Loans (234.2**)	80% of market value (234.2**) 90% of purchase price (234.2**)	36 months construction 6 months if 1-to-4 residential as trade-in or exchange 3 months all others (7151)	Monthly (5074)
HOAP loans, improved real property, SFR, owner-occupied, no other liens permitted (7153.7) (See Part 527, Title 12, Code of Federal Regulations)	(See Federal Regulations)	Lesser of 100% of market value, purchase price, or $25,000 (7153.7) (See Section 12640.02, Insurance Code, for mortgage guarantee insurance requirement)	(See Federal Regulations)	(See Federal Regulations)

*. From due date of first principal installment
** S&L Commissioner's Regulations

TYPE OF LOAN	MAXIMUM TERM	MAXIMUM % TO VALUE	PRINCIPAL PAYMENT MUST START WITHIN	PRINCIPAL PAYMENT MADE
Alternative Mortgage Instruments. Improved real property, residential, owner-occupied, 1-to-4 units, condominium, co-op and cluster-type units included. Such loans limited to 10% of association's assets (7153.9 effective 1-1-78 to 1-1-83) (See Subchapter 7.8**, which applies to loans made within 4 years of 2-10-78 effective date of subchapter)				
Flexible payment loan (178.4(b)**)	30 years (178.4(b)**)	Lesser of (1) for 1-family structures, $93,750, and for 2-to-4 family structures, greater of $60,000 per dwelling unit or amount allowable under Section 207 (c)(3) of National Housing Act, as amended, or (2) 95% of value, or (3) 95% of purchase price—private mortgage guarantee insurance required on unpaid balance of loan in excess of 90% or specific reserve of 1% of unpaid principal balance until unpaid principal balance reduced to amount not in excess of 90% (178.4(b)**)	Interest only may be paid during an initial period not to exceed five years (See Section 178.4(b)** for additional information re payments)	Monthly by maturity (178.4(b)**)
Graduated payment loan (savings account may be pledged as additional security) (178.4(c)**)	30 years (178.4(c)**)	Same as for flexible payment loan above (178.4(c)**)	No requirement (See Section 178.4(c)** for two possible mortgage payment plans)	Monthly by maturity (178.4(c)**)
Reverse annuity loan, unamortized (178.4(d)**)	Repayable in full upon borrower's or last surviving borrower's death or upon prior sale of property securing loan (178.4(d)**)	95% of value (178.4(d)**)	No requirement (See Section 178.4(d)** for information re purchase of annuity contract for borrower)	No requirement (178.4(d)**)
90% loans plus 15% for rehabilitation, improved real property, residential, condominium, co-op and cluster-type units included, SFR, owner-occupied, no other liens permitted, insured or guaranteed by California Housing Finance Agency or by State of California or any instrumentality of the United States. Such loans limited to 30% of association's total assets (7153.10)	*35 years (7153.10)	90% of appraised value plus an additional 15% for rehabilitation, or 90% of purchase price plus an additional 15% for rehabilitation, not to exceed $60,000 (7153.10)	36 months construction 6 months if 1-to-4 residential as trade-in or exchange 3 months all others (7151)	Monthly plus impounds for taxes in advance until unpaid balance of loan reduced to 80% of lesser of appraised value or purchase price (7153.10)
Energy conservation equipment loans, improved real property, residential, 1-to-4 units, purchase and installation of energy conservation equipment. Such loan to be made in connection with concurrent loan authorized under Section 7153 (7153.11)	*30 years (term of variable interest rate loan may be extended to maximum of 40 years on mutual agreement between lender and borrower) (7150)	10% of loan made under authority of Section 7153 (7153.11)	36 months construction 3 months all others (7151)	Monthly (5074)
Additional advances or additional loans to existing borrower for purposes stated above (7153.11)	*30 years (term of variable interest rate loan may be extended to maximum of 40 years on mutual agreement between lender and borrower) (7150)	Aggregate of additional advance or loan and unpaid balance of existing loan will not exceed 80% of appraised value after purchase and installation of energy conservation equipment (7153.11)	36 months construction 3 months all others (7151)	Monthly (5074)

* From due date of first principal installment
** S&L Commissioner's Regulations

TYPE OF LOAN	MAXIMUM TERM	MAXIMUM % TO VALUE	PRINCIPAL PAYMENT MUST START WITHIN	PRINCIPAL PAYMENT MADE
Unamortized, improved real property (7154) (See Comments, Item 2, for limitation on unamortized loan)	3 years (7154)	60% of appraised value (7154)	No requirement (7154)	By maturity
	2 years (7154)	70% of appraised value (7154)	No requirement (7154)	By maturity
Swing loan (on principal residence of borrower at time of loan) to purchase property to be occupied by borrower as principal residence (prepayment fee prohibited) (7154)	1 year (7154)	80% of market value, including any amount already recorded by deed of trust on such property (7154)	No requirement (7154)	By maturity
Rehabilitation, improved real property, residential—combined value and disbursement of funds (7154.1)	36 months (7154.1) Permanent loan under Chapter 10 of S&L Association Law may be combined into single loan with loan under Section 7154.1 and term of permanent loan shall begin at end of term allowed under Section 7154.1 for rehabilitation	Up to 80%, 90% or 95% of value (percentage permissible under Chapter 10 of S&L Association Law)— disbursement of funds in excess of 80% of value shall not be made until completion of rehabilitation and compliance with applicable provisions of Section 7153.2 or 7153.8 (7154.1)	No requirement (7154.1)	No requirement, but interest payable at least semiannually (7154.1)
Combination of commercial farming enterprise and farm residence (to be used as principal residence of owner of commercial farming enterprise) (7154.5) (See also Section 7155.3 re loans on real property used for commercial farming enterprises which are not otherwise authorized)	25 years (7154.5)	80% of appraised value (7154.5)	Principal and interest payable at least annually (7154.5)	By maturity
Unimproved real property (before foundation completed - 5072), unamortized (7155)	2 years (7155)	70% of appraised value (7155)	No requirement (7155)	By maturity
Construction, SFR or mobilehome park development as defined in Section 7187.1. Such loans limited to 5% of association's assets (7155)	3 years (7155) Such loan may be extended an additional 3 years provided interest is current and balance of loan is reduced to amount not in excess of 75% of current appraised value (7155)	75% of appraised value (7155)	No requirement (7155)	By maturity or after 3-year extension (7155)
Construction, SFR, owner-occupied, no other liens permitted (7155)	5 years (7155)	75% of appraised value (7155)	Not more than 60 days after disbursement of loan (7155)	Monthly to amortize at least 40% of original principal amount of loan by maturity (7155)
Property improvement or equipment, except furnishings, includes energy conservation equipment (Secured or Unsecured). All such loans limited to 20% of association's total assets—loans for financing equipment limited to 5% of association's assets (7184 as amended by 235.24**)	20 years (235.24**)	No limit on loans financing repairs, alterations, or improvements; $15,000 on any one loan for equipping of any real property when aggregated with balance of all outstanding equipment loans relating to same real property made under sole authority of Section 7184 (235.24**)	3 months (7151)	Monthly (5074)
	FHA Title 1 (7200)	FHA limit	FHA Regulation	FHA Regulation
Education loans—college, university or vocational school (Secured or Unsecured) Such loans limited to 5% of association's total assets (7185)	No limitation (7185)	Amount of expenses of such education as certified by borrower. Association may require co-maker, insurance guaranty under a government student loan guarantee plan, or other protection (7185)	No requirement (7185)	By maturity

* From due date of first principal installment
** S&L Commissioner's Regulations

TYPE OF LOAN	MAXIMUM TERM	MAXIMUM % TO VALUE	PRINCIPAL PAYMENT MUST START WITHIN*	PRINCIPAL PAYMENT MADE
Mobilehomes, minimum width-10 ft., minimum area-400 sq. ft. (7187) (See Subchapter 15**) Such loans limited to 20% of association's total assets (233.2**)				
Mobilehome chattel paper that finances mobilehome dealer's acquisition of inventory (inventory held for sale by dealer in ordinary course of business within state and loan evidenced by chattel paper is dealer's obligation) (233.4**)	Inventory Financing New Mobilehome No requirement (233.4**) Used Mobilehome No requirement (233.4**)	100% of manufacturer's invoice price for each mobilehome and equipment to be installed by dealer 75% of appraised market value, including installed equipment (233.4**)	No requirement (233.4**) No requirement (233.4**)	By maturity By maturity
Conventional retail mobilehome chattel paper (mobilehome to be maintained as residence of owner (or beneficial owner) or owner's (or beneficial owner's) relative or employee, and located at mobilehome park or other permanent or semipermanent site within the state or within 100 miles of an office of association's service corporation (233.5**)	Retail Financing 30 years on new mobilehome (233.5**) 20 years on used mobilehome (233.5**)	90% of buyer's total costs (excluding time-price differential or interest, however computed)— insurance premiums may be financed for customary physical damage insurance and vendor's single-interest coverage on mobilehome for an initial policy term not to exceed 3 years (233.5**)	Substantially equal monthly installments (233.5**)	By maturity
Association may also invest in retail mobilehome chattel paper insured or guaranteed under National Housing Act or Chapter 37 of Title 38, U.S. Code, as amended, if satisfactory local servicing of that paper is arranged (233.5**)				
Loans to rehabilitate used mobilehomes (Secured or Unsecured) to enable borrower to comply with minimum health and safety code standards (such loans limited to 5% of association's total assets and together with property improvement loans made under Section 7184 shall not aggregate at any one time more than 20% of association's total assets) (233.8**) (See Comments, Items 11(f) and 12(d))	10 years (233.8**)	$5,000 and shall not be used to refinance existing loans (233.8**)	3 months (7151)	Monthly (5074)
Mobilehome park, improved (area of land where two or more mobilehome sites are rented to accommodate mobilehomes) (7187.1)	31 years (7187.1)	80% of appraised value (7187.1)	3 months (7151)	Monthly (5074)
Federal funds (unsecured loan of funds from deposit of association to member bank of FDIC) (7188)	6 months (7188)	Total of all time deposits and federal funds loans in same bank not to exceed greater of 1/4 of 1% of bank's total deposits or $40,000 (7188)	No requirement (7188)	By maturity
Foreign countries—real property and securities in foreign countries—AID (6702(n)) (See Subchapter 13**) Such loans limited to 1% of association's total assets, prior written approval of Commissioner required (231.4**)	Loans Guaranteed AID	AID	AID	AID
Unimproved real property (before foundation completed - 5072) Sale of 6705 property with or without amortization (6705.1)	2 years (6705.1)	95% of market value (6705.1) (See Comments, Item 4, for limitations)	No requirement— interest to be paid at least semiannually (6705.1)	By maturity
Improved land with offsite improvements but no buildings. Sale of 6705 property (6705.2)	5 years (6705.2)	90% of market value (6705.2) (See Comments, Item 4, for limitations)	3 months (7151)	Monthly at rate of not less than 1% per month but by maturity—payments shall be accelerated if subsequent lien placed on property (6705.2)

* From due date of first principal installment
** S&L Commissioner's Regulations

TYPE OF LOAN	MAXIMUM TERM	MAXIMUM % TO VALUE	PRINCIPAL PAYMENT MUST START WITHIN	PRINCIPAL PAYMENT MADE
FHA pursuant to Titles 1, 2 and 6, National Housing Act, if insured by FHA (Secured or Unsecured) (7200, 7201)	FHA limit (7150)	FHA limit	FHA Regulation	FHA Regulation
VA pursuant to Title 3 of Servicemen's Readjustment Act of 1944 or Veteran's Readjustment Assistance Act of 1952 if guaranteed or insured by Administrator of Veterans' Affairs (Secured or Unsecured) (7202 thru 7206)	VA limit (7150)	VA limit	VA Regulation	VA Regulation
Farmers Home Administration Rural Housing Program (loans guaranteed under) Residential real property. Aggregate outstanding balance of nonguaranteed portions of all loans made under program shall not exceed greater of 2.5% of total assets or 1/2 of association's statutory net worth (235.25**)	Farmers Home Administration limit (235.25**)	Farmers Home Administration limit—at least 80% of principal amount and accrued interest shall be guaranteed (235.25**)	Farmers Home Administration requirement	Farmers Home Administration requirement

* From due date of first principal installment
** S&L Commissioner's Regulations

This Guide to Loan Limitations, prepared by the California Savings and Loan League, is revised to 6-15-80.

ADDITIONAL COMMENTS
ON SOME STATUTORY LOAN LIMITATIONS

(Unless otherwise indicated, section references
are to the California Financial Code)

1. LIMITATION ON AMOUNT OF LOAN

Without consent of Commissioner, no loan can exceed $125,000 principal if loan exceeds 1% of book value of association's assets—subject to provisions of Section 7104 (7172).

2. LIMITATION ON UNAMORTIZED LOAN

No unamortized loan may be made unless at least 90% of unpaid principal of all loans then in force are amortized loans. Notwithstanding this limitation, unamortized loans may be made in an amount equal to 20% of unpaid principal of all loans in effect provided 10% of such loans are made pursuant to Section 7153.9 and during such time as Section 7153.9 is in effect (7170).

3. SECURITY FOR LOANS

(a) Loans may be secured by a first trust deed upon real property, the pledge of shares or investment certificates of such association (7157), or the pledge of bonds or other collateral (7159) (7102). A leasehold interest in real property under a lease which does not expire, or which has been extended or renewed so that it does not expire for at least 10 years beyond maturity date of loan, can also be security for a loan (7100, 7101).

(b) Two or more successive trust deeds on the same real property, if one of them is a first trust deed, are collectively deemed to be a first trust deed when they are owned or purchased by the same association (7103).

(c) In lieu of making two or more separate loans secured by trust deed, etc., in permitted amounts, a single loan secured by all such properties may be made if it does not exceed aggregate of principal amounts permitted for separate loans (7104).

(d) Any security may be taken at any time and without limit as additional security for any loan held by association (7105).

(e) When borrower is in arrears in payment of obligation, the whole loan shall become due at the option of the association, and association may proceed to enforce collection or foreclose on securities held (7106).

(f) Several types of eligible security may be combined to secure a single loan (A. G. Opinion No. 60-191).

(g) Loans may also be secured by a first security interest in stock or membership certificate issued to tenant-stockholder or resident-member by nonprofit cooperative housing organization (235.26, S&L Commissioner's Regulations, which repeals 7153.4); and by the pledge of notes evidencing loans which at the time of pledge are not in excess of association loan limits and which are secured by property upon which the association might make a direct loan, if such collateral loans at no time exceed 90% of unpaid principal of notes pledged as collateral security (7158).

(h) An association may make loans upon the "mutual plan" (accompanied by pledge of shares having a matured or par value equal to principal of loan) or upon the "definite contract plan" (repayable at designated time or in installments specified in notes or other obligations evidencing such loans). See Sections 7160-7167 for information pertaining to these loans.

4. SOME LIMITATIONS ON LAND LOANS AND CONSTRUCTION LOANS

Construction loans may be made to borrowers who purchased land held by association under Section 6705, the purchase of which was financed under Section 6705.1 or 6705.2 (6705.4). Except with consent of Commissioner, total amounts loaned on security of such property shall not exceed 85% of fair market value of completed improved property (6705.4). Investments of an association under Section 6705 and loans by an association under Sections 6705.1, 6705.2, 6705.4 and 6705.6 (with certain exceptions) shall not aggregate more than lesser of 5% of total assets or association's statutory net worth (6705). Section 6705.5 sets forth restrictions pertaining to investments authorized by Sections 6705.1, 6705.2, 6705.3, 6705.4 and 6705.6 and in unimproved property authorized in Section 6705. See also Subchapter 21, S&L Commissioner's Regulations. In addition, an association shall not make any loan upon security of unimproved real property made under Sections 6705.1, 6705.2 and 7155(a) if unpaid principal of all its loans then in force on unimproved real property exceeds 5% of unpaid principal of all its loans of all classes then in force (7171).

5. LIMITATION ON LOANS TO ONE BORROWER, ETC.
Without consent of Commissioner, loans to any one borrower or under any one transaction or applicable to any one project or tract may not be held by an association if such loans exceed the lesser of 10% of its total assets or the statutory net worth of the association (7174). See Section 7175 for exceptions.

6. LOANS WITHOUT SPECIFIC LIMITATIONS (Salvage Powers)
Regardless of any other provisions, excepting those provisions of Sections 5613, 7177 to 7180, inclusive, and 7182, an association may make additional advances or loans on property securing a loan to protect such property or to preserve the security of the loan; may make loans to facilitate the sale of property acquired by foreclosure or by conveyance in lieu of foreclosure; may take such other action as is reasonably and prudently necessary for the salvage of any loan; may, with

prior consent of Commissioner, make loans to facilitate the sale of property acquired by foreclosure, etc., to persons enumerated in Section 7177 (6701). Regardless of any other provisions, with prior written approval of Commissioner, an association may take such action as is reasonably and prudently necessary to protect the association or any of its interests or investments (6701).

7. PURCHASE OF LOANS
An association may purchase any loan it would be authorized to make, except for the original amount and term thereof, if the purchase price and remaining term thereof at time of purchase do not exceed association's loan limits (6711).

8. LENDING AREA
There is no restriction in California law that loans must be made within any distance of the association's home office. However, insured state-licensed associations are restricted by Section 561.22 of FSLIC's Insurance of Accounts Regulations re normal lending territory. See also Section 563.9 re nationwide lending.

9. RESTRICTIONS AS TO BORROWERS (Loans to Officers, etc.)
(a) Except as provided in Section 7177.5, no loans (other than those wholly secured by pledge of its shares or investment certificates) may, directly or indirectly, be made to, acquired from or inure to the benefit of any substantial stockholder, or any officer, director or employee of such association or such substantial stockholder, or to any member of the immediate family of such enumerated persons, except that a loan may be made to a purchaser of a single-family dwelling or mobilehome owned and occupied as principal residence by salaried officer or employee (7177). See Section 5073 for definition of member of immediate family.
(b) Section 7177.5 permits loan to salaried officer or employee of

association if loan is secured by single-family dwelling or mobile-home owned and occupied by borrower as principal residence, and, if borrower is an officer, loan is approved in advance by resolution approved by majority of directors, with no director interested in transaction voting.

(c) Loans may be made to corporations in which such persons have, or control, less than a 10% interest upon authorization of association's disinterested directors (7179). See Section 7180 for required reports.

(d) With consent of Commissioner, loans may be made to corporations in which such persons have greater than a 10% interest (7178).

(e) No loans shall be made on security of association's own stock (7181).

(f) No loans shall be made to or purchased from Commissioner or specified employees (7182).

(g) Violators are guilty of a felony (7183).

10. APPRAISALS

(a) In determining appraised value, unimproved real property without offsite improvements shall be evaluated as though offsite improvements have been installed if a subdivision map has been recorded and a bond guaranteeing installation of such offsite improvements has been accepted by governing authorities (7155.1).

(b) If loan is made upon security of real property where it is agreed or contemplated that improvements will be made to the property which shall become a part of such security, the real property shall be deemed improved real property and value of proposed improvements shall be included in appraised value of such real property (7156).

(c) No loan shall be made upon the appraisement of, nor shall compensation for any appraisement be paid to, any appraiser, officer or member of any committee who has not been first approved in writing by Commissioner (7250).

(d) Records written in ink or typewritten. and appropriately

signed shall be kept showing appraised values of real estate securing loans (8703).

11. LIMITATIONS ON TYPES OF LOANS

(a) Section 6705.7 provides an association may invest an amount not in excess of 2% of its total assets in loans secured by commercial real property which are not otherwise authorized.

(b) Section 7153.2 permits construction loans to 90%, provided, among other things, amount in excess of 80% of appraised value shall not be disbursed until construction is completed, and, if loan is made to finance construction for sale, the property is sold and title conveyed to a purchaser who has assumed and agreed to pay the loan and there is compliance with other applicable requirements.

(c) Section 7153.8 requires private mortgage guarantee insurance on unpaid balance of loan in excess of 90% or specific reserve of 1% of unpaid principal balance until unpaid principal balance reduced to amount not in excess of 90%.

(d) Section 7155.3 provides no association shall make nonconforming secured loans (on security of residential real property and real property used or to be used for commercial farming enterprises — includes equity loans) aggregating at any one time more than an amount equal to lesser of 2% of its total assets plus 1/2% of total assets for each percentage point of statutory net worth in excess of 4% of assets or 5% of its total assets. A secured investment will be deemed to be unsecured to extent it exceeds lesser of appraised value or purchase price at time loan is made.

(e) Section 7184.1 provides an association may make other secured or unsecured loans for constructing, improving, etc., what is expected to become residential real property or for financing purchases of modular housing units where the association relies substantially for repayment on borrower's general credit standing and forecast of income or association relies on other assurances for repayment, including a third-party guaranty. Such loans are limited to the lesser of 2% of association's total assets plus 1/2% of total assets for each percentage point of statutory net worth in excess of 4% of assets or 5% of association's total assets.

(f) Section 233.6, S&L Commissioner's Regulations, sets forth provisions for the purchase and sale of participation interests in mobilehome chattel paper and sale of mobilehome chattel paper. It also provides that no association may sell mobilehome loans or participations in such loans if, at the close of its most recent semi-annual period, it has mobilehome loan scheduled items (other than assets acquired in a supervisory merger) in excess of 5% of its total mobilehome loan portfolio (association may apply to Commissioner for waiver of this restriction).

12. LOAN DOCUMENTATION REQUIRED

(a) Each association granting a single loan for more than $150,000, or total loans to one borrower in excess of $250,000, shall obtain financial statement from borrower properly signed and containing certain information (8703.2).

(b) Each association making construction loans shall prepare and maintain in its files signed and approved inspection records with sufficient detail to determine whether amount advanced by association conforms to ratio of loan to value set forth in Section 7156 (8703.1).

(c) Subchapter 1.3, S&L Commissioner's Regulations, Section 118, et seq., lists loan register requirements and other required documents supporting loans.

(d) Section 233.9, S&L Commissioner's Regulations, lists documents and information to be maintained by association in connection with making or buying whole loans or installment sales contracts on mobilehomes, including inventory financing and other transactions.

13. VARIABLE INTEREST RATE LOANS

Sections 1916.5 and 1916.6, Civil Code, set forth various provisions pertaining to variable interest rate loans. See also Subchapter 18, S&L Commissioner's Regulations.

14. MORTGAGE OF REAL PROPERTY

Sections 2947-2955, Civil Code, pertain to mortgage of real property and include such items as acceleration, impound accounts, late payment charges, and prepayments. Section 7186 also pertains to prepayment of loans.

15. OTHER LOAN REFERENCES

We call your attention to the following sections in the Financial Code, which are especially pertinent to this Guide to Loan Limitations:

5072 Offsite improvements and improved real property defined
5074 Amortized loan defined
5076 Statutory net worth defined
6700-6719 Authorized investments and borrowings
7100-7106 Security required for loans
7150-7188 Loan limitations
7200-7206 Insured and guaranteed loans (FHA and VA)
7250-7255 Appraisal of properties securing loans

The following subchapters of the S&L Commissioner's Regulations also contain pertinent loan and investment information:

Subchapter 1.3 - Supplementary Loan Report and Documentation Requirements
Subchapter 1.5 - Statutory Net Worth Requirements
Subchapter 7 - Sale of Loans or Participating Interests Therein
Subchapter 7.5 - Modification Agreements
Subchapter 7.6 - Wrap-around Loans
Subchapter 7.8 - Alternative Mortgage Instrument Loans

Subchapter 12 - Investments—Service Corporations and Business Development Credit Corporations

Subchapter 13 - Investments and Borrowings

Subchapter 14 - Other Amortized Loans

Subchapter 15 - Loans on Mobile Dwellings

Subchapter 16 - Loans on Low-Rent Housing

Subchapter 17 - Extension to State-Licensed Associations of Right, Power, Privilege or Duty Extended to Federal Institutions

Subchapter 18 - Loans—Variable Interest Rate Provisions

Subchapter 19 - Insurance in Connection with Sales, Loans and Advances of Credit

Subchapter 21 - Real Estate Owned

Also, a reminder that the following material in the CALIFORNIA GUIDE does contain relevant information regarding loans that can be made by state-licensed associations and should be referred to when necessary:

BOOK 1

Savings and Loan Association Law

Regulations of the Savings and Loan Commissioner

Legal Opinions—Department of Savings and Loan

BOOK 2

Related Code Sections

Selected Attorney General Opinions

Selected Regulations of Related State Agencies (contains Business and Transportation Agency's Regulations Pursuant to the Housing Financial Discrimination Act of 1977)

Department Procedures

Commissioner's Accounting Instruction Letters

Commissioner's Directives

This Guide to Loan Limitations is revised to 6-15-80.

Appendix F LENDING POLICY AND PROCEDURES GUIDE

The Board of Directors of _____ adopts this "LENDING POLICY AND PROCEDURES GUIDE" respecting lending and related matters set forth herein.

It is hereby declared the basic policy of this association:

To give prompt, efficient service to prospective borrowers, real estate brokers and builders, enlisting and encouraging their good will for future business, both loans and savings and to aid in the creation of additional single family residences in order to assure an adequate future supply of homes to satisfy the demand of our area population.

This "Lending Policy and Procedures Guide" includes:

I	*General Lending Policies*
II	*Construction Loans*
III	*Appraisal Policies*
IV	*Credit Policy*
V	*Title Insurance*
VI	*Impound Accounts*
VII	*Hazard Insurance*
VIII	*Loan Approval Procedures*
IX	*Loan Committee*
X	*Collection Procedures*
XI	*Assumptions*
XII	*Modifications*
XIII	*Additional Advances*

I GENERAL LENDING POLICIES

Lending policies shall coincide with available capital and with the requirements of the local loan market. Undue concentration of loans to any one borrower or his interlocking interest shall be avoided and loans on the security of other than owner-occupied home type properties shall be kept within reasonable limits. Emphasis shall be on single-family dwellings.

Mortgage loan plans shall be carefully formulated to avoid undue concentration of loans with junior financing behind the association's mortgage to avoid the possibility of inflating prices and creating unsafe loans. Loans on property which an officer or director owned immediately prior to making the loan, or the property on which any officer or director, his family or any business affiliation provides any secondary financing shall be avoided.

A limitation shall be set on loans made from referrals from any one source of loans. An officer or director connected with a business from which loans may be derived shall be required to disclose to the directors the loan(s) in question and refrain from taking part in any action to approve the loan.

Loans will be granted to applicants without consideration of race, color, or creed and primary consideration of accepting of rejecting a loan application will be confined to evidence of an applicant's willingness and financial ability to repay the loan, to evidence of the sufficient market value of the security and to evidence of good and sufficient lien title to the security.

Interest rates on loans shall be set at a level consistent with the best loans which are available in the market from time to time. There shall be avoidance of rates which are higher than normal since a safe and prudent borrower would not ordinarily pay more than a prevailing rate. Loan fees and the initial charges shall be generally not more than the prevailing charges in the market to enable the assoication to provide the services required in its Charter for economical home-financing and to ensure that the general quality of the loans will be the best available.

The general loan policies will be:

(*a*)   The association will not reject any loan to any person simply because of his race, color, creed or sex.

(*b*)   The association will not commit itself to grant loans in excess of its available capital nor in excess of its borrowing capacity for loan expansion.

(*c*)   The association intends to loan on all types of property legally accepted for security and at ratios of loan value to appraisals not in excess of the California law. However, since the association is new and its capacity to grant certain types of loans is limited by available capital and qualified personnel, it shall limit itself to 1–4 family units and make a concerted effort to place strong emphasis on single family owner occupied dwellings. This does not preclude the association from granting a reasonable amount of construction loans on the basis hereinafter described.

(d) Concentration of loans to one borrower or to any of his interlocking interests or referrals from any one source shall be discouraged along with a concentration of loans within a small area or tract.

(e) Loans will not be granted outside the normal service area of the association, which, until changed by resolution of the Board of Directors, shall include only the counties of . . .

(f) To avoid a concentration of loans on property on which there is secondary financing and not to grant any loans on property which an officer, director or substantial stockholder owned immediately prior to making the loan or on any property on which any officer, director or substantial stockholder, his family or any business affiliation provides any secondary financing.

(g) The association intends to grant loans on single family residences that will be insured under the FHA program or guaranteed by the Veterans Administration or insured by Private Mortgage Insurance companies.

(h) The general association loan policy for acquisition, appraisal, approval, documentation, insurance, service and file maintenance will be so governed by, but not limited to, complying with the guidelines for acceptance within the Real Estate Settlement Act of 1974, as to allow the association the flexibility of a loan portfolio acceptable for sale or participation within existing GNMA, FNMA, FHLMC, or succeeding programs.

(i) It will be general association policy to require all borrowers to establish a preauthorized loan payment procedure, such as Transmatic, except in those cases where the borrower's income-to-payment ratio clearly warrants a waiver of this policy or in the case of a short-term construction loan. A preauthorized payment procedure on a loan for a nonowner occupied property may only be waived under special conditions as set from time to time by the loan committee.

(j) In order to provide:

A sound financial base for future operations of the association

A greater assurance of the availability of loan funds for future borrowers

That future borrowers need not subsidize earlier borrowers

Greater liquidity during future periods of disintermediation and "tight money"

A more stable relationship between the return on loans and the current costs of savings and borrowings thereby enabling lower loan interest rates at all times

A loan program which, through allowing competitive loan interest rates at all times, will provide the association the opportunity to build a loan portfolio comprised of high quality loans

It shall be the policy of . . . to make loans exclusively on a variable interest rate basis except as provided below. All such loans will fully comply with California law regulating variable interest rate notes. The law includes provisions which allow interest rate increases, require interest rate decreases, limit the amounts and frequencies of increases and decreases and which safeguard the rights of borrowers.

In addition to the provisions of California law it shall be the policy of this association to accept variable rate notes which provide that the loan interest rate will never increase more than 2.5 per cent per annum above the original loan rate regardless of any greater increase in the index. As provided in California law the index will be the average cost of funds (savings and borrowings) for all insured savings and loan associations in California as published from time to time by the Federal Home Loan Bank of San Francisco.

It shall further be the policy of this association to waive all prepayment penalties where a borrower is paying off or otherwise reducing his obligations on his own home from his own funds and no loan from any other source is replacing the association's loan. There shall also be no prepayment penalty where the association retains the loan on a property subject to a sale if the new owner has complied with association policy for assumption or has obtained a new loan from the association to replace the existing loan nor will there be a prepayment penalty where the association is providing financing on the borrower's new home even if the loan on the previous home is paid off by the buyer with loan funds from another lender.

An acceptable alternative to a variable rate loan shall be, when the following or a similar procedure is approved by the Department of Savings and Loan, a fixed interest rate loan which, regardless of the term used for the calculation of amortizing monthly payments, is all due and payable five years from the date of the note. On such loans the borrower may pay off the loan on the due date or may exercise a personal option to renew the loan for successive five-year periods at an interest rate equal to the association's then current rate for such loans on such properties with no stated or implied limit on increases or decreases in interest rates which may exist at the original or successive due dates. Such initial fixed rate loans will generally be written at rates higher than prevail for similar loans with a variable rate.

The association recognizes that the two loan plans discussed above may not be appropriate for all borrowers. Specifically, it is recognized that individuals with fixed incomes and individuals with no prospects for income increases eqaul to possible inflation would be unwise to purchase a home without the assurance of a long-term level-payment loan such as provided under a long-term fixed-rate loan. Therefore, to assist such individuals in purchasing and owning homes under circumstances and on terms which will truly enable them to make the commitment to home ownership with the actual potential of affording such ownership, it shall be the policy of . . . to accept and approve loan applications for long-term fixed-rate loans from such individuals in every case where there is also submitted evidence that the other determinable costs of the home ownership including real estate taxes, water, gas, electricity, maintenance and hazard insurance, have also been set at fixed amounts for a time period at least equal to the requested loan term. It is not believed to be in the public interest to encourage the assumption of the burdens of home ownership by such individuals without such safeguards for their ability to afford and maintain the home.

II CONSTRUCTION LOANS

The policy with respect to construction loans shall be:

1. The association intends to grant construction loans on all types of property legally accepted for security and at ratios of loan value to appraisal not in excess of California law.

2. Since the association is new and is limited by available capital and qualified personnel, it shall limit all such loans to single family dwellings and then only on a limited basis and amount, as established by the loan committee from time to time.

3. Plans, specifications, cost breakdown, and in case of a contract to build, a firm building contract between a licensed contractor and borrower, must accompany the loan application.

4. The cash difference between the complete cost of the building contract and the net proceeds of the construction loan shall be deposited with the association prior to the closing of the construction loan.

5. Inspection, during the course of construction, will be made periodically and a progress report will be kept on each construction loan. No progress payments will be made without an inspection first being made warranting that the payment is due.

6. All inspection reports must be in writing and signed by the inspector.

7. Construction payments will be made based on the usual 5-pay construction draw or by the payment of bills submitted by the borrower along with lien waivers from subcontractors and suppliers. Management will recommend and the loan committee will decide as to which plan to use an all construction loans granted.

III APPRAISAL POLICIES

The following policies govern the appraisal practice of the association:

1. The appraiser will submit to management a written report, on a form(s) proven in use by the industry, indicating market value as of a given inspection date.

2. In arriving at the market value conclusion the appraiser will correlate at least two of the appropriate following valuation approaches: Cost Approach; Market Approach; Income Approach.

3. Appropriate tests, investigation and weighted consideration are to be given, and so noted when applicable, to the following appraisal subject material as it relates to current highest and best use, value, and acceptability of the risk for the association portfolio: (a) Economic stability of the city, community and neighborhood of the subject property; (b) Growth rate, type of growth, and direction of growth development within the areas affecting the subject property; (c) Owner occupancy and tenant occupancy factors as they relate to neighborhood value; (d) Vacancy factors, supply and demand of like properties on the market including new starts and projected new starts based on current land so zoned to

compete within the market; (*e*) The general convenience amenities of the area; i.e., schools, shopping, churches, recreation, transportation and road systems; (*f*) Any limiting factors shown in the title search, or any evidence the subject property lies within a HUD designated flood or earthquake zone will be so noted in bold script on all appraisals and proper notation of consideration included on the loan approval form.

4. As cost and market change, lending policies will accordingly be established by the joint judgment of management and the loan committee rather than by the judgment of the appraisers.

5. Appraisals made for the association will be made without any regard to the amount of the loan which in the judgment of the appraisers should be made as a maximum.

6. No loans secured by real estate shall be made by the association except on the basis of an appraisal made within three months prior to the date of the loan application, excepting that the permanent financing on a construction loan may be made on the basis of the original construction loan appraisal if made within twelve months.

7. No loan will be granted or any loan purchased without it first being inspected by an approved appraiser and a written appraisal furnished to the association signed and certified by him. The association will use only appraisers who have first been approved by the Savings and Loan Commissioner.

8. Appraisal practices and procedures together with final loan consummation will conform to the best established practices of the industry and appraisal practices will be closely reviewed with due diligence to the Statement of Policy (Section 571.1 of Insurance Regulations).

IV   CREDIT POLICY

All applications for a loan from the association will be accepted or rejected on the following credit basis:

1. Collateral or security of property offered and its marketability
2. Capacity or ability of the borrower to repay the credit extended
3. Credit or the character of borrower showing his willingness to acknowledge his financial obligations
4. Credit check to be in the form of a written credit report from a reputable credit reporting firm

V TITLE INSURANCE

All loans granted by the association must have their deeds of trust insured as a first lien, for no less than the amount of the loan, through a title company whose insurance underwriter is acceptable to the association and to GNMA, FNMA and FHLMC.

The minimum coverage consists of an ALTA policy with endorsements 100 and 116. Other endorsements may be required by the association for construction loans, condominium units, leases, mechanics liens and any other endorsements that may fit a particular situation.

Any lien created by an improvement or assessment bond must be paid in full prior to the recording of the association's deed of trust. The association's deed of trust must be the primary lien on all property given as security for a real estate loan.

VI IMPOUND ACCOUNTS

Impounds for insurance and taxes will be required on all loans except loans on single family dwellings.

On single family dwellings it will be optional for the borrower; however, every attempt will be made to secure approval from the borrower to hold impounds.

On any loans, where impounds are not secured, that become delinquent in taxes for a period of three consecutive tax periods (1½ years), the association will require future tax impounds.

Any borrower who fails to pay his insurance when due and who does not pay into an impound account, will be required to establish such an impound for future insurance premiums.

A Realty Tax service will be hired to search and report to the association the realty tax status of all real estate loans held by the association. The borrower will be required to pay for this service.

VII HAZARD INSURANCE

The policy with respect to hazard insurance shall be:

1. The amount of insurance must be equal to the amount of the loan exposure.
2. Fire and Special Form Coverage and/or extended coverage with loss payable to the association.

3. Other insurance that may be required is vandalism, earthquake, flood, protection from "slide" areas.

4. Other insurance requirements will be established depending on the security offered and its location; i.e., condominiums, apartments, commercial or construction loans. In locations that may be designated a flood plain zone, earthquake area, slide area or any area subject to other hazards.

5. All insurance policies must be written by an acceptable insurance company recognized by the mortgage industry.

6. Proof that at least the first year's premium is paid in full.

The borrower, by a written statement to the association, declares he was given free choice of selecting an agency or broker and that the granting of the loan was not conditioned on the placement of the insurance through any particular agent or broker.

The association through its accounting or loan servicing department establishes for each loan a cross index file in part for hazard insurance so that at least 30 days before a subsequent premium payment is due or a policy lapses the borrower and/or his agent is notified that the association requires continuous paid-up coverage in an amount at least equal to the unpaid balance of its loan.

VIII   LOAN APPROVAL PROCEDURES

Loans based upon borrowers, appraisals and properties which meet or exceed the requirements of the foregoing Loan Policies and which may be secured within the requirements of the foregoing security guidelines as to the sufficiency of the association's lien and proper hazard insurance, may be approved, subject to the association's legal lending limit as such limit exists from time to time, by the President or any Vice President provided: that the appraisal of the underlying security property shall have been made by an approved appraiser other than the officer approving the loan.

IX   LOAN COMMITTEE

The loan committee will be composed of the President and three other qualified individuals, at least two of which shall be members of the Board of Directors. The loan committee shall meet monthly to review all loans granted by the association, including vertification that loan documentation complies with this "Guide" and applicable regulations, together with an inspection of such of the underlying security properties as the committee deems necessary to ensure that lending procedures, appraisals and loan documentation are in conformity with these Lending Policies and Procedures as well as with good business practices. The loan committee shall submit its report monthly to the Board of Directors and shall in addition be charged with recommending changes both in operating practices and in association policy. Any person apopinted to the loan committee must be approved by the Savings and Loan Commissioner.

Management is charged with submitting a separate monthly loan report containing statistical and other data including information as to loan volume, fees, interest rates, loan-to-value ratios, etc. In addition, management will furnish the loan committee with all information necessary for the committee's review of loans granted.

X COLLECTION PROCEDURES

The policy with respect to collection procedures shall be:

1. When a payment has not been received within fifteen days of its due date, a form "reminder notice including late penalty" will be sent to the borrower. If no response it received within 10 days of the first notice, a telephone call will be made to the borrower with a follow-up letter sent to the borrower.

2. Depending upon the response to the letter, a personal visit will be attempted to ascertain the cause of delinquency and the condition of the property. The results of this visit will be reported to management for further action.

3. On the 30th day of delinquency, a delinquent billing notice will be sent to the borrower showing 2 payments due plus late penalties.

4. On the 45th day of delinquency a reminder notice and/or letter of intention to foreclose will be sent to the borrower.

5. No loan will be allowed to become 60 days contractually delinquent without the filing of a notice of default unless a "work out" with the borrower has been approved by management.

6. Provided a "work out" has been arranged, a continuous servicing of the loan will be made to assure that the arrangements are being adhered to and, if not, management must be notified for further action.

7. The above procedure is basically written for loans on single family dwellings. Other loans may be modified or enhanced, depending on the type of security or circumstances.

8. After filing a notice of default on any property, a periodic field trip will be made to ascertain the condition of the property.

9. All loans contractually delinquent in excess of 30 days will be reported to the Board of Directors at their monthly meeting following the delinquency.

10. Appropriate records will be kept on all delinquency correspondence, telephone contacts, notice of default and other documentation sufficient to provide a complete history and status review at any time.

XI ASSUMPTIONS

An assumption of an association loan by a third party will be permitted, provided that the following procedure is followed: the new owner furnishes the association

1. A loan application and financial statement
2. A credit report
3. Copy of any escrow documents
4. An assumption agreement
5. Meets any other requirements established by the association
6. The property is reappraised prior to approval of the assumption
7. The loan assumption application is approved in accordance with loan approval procedure

XII   MODIFICATIONS

Due to a borrower's unexpected financial problems or other extenuating circumstances it may be to the best interest of the association and the borrower to temporarily modify the repayment of a loan. In such a case management must take into consideration:

1. All regulatory laws
2. Whether the loan is insured, guaranteed or sold in whole or in part

3. Subordinate liens

4. The circumstances of the request for modification

XIII ADDITIONAL ADVANCES

The policy with respect to additional advances shall be:

1. No additional optional advances may be made on any insured loans, or any loan sold in whole or in part to any other investor.

2. No additional optional advances will be made on any loan granted by the association that has not had at least 24 consecutive payments, all made on their due dates and then only on owner-occupied single family residences.

3. All additional optional advances must be further secured by a note and title insurance on the advance.

4. No additional optional advance will be granted on property where there is secondary financing unless the advance is given to pay off such a lien.

5. No additional optional advance will be given if there has been a previous advance granted or if the loan is more than 30 days delinquent.

6. It is preferred that a loan be completely rewritten if the advance request is more than $2,500.00. It will be required to be rewritten if the advance, when added to the unpaid balance, exceeds the original amount of the initial note and deed of trust.

7. The property be reappraised when the advance is for more than $500.00 or if the property has not been appraised within the previous year.

STATEMENT OF POLICY ADOPTED BY MIDWEST SECURITIES COMMISSIONERS ASSOCIATION ON FEBRUARY 28, 1973 (amended February 26, 1974, July 22, 1975)

I INTRODUCTION

A Application

1. The rules contained in these guidelines apply to qualifications and registrations of real estate programs in the form of limited partnerships (herein sometimes called "programs" or "partnerships") and will be applied by analogy to real estate programs in other forms. While applications not conforming to the standards contained herein shall be looked upon with disfavor, where good cause is shown certain guidelines may be modified or waived by the Administrator.

2. Where the individual characteristics of specific programs warrant modification from these standards they will be accommodated, insofar as possible while still being consistent with the spirit of these Rules.

3. Where these guidelines conflict with requirements of the Securities Exchange Commission, the guidelines will not apply.

B Definitions

1 *Acquisition Fee* The total of all fees and commissions paid by any party in connection with the purchase or development of property by a program, except a development fee paid to a person not affiliated with a sponsor, in connection with the actual development of a project after acquisition of the land by the program. Included in the computation of such fees or commissions shall be any real estate commission, acquisition fee, selection fee, development fee, nonrecurring management fee, or any fee of a similar nature, however designated.

2 *Administrator* The official or agency administering the securities law of a state.

3 Affiliate   Means (i) any person directly or indirectly controlling, controlled by or under common control with another person, (ii) any person owning or controlling 10% or more of the outstanding voting securities of such other person (iii) any officer, director, partner of such person and (iv) if such other person is an officer, director or partner, any company for which such person acts in any such capacity.

4 Appraised Value   Value according to an appraisal made by an independent qualified appraiser.

5 Assessments   Additional amounts of capital which may be mandatorily required of or paid at the option of a participant beyond his subscription commitment.

6 Audited Financial Statements   Financial statements (balance sheet, statement of income, statement of partners' equity, and statment of changes in financial position) prepared in accordance with generally accepted accounting principles and accompanied by an auditor's report containing an opinion acceptable to the Administrator of an independent certified public accountant or independent public accountant.

7 Capital Contribution   The gross amount of investment in a program by a participant, or all participants as the case may be.

8 Cash Flow   Program cash funds provided from operations, including lease payments on net leases from builders and sellers, without deduction for depreciation, but after deducting cash funds used to pay all other expenses, debt payments, capital improvements and replacements.

9 Cash Available for Distribution   Cash flow less amount set aside for restoration or creation of reserves.

10 Construction Fee   A fee for acting as general contractor to construct improvements on a program's property cither initially or at a later date.

11 Development Fee   A fee for the packaging of a program's property, including negotiating and approving plans, and undertaking to assist in obtaining zoning and necessary variances and necessary financing for the specific property, either initially or at a later date.

12 Net Worth   The excess of total assets over total liabilities as determined by generally accepted accounting principles, except that if any of such assets have been depreciated, then the amount of depreciation relative to any particular asset may be added to the depreciated cost of such asset to compute total assets, provided that the amount of depreciation may be added only to the extent that the amount resulting after adding such depreciation does not exceed the fair market value of such asset.

13 Nonspecified Property Program   A program where, at the time a securities registration is ordered effective, less than 75% of the net proceeds from the sale of program interests is allocable to the purchase, construction, or improvement of specific properties, or a program in which the proceeds from any sale or refinancing of properties may be reinvested. Reserves shall be included in nonspecified 25%.

14 Organization and Offering Expenses   Those expenses incurred in connection with and in preparing a program for registration and subsequently offering and distributing it to the public, including sales commissions paid to broker-dealers in connection with the distribution of the program.

15 Participant   The holder of a program interest.

16 Person   Any natural person, partnership, corporation, association or other legal entity.

17 Program   A limited or general partnership, joint venture, unincorporated association or similar organization other than a corporation formed and operated for the primary purpose of investment in and the operation of or gain from an interest in real property.

18 Program Interest   The limited partnership unit or other indicia of ownership in a program.

19 Program Management Fee   A fee paid to the sponsor or other persons for management and administration of the program.

20 Property Management Fee   The fee paid for day to day professional property management services in connection with a program's real property projects.

21 Prospectus   Shall have the meaning given to that term by Section 2(10) of the Securities Act of 1933, including a preliminary prospectus; provided, however, that such term as used herein shall also include an offering circular as described in Rule 256 of the General Rules and Regulations under the Securities Act of 1933 or, in the case of an intrastate offering, any document by whatever name known, utilized for the purpose of offering and selling securities to the public.

22 Purchase Price of Property   The price paid upon the purchase or sale of a particular property, including the amount of acquisition fees and all liens and mortgages on the property, but excluding points and prepaid interest.

23 Sponsor   A "sponsor" is any person directly or indirectly instrumental in organizing, wholly or in part, a program or any person who will manage or participate in the management of a program, and any affiliate of any such person, but does not include a person whose only relation with the program is as that of an independent property manager, whose only compensation is as such. "Sponsor" does not include wholly independent third parties such as attorneys, accountants, and underwriters whose only compensation is for professional services rendered in connection with the offering of syndicate interests.

24 Standard Real Estate Commission   That real estate or brokerage commission paid for the purchase or sale of property which is reasonable, customary and competitive in light of the size, type and location of the property.

II REQUIREMENTS OF SPONSORS

A Experience

The sponsor and the general partner or their chief operating officers shall have at least two years relevant real estate or other experience demonstrating the knowledge and experience to acquire and manage the type of properties being acquired, and they or any affiliate providing services to the program shall have had not less than four years relevant experience in the kind of service being rendered or otherwise must demonstrate sufficient knowledge and experience to perform the services proposed.

B Net Worth Requirement of General Partner

The financial condition of the general partner or general partners must be commensurate with any financial obligations assumed in the offering and in the operation of the program. As a minimum, the general partners shall have an aggregate financial net worth, exclusive of home, automobile and home furnishings, of the greater of either $50,000 or an amount at least equal to 5% of the gross amount of all offerings sold within the prior 12 months plus 5% of the gross amount of the current offering, to an aggregate maximum net worth of the general partners of one million dollars. In determining net worth for this purpose, evaluation will be made of contingent liabilities to determine the appropriateness of their inclusion in computation of net worth.

C Reports to Administrator

The sponsor shall submit to the Administrator any information required to be filed with the Administrator, including, but not limited to, reports and statements required to be distributed to limited partners.

D Liability

Sponsors shall not attempt to pass on to limited partners the general liability imposed on them by law except that the partnership agreement may provide that a general partner shall have no liability whatsoever to the partnership or to any limited partner for any loss suffered by the partnership which arises out of any action or inaction of the general partner, if the general partner, in good faith, determined that such course of conduct was in the best interests of the partnership, and such course of conduct did not constitute negligence of the general partner. The sponsor may be indemnified by the program against losses sustained in connection with the program, provided the losses were not the result of negligence or misconduct on the part of the sponsors.

III SUITABILITY OF THE PARTICIPANT

A Standards to be Imposed

Given the limited transferability, the relative lack of liquidity, and the specific tax orientation of many real estate Programs, the Sponsor and its selling representatives should be cautious concerning the Persons to whom such securities are marketed. Suitability standards for investors will, therefore, be imposed which are reasonable in view of the foregoing and of the type of Program to be offered. Sponsors will be required to set forth in the Prospectus the investment objectives as a program, a description of the type of person who could benefit from the program and the suitability standards to be applied in marketing it. The suitability standards proposed by the sponsor will be reviewed for fairness by the Administrator in processing the application. In determining how restrictive the standards must be, special attention will be given to the existence of such factors as high leverage, substantial prepaid interest, balloon payment financing, excessive investments in unimproved land, and uncertain or no cash flow from program property. As a general rule, programs structured to give deductible tax losses of 50% or more of the capital contribution of the participant in the year of investment should be sold only to persons in higher income tax brackets considering both state and federal income taxes. Programs which involve more than ordinary investor risk should emphasize suitability standards involving substantial net worth of the investor.

B Sales to Appropriate Persons

1 The sponsor and each person selling limited partnership interests on behalf of the sponsor or program shall make every reasonable effort to assure that those persons being offered or sold the limited partnership interests are appropriate in light of the suitability standards set forth as required above and are appropriate to the customers' investment objectives and financial situations.

2 The sponsor and/or his representatives shall ascertain that the investor can reasonably benefit from the program, and the following shall be evidence thereof:

a. The investor has the capacity of understanding the fundamental aspects of the Program, which capacity may be evidenced by the following:

   (1) The nature of employment experience

   (2) Educational level achieved

   (3) Access to advice from qualified sources, such as, attorney, accountant and tax adviser

   (4) Prior experience with investments of a similar nature

b. The sponsor and/or his representatives shall ascertain that the investor has apparent understanding:

   (1) Of the fundamental risks and possible financial hazards of the investment

   (2) Of the lack of liquidity of this investment

   (3) That the investment will be directed and managed by the sponsor and

   (4) Of the tax consequences of the investment

c. The participant is able to bear the economic risk of the investment. For purposes of determining the ability to bear the economic risk, unless the Administrator approves a lower suitability standard, participants shall have a minimum annual gross income of $20,000 and a net worth of $20,000, or in the alternative, a net worth of $75,000. Net worth shall be determined exclusive of home, home furnishings and automobiles. In high risk or principally tax oriented offerings, higher suitability standards may be required. In the case of sales to fiduciary accounts, the suitability standards shall be met by the fiduciary or by the fiduciary account or by a donor who directly or indirectly supplies the funds to purchase the interest in the program.

C   Maintenance of Records

The sponsor shall maintain a record of the information obtained to indicate that a participant meets the suitability standards employed in connection with the offer and sale of its interests and a representation of the participant that he is purchasing for his own account or, in lieu of such representation, information indicating that the participants for whose account the purchase is made meet such suitability standards. Such information may be obtained from the participant through the use of a form which sets forth the prescribed suitability standards in full and which includes a statement to be signed by the participant in which he represents that he meets such suitability standards and is purchasing for his own account. However, where the offering is underwritten or sold by a broker-dealer, the sponsor shall obtain a commitment from the broker-dealer to maintain the same record of information required of the sponsor.

D   Minimum Investment

A minimum initial cash purchase of $2,500 per investor shall be required. Subsequent transfers of such interests shall be limited to no less than a minimum unit equivalent to an initial minimum purchase, except for transfers by gifts, inheritance, intra-family transfers, family dissolutions, and transfers to affiliates.

IV   FEES—COMPENSATION—EXPENSES

A   Fees, Compensation and Expenses to be Reasonable

1   The total amount of consideration of all kinds which may be paid directly or indirectly to the sponsor or its affiliates shall be reasonable, considering all aspects of the syndication program and the investors. Such consideration may include, but is not limited to:

   a.   Organization and offering expenses.

   b.   Compensation for acquisition services.

   c.   Compensation for development and/or construction services.

   d.   Compensation for program management.

   e.   Additional compensation to the sponsor/subordinated interests and promotional interests.

   f.   Real estate brokerage commissions on resale of property.

   g.   Property management fee.

2   Except to the extent that a subordinated interest is permitted for promotional activities pursuant to Subdivision E, hereof, consideration may only be paid for reasonable and necessary goods, property or services.

3   The application for qualification or registration and the Prospectus must fully disclose and itemize all consideration which may be received from the program directly or indirectly by the sponsor, its affiliates and underwriters, what the consideration is for and how and when it will be paid. This shall be set forth in one location in tabular form.

B   Organization and Offering Expenses

All Organization and Offering Expenses incurred in order to sell program interests shall be reasonable and shall comply with all statutes, rules and regulations imposed in connection with the offering of other securities in the state.

C   Compensation for Acquisition Services

Payment of an acquisition fee shall be reasonable and shall be payable only for services actually rendered and to be rendered directly or indirectly and subject to the following conditions:

1   The total of all such compensation paid to everyone involved in the transaction by the program and/or any other person shall be deemed to be presumptively reasonable if it does not exceed the lesser of such compensation customarily charged in arm's length transactions by others rendering similar services as an ongoing public activity in the same geographical location and for comparable property or an amount equal to 18% of the gross proceeds of the offering. The acquisition fee to be paid to the sponsor shall be reduced to the extent that other real estate commissions, acquisition fees, finder's fees, or other similar fees or commissions are paid by any person in connection with the transaction. For purposes of this section, a standard real estate commission shall be based on the purchase price of the property.

2   The sponsor shall set forth on the face of the prospectus the amount of all acquisition fees which may be paid. This amount shall be expressed in both absolute dollars and as a percentage of the gross proceeds of the offering and may, in addition, be ex-

pressed as a percentage of the sum of the purchase price of the property, plus the acquisition fee.

3   The sum of the purchase price of the program's properties plus the acquisition fees paid shall not exceed the appraised value of the properties.

D   Program Management Fee

1   A general partner of a Program owning unimproved land shall be entitled to annual compensation not exceeding ¼ of 1% of the cost of such unimproved land for operating the Program until such time as the land is sold or improvement of the land commences by the limited partnership. In no event shall this fee exceed a cumulative total of 2% of the original cost of the land regardless of the number of years held.

2   A general partner of a Program holding property in government subsidized projects shall be entitled to annual compensation not exceeding ½ of 1% of the cost of such property for operating the Program until such time as the property is sold.

3   Program management fees other than as set forth above shall be prohibited.

E   Promotional Interest

An interest in the limited partnership will be allowed as a promotional interest and partnership management fee, provided the amount or percentage of such interest is reasonable. Such an interest will be considered presumptively reasonable if it is within the limitations expressed in either subparagraph 1 or 2 below:

1   An interest equal to 25% in the undistributed cash amounts remaining after payment to investors of an amount equal to 100% of capital contribution; or

2   An interest equal to:
   a.   10% of distributions from cash available for distribution
   b.   15% of cash distributions to investors from the proceeds remaining from the sale or refinancing of properties after payment to investors of an amount equal to 100% of capital contributions, plus an amount equal to 6% of capital contributions per annum cumulative, less the sum of prior distributions to investors from cash available for distribution.

3 For purposes of this Section, the capital contribution of the investors shall only be reduced by a cash distribution to investors of the proceeds from the sale or refinancing of properties.

4 Dissolution and liquidation of the partnership. The distribution of assets upon dissolution and liquidation of the partnership shall conform to the applicable subordination provisions of subsections 1 and 2b herein, and appropriate language shall be included in the partnership agreement.

F   Real Estate Brokerage Commissions on Resale of Property

Payment of all real estate commissions or similar fees to the sponsor on the resale of property by a program shall not exceed the lesser of 9% of the gross proceeds of the offering or 50% of the standard real estate commission. Such commission shall be paid only for services actually performed, and shall be subordinated as in E. 2. above. If the sponsor participates with an independent broker on resale, the subordination requirement shall apply only to the commission earned by the sponsor.

V   CONFLICTS OF INTEREST AND INVESTMENT RESTRICTIONS

A   Sales, Leases and Loans

1 *SALES AND LEASES TO PROGRAM.*   A program shall not purchase or lease property in which a sponsor has an interest unless:

a. The transaction occurs at the formation of the program and is fully disclosed in its prospectus or offering circular.

b. The property is sold upon terms fair to the program and at a price not in excess of its appraised value.

c. The cost of the property and any improvements thereon to the sponsor is clearly established. If the sponsor's cost was less than the price to be paid by the program, the price to be paid by the program will not be deemed fair, regardless of the appraised value, unless some material change has occurred to the property which would increase the value since the sponsor acquired the property. Material factors may include the passage of a significant amount of time (but in no event less than 2 years), the assumption by the promoter of the risk of obtaining a re-zoning of the property and its subsequent re-zoning, or some other extraordinary event which in fact increases the value of the property.

d. The provisions of this subsection notwithstanding, the sponsor may purchase property in its own name (and assume loans in connection therewith) and temporarily hold title thereto for the purpose of facilitating the acquisition of such property or the borrowing of money or obtaining of financing for the program, or completion of construction of the property, or any other purpose related to the business of the program, provided that such property is purchased by the program for a price no greater than the cost of such property to the sponsor, except compensation in accordance with Section IV above of these Rules, and provided there is no difference in interest rates of the loans secured by the property at the time acquired by the sponsor and the time acquired by the program, nor any other benefit arising out of such transaction to the sponsor apart from compensation otherwise permitted by these Rules.

2 SALES AND LEASES TO SPONSOR.   The program will not ordinarily be permitted to sell or lease property to the sponsor except that the program may lease property to the sponsor under a lease-back arrangement made at the outset and on terms no more favorable to the sponsor than those offered other persons and fully described in the prospectus.

3 LOANS.   No loans may be made by the program to the sponsor or affiliate.

4 DEALINGS WITH RELATED PROGRAMS.   A program shall not acquire property from a program in which the sponsor has an interest.

B   Exchange of Limited Partnership Interests

The program may not acquire property in exchange for limited partnership interests, except for property which is described in the prospectus which will be exchanged immediately upon effectiveness. In addition, such exchange shall meet the following conditions:

1   A provision for such exchange must be set forth in the partnership agreement, and appropriate disclosure as to tax effects of such exchange are set forth in the prospectus.
2   The property to be acquired must come within the objectives of the program.

3   The purchase price assigned to the property shall be no higher than the value supported by an appraisal prepared by an independent, qualified appraiser.

4   Each limited partnership interest must be valued at no less than:

   a.   Market value if there is a market or if there is no market

   b.   Fair market value of the program's assets as determined by an independent appraiser within the last 90 days, less its liabilities, divided by the number of interests outstanding.

5   No more than one-half of the interests issued by the program shall have been issued in exchange for property.

6   No securities sales or underwriting commissions shall be paid in connection with such exchange.

7   Such exchange, however, is prohibited between the program and the sponsor.

C   Exclusive Agreement

A program shall not give a sponsor an exclusive right to sell or exclusive employment to sell property for the program.

D   Commissions on Reinvestment

A program shall not pay, directly or indirectly, a commission or fee to a sponsor in connection with the reinvestment of the proceeds of the resale, exchange, or refinancing of program property.

E   Services Rendered to the Program by the Sponsor

1   *PROPERTY MANAGEMENT SERVICES.*   The sponsor or his affiliates may perform property management services for the program provided that the compensation to the sponsor therefor is competitive in price and terms with other non-affiliated persons rendering comparable services. All such self-dealing and the compensation paid therefor shall be fully disclosed in the prospectus or offering circular.

2   *OTHER SERVICES.*   Any other services performed by the sponsor for the program will be allowed only in extraordinary circumstances fully justified to the Administrator. As a minimum, self-dealing arrangements must meet the following criteria:

a. The compensation, price or fee therefor must be comparable and competitive with the compensation, price or fee of any other person who is rendering comparable services or selling or leasing comparable goods which could reasonably be made available to the programs and shall be on competitive terms.

b. The fees and other terms of the contract shall be fully disclosed in the prospectus.

c. The sponsor must be previously engaged in the business of rendering such services or selling or leasing such goods, independently of the program and as an ordinary and ongoing business.

d. All services or goods for which the sponsor is to receive compensation shall be embodied in a written contract which precisely describes the services to be rendered and all compensation to be paid, which contract may only be modified by a vote of the majority of the limited partners. Said contract shall contain a clause allowing termination without penalty on 60 days notice.

F   Rebates, Kickbacks and Reciprocal Arrangements

1 No rebates or give-ups may be received by the sponsor nor may the sponsor participate in any reciprocal business arrangements which would circumvent these Rules. Furthermore the prospectus and program charter documents shall contain language prohibiting the above as well as language prohibiting reciprocal business arrangements which would circumvent the restrictions against dealing with affiliates or promoters.

2 No sponsor shall directly or indirectly pay or award any commissions or other compensation to any person engaged by a potential investor for investment advice as an inducement to such advisor to advise the purchaser of interests in a particular program; provided, however, that this clause shall not prohibit the normal sales commissions payable to a registered broker-dealer or other properly licensed person for selling program interests.

G   Commingling of Funds

The funds of a Program shall not be commingled with the funds of any other person.

H   Expenses of Program

All expenses of the programs shall be billed directly to and paid by the program. Reimbursements (other than for organization and offering expenses) to any sponsor shall not be allowed, except for reimbursement of the actual cost to the sponsor of goods and materials used for or by the program. Expenses incurred by the sponsor or any affiliate in connection with his administration of the program, including but not limited to salaries, rent, travel expenses and such other items generally falling under the category of sponsor's overhead, shall not be charged to the program.

I Investments in Other Programs

Investments in limited partnership interests of another program shall be prohibited; however, nothing herein shall preclude the investment in general partnerships or ventures which own and operate a particular property provided the program acquires a controlling interest in such other ventures or general partnerships. In such event, duplicate property management or other fees shall not be permitted. Such prohibitions shall not apply to programs under Sections 236 or 221(d)(3) of the National Housing Act or any similar programs that may be enacted, but unless prohibited by the applicable federal statute, such partnership (herein referred to as lower tier partnership) shall provide for its limited partners all of the rights and obligations required to be provided by the original program in Section VII of these Rules.

J Lending Practices

1   On financing made available to the program by the sponsor, the sponsor may not receive interest and other financing charges or fees in excess of the amounts which would be charged by unrelated lending institutions on comparable loans for the same purpose in the same locality of the property. No prepayment charge or penalty shall be required by the sponsor on a loan to the program secured by either a first or a junior or all-inclusive trust deed, mortgage or encumbrance on the property, except to the extent that such prepayment charge or penalty is attributable to the underlying encumbrance. Except as permitted by subsection 2. of this Section, the sponsor shall be prohibited from providing permanent financing for the program.

2   An "all-inclusive" or "wrap-around" note and deed of trust (the "all-inclusive note" herein) may be used to finance the purchase of property by the program only if the following conditions are complied with:

a. The sponsor under the all-inclusive note shall not receive interest on the amount of the underlying encumbrance included in the all-inclusive note in excess of that payable to the lender on that underlying encumbrance.

b. The program shall receive credit on its obligation under the all-inclusive note for payments made directly on the underlying encumbrance.

c. A paying agent, ordinarily a bank, escrow company, or savings and loan, shall collect payments (other than any initial payment of prepaid interest or loan points not to be applied to the underlying encumbrance) on the all-inclusive note and make disbursements therefrom to the holder of the underlying encumbrance prior to making any disbursement to the holder of the all-inclusive note, subject to the requirements of subparagraph a. above, or, in the alternative, all payments on the all-inclusive and underlying note shall be made directly by the program.

K   Development or Construction Contract

The sponsor will not be permitted to construct or develop properties, or render any services in connection with such development or construction unless all of the following conditions are satisfied:

1 The transactions occur at the formation of the program.

2 The specific terms of the development and construction of identifiable properties are ascertainable and fully disclosed in the prospectus.

3 The purchase price to be paid by the program is based upon a firm contract price which in no event can exceed the sum of the cost of the land and the sponsor's cost of construction. For the purposes of this subdivision, cost of construction includes the contractor or construction fee customarily paid for services as a general contractor, provided, however, than any overhead of the general contractor is not charged to the program or included in the cost of construction.

4 In the case of construction, the only fees paid to the sponsor in connection with such project shall consist of a construction fee for acting as a general contractor, which fee must be comparable and competitive with the fee of disinterested persons rendering comparable services (excluding, however, any overhead of the

contractor) and a real estate commission in connection with the acquisition of the land, if appropriate under the circumstances. Any such real estate commission shall be subject to the provisions of Section IV C. of these Rules.

5 The sponsor demonstrates the presence of extraordinary circumstances as required by subsection 2 of Section V E and otherwise complies with subdivisions *b, c,* and *d* thereunder.

L   Completion Bond Requirement

The completion of property acquired which is under construction should be guaranteed at the price contracted by an adequate completion bond or other satisfactory arrangements.

M   Requirement for Real Property Appraisal

All real property acquisitions must be supported by an appraisal prepared by a competent, independent appraised. The appraisal shall be maintained in the sponsor's records for at least five years, and shall be available for inspection and duplication by any participant. The prospectus shall contain notice of this right.

VI   NONSPECIFIED PROPERTY PROGRAMS

The following special provisions shall apply to nonspecified property programs:

A   Minimum Capitalization

A nonspecified property program shall provide for a minimum gross proceeds from the offering of not less than $1,000,000.00 after payment of all marketing and organization expenses before it may commence business.

B   Experience of Sponsor

For nonspecified property programs, the sponsor or at least one of its principals must establish that he has had the equivalent of not less than five years experience in the real estate business in an executive capacity and two years experience in the management and acquisition of the type of properties to be acquired or otherwise must demonstrate to the satisfaction of the Administrator that he has sufficient knowledge and experience to acquire and manage the type of properties proposed to be acquired by the nonspecified property program.

C   Statement of Investment Objectives

A nonspecified property program shall state types of properties in which it proposes to invest, such as first-user apartment projects, subsequent-user apartment projects, shopping centers, office buildings, unimproved land, etc., and the size and scope of such projects shall be consistent with the objectives of the program and the experience of the sponsors. As a minimum the following restrictions on investment objectives shall be observed:

1   Unimproved or nonincome producing property shall not be acquired except in amounts and upon terms which can be financed by the program's proceeds or from cash flow.

2   Investments in junior trust deeds and other similar obligations shall be limited. Normally such investments shall not exceed 10% of the gross assets of the program.

3   The manner in which acquisitions will be financed, including the use of an all-inclusive note or wrap-around, and the leveraging to be employed shall all be fully set forth in the statement of investment objectives.

4   The Statement shall indicate whether the program will enter into joint venture arrangements and the projected extent thereof.

D   Period of Offering and Expenditure of Proceeds

No offering of securities in a nonspecified property program may extend for more than one year from the date of effectiveness. While the proceeds of an offering are awaiting investment in real property, the proceeds may be temporarily invested in short-term highly liquid investments where there is appropriate safety of principal, such as U.S. Treasury Bonds or Bills. Any proceeds of the offering of securities not invested within two years from the date of effectiveness (except for necessary operating capital) shall be distributed pro rata to the partners as a return of capital.

E   Special Reports

At least quarterly, a "Special Report" of real property acquisitions within the prior quarter shall be sent to all participants until the proceeds are invested or returned to the partners as set forth in paragraph D above. Such notice shall describe the real properties, and include a description of the geographic locale and of the market upon which the sponsor is relying in projecting successful operation of the properties. All facts which reasonably appear to the sponsor to materially influence the value of the property should be disclosed. The "Special Report" shall include, by way of illustration and not of limitation, a statement of the date and amount of the appraised value, if applicable, a statement of the actual purchase price including terms of the purchase, a statement of the total amount of cash expended by the program to acquire each property, and a statement regarding the amount of proceeds in the program which remain unexpended or uncommitted. This unexpended or uncommitted amount shall be stated in terms of both dollar amount and percentage of the total amount of the offering of the program.

F   Assessments

Plans calling for assessments shall not be allowed.

G   Multiple Programs

Sponsors shall be discouraged from offering for sale more than one unspecified property program at any point in time unless the programs have different investment objectives. Similarly, the continuance of new offerings by the same sponsor shall not be looked upon with favor if that sponsor has not substantially committed or placed the funds raised from preexisting unspecified property programs.

H   Allocation of Acquisition Fee

Sponsors of a nonspecified property syndication shall not collect an acquisition fee until properties are acquired by the program and the purchase has closed. The acquisition fee shall be reasonable in light of the services performed; shall be based on the purchase price of the property; and shall not exceed, at any time, 18% of the gross proceeds of the offering, applied on the purchase of specific properties by the program.

VII   RIGHTS AND OBLIGATIONS OF PARTICIPANTS

A   Meetings

Meetings of the limited partnership may be called by the general partner(s) or the limited partner(s) holding more than 10% of the then outstanding limited partnership interests, for any matters for which the partners may vote as set forth in the limited partnership agreement. A list of the names and addresses of all limited partners shall be maintained as part of the books and records of the limited partnership and shall be made available on request to any limited partner or his representative at his cost. Upon receipt of a written request either in person or by registered mail stating the purpose(s) of the meeting, the general partner shall provide all partners, within ten days after receipt of said request, written notice (either in person or by registered mail) of a meeting and the purpose of such meeting to be held on a date not less than fifteen nor more than sixty days after receipt of said request, at a time and place convenient to participants.

B   Voting Rights of Limited Partners

To the extent the law of the state in question is not inconsistent, the limited partnership agreement must provide that a majority of the then outstanding limited partnership interests may, without the necessity for concurrence by the general partner, vote to (1) amend the limited partnership agreement, (2) dissolve the program, (3) remove the general partner and elect a new general partner, and (4) approve or disapprove the sale of all or substantially all of the assets of the program. The agreement should provide for a method of valuation of the general partner's interest, upon removal of the general partner, that would not be unfair to the participants. The agreement should also provide for a successor general partner where the only general partner of the program is an individual.

C   Reports to Holders of Limited Partnership Interests

The partnership agreement shall provide that the sponsor shall cause to be prepared and distributed to the holders of program interests during each year the following reports:

1   In the case of a program registered under Section 12 (g) of the Securities Exchange Act of 1934, within sixty days after the end of each quarter of the program, a report containing:
   a.   A balance sheet, which may be unaudited
   b.   A statement of income for the quarter then ended, which may be unaudited

    c. A cash flow statement for the quarter then ended, which may be unaudited

    d. Other pertinent information regarding the program and its activities during the quarter covered by the report

2 In the case of all other programs in addition to the annual report required by paragraph 4 hereof, within sixty days after the end of the program's first six-month period, a semiannual report containing the same information as to the preceding six-month period as that required in quarterly reports under paragraph 1 hereof.

3 In the case of all programs, within 75 days after the end of each program's fiscal year, all information necessary for the preparation of the limited partners' federal income tax returns.

4 In the case of all programs, within 120 days after the end of each program's fiscal year, an annual report containing (1) a balance sheet as of the end of its fiscal year and statements of income, partners' equity, and changes in financial position and a cash flow statement, for the year then ended, all of which, except the cash flow statement, shall be prepared in accordance with generally accepted accounting principles and accompanied by an audtior's report containing an opinion of an independent certified public accountant or independent public accountant, (2) a report of the activities of the program during the period covered by the report, and (3) where projections have been provided to the holders of limited partnership interests, a table comparing the projections previously provided with the actual results during the period covered by the report. Such report shall set forth distributions to limited partners for the period covered thereby and shall separately identify distributions from (*a*) cash flow from operations during the period, (*b*) cash flow from operations during a prior period which had been held as reserves, (*c*) proceeds from disposition of property and investments, (*d*) lease payment on net leases with builders and sellers, and (*e*) reserves from the gross proceeds of the offering originally obtained from the limited partners.

5 Where assessments have been made during any period covered by any report required by paragraphs 1, 2 and 4 hereof, then such report shall contain a detailed statement of such assessments and the application of the proceeds derived from such assessments.

6 Where any sponsor receives fees for services, including acquisition fees from the program, then he shall, within 60 days of the end of each quarter wherein such fees were received, send to each limited partner a detailed statement setting forth the services rendered, or to be rendered by such sponsor and the amount of the fees received. This requirement may not be circumvented by lump-sum payments to management companies or other entities who then disburse the funds.

D   Access to Records

The limited partners and their designated representatives shall be permitted access to all records of the program at all reasonable times.

E   Admission of Participants

Admission of participants to the program shall be subject to the following:

1   ADMISSION OF ORIGINAL PARTICIPANTS.   Upon the original sale of partnership units by the program, the purchasers should be admitted as limited partners not later than 15 days after the release from impound of the purchaser's funds to the program, and thereafter purchasers should be admitted into the program not later than the last day of the calendar month following the date their subscription was accepted by the program. Subscriptions shall be accepted or rejected by the program within 30 days of their receipt; if rejected, all subscription monies should be returned to the subscriber forthwith.

2   ADMISSION OF SUBSTITUTED LIMITED PARTNERS AND RECOGNITION OF ASSIGNEES.   The program shall amend the certificate of limited partnership at least once each calendar quarter to effect the substitution of substituted participants, although the sponsor may elect to do so more frequently. In the case of assignments, where the assignee does not become a substituted limited partner, the program shall recognize the assignment not later than the last day of the calendar month following receipt of notice of assignment and required documentation.

F   Redemption of Program Interests

Ordinarily, the program and the sponsor may not be mandatorily obligated to redeem or repurchase any of its program interests, although the program and the sponsor may not be precluded from purchasing such outstanding interests if such purchase does not impair the capital or the operation of the program. Notwithstanding the foregoing, a real estate program may provide for mandatory redemption rights under the following necessitous circumstances:

1 Death or legal incapacity of the owner
2 A substantial reduction in the owner's net worth or income provided that (1) the program has sufficient cash to make the purchase, (2) the purchase will not be in violation of applicable legal requirements and (3) not more than 15% of the outstanding units are purchased in any year.

G Transferability of Program Interests

Restrictions on assignment of limited partnership interests will not be allowed. Restrictions on the substitution of a limited partner are generally disfavored and will be allowed only to the extent necessary to preserve the tax status of the partnership and any restriction must be supported by opinion of counsel.

H Assessability

Except as provided in Section VI F, herein in the case of nonspecified property programs, if the anticipated income cash flow from property (after payment of debt service and all operating expenses) is not sufficient to pay taxes and/or special assessments imposed by governmental or quasi-governmental units, the program agreement may include a provision for assessability to meet such deficiencies, including those obligations of a defaulting participant. Assessability must be limited to the foregoing obligations, and all amounts derived from such assessments must be applied only to satisfaction of said obligations.

I Defaults

In the event of a default in the payment of assessments by a limited partner, his interests shall not be subject to forfeiture, but may be subject to a reasonable penalty for failure to meet his commitment. Provided that the arrangements are fair, this may take the form of reducing his proportionate interest in the program, subordinating his interest to that of nondefaulting partners, a forced sale complying with applicable procedures for notice and sale, the lending of the amount necessary to meet his commitment by the other participants or a fixing of the value of his interest by independent appraisal or other suitable formula with provision for a delayed payment to him for his interest not beyond a reasonable period, but a debt security issued for such interest should not have a claim prior to that of the other investors in the event of liquidation.

VIII DISCLOSURE AND MARKETING REQUIREMENTS

A   Sales Promotional Efforts

1 SALES LITERATURE.   Sales literature, sales presentations (including prepared presentations to prospective investors at group meetings) and advertising used in the offer or sale of partnership interests shall conform in all applicable respects to requirements of filing, disclosure and adequacy currently imposed on sales literature, sales presentations and advertising used in the sale of corporate securities.

2 GROUP MEETINGS.   All advertisements of and oral or written invitations to "seminars" or other group meetings at which program interests are to be described, offered or sold shall clearly indicate that the purpose of such meeting is to offer such program interests for sale, the minimum purchase price thereof, and the name of the sponsor, underwriter or selling agent. No cash, merchandise or other item of value shall be offered as an inducement to any prospective participants to attend any such meeting. In connection with the offer or sale of program interests, no general offer shall be made of "free" or "bargain price" trips to visit property in which the program or proposed program has invested or intends to invest. All written or prepared audio-visual presentations (including scripts prepared in advance for oral presentations) to be made at such meetings must be submitted in advance to the Administrator not less than three business days prior to the first use thereof. The foregoing paragraphs 1 and 2 shall not apply to meetings consisting only of representatives of securities broker-dealers.

B   Offerings Registered With the Securities and Exchange Commission ("SEC")

With respect to offerings registered with the Securities and Exchange Commission under the Securities Act of 1933, as amended, and qualified with the Administrator by coordination, a Prospectus which is part of a Registration Statement which has been declared effective by said Commission shall be deemed to comply with all requirements as to form of this Rule; provided, however, that the Administrator reserves the right to require additional disclosure of substance in his discretion.

C   Contents of Prospectus

The following information shall be included in the prospectus of the program:

1   INFORMATION ON COVER PAGE.   There should be set forth briefly on the cover page of the Prospectus a summary which should include the following:

The title and general nature of the securities (interests in the proposed program) being offered; the maximum aggregate amount of the offering; the minimum amount of net proceeds; the minimum subscription price; the period of the offering; the maximum amount of any sales or underwriting commissions to be paid (or if none, or if such commissions are paid by the sponsor), the maximum acquisition fee, or development and/or construction fee; the estimated amount of organization and offering expenses.

2   DEFINITIONS.   Technical terms used in the Prospectus should be defined either in a glossary or as they appear in the Prospectus.

3   RISK FACTORS.   The investor should be advised in a carefully organized series of short, concise paragraphs, under subcaptions where appropriate, of the risks to be considered before making an investment in the program. These paragraphs should include a cross-reference to further information in the Prospectus. Possible disadvantageous tax consequences such as potential inability to deduct prepaid interest in the year paid, tax liability for potential depreciation recapture, depreciation recapture greater than cash distributions and tax liability in the event of foreclosure shall be disclosed.

4   BUSINESS EXPERIENCE.   The business experience of the sponsor(s), general partner(s), principal officers of a corporate general partner (Chairman of the Board, President, Vice President, Treasurer, Secretary or any person having similar authority or performing like functions) and other managers of the program, shall be prominently disclosed in the Prospectus, such disclosure indicating their business experience for the past ten years. The lack of experience or limited experience of the sponsor, general partner, principal officer of a corporate general partner, or other manager of a real estate program shall be prominently disclosed in the Prospectus.

5 COMPENSATION. All indirect and direct compensation which may be paid by the program to the sponsor of every type and from every source shall be summarized in tabular form in one location in the forepart of the Prospectus.

6 USE OF PROCEEDS. State the purposes for which the net proceeds to the program are intended to be used and the approximate amount intended to be used for each such purpose. Also state the minimum aggregate amount necessary to initiate the program and the disposition of the funds raised if they are not sufficient for that purpose.

7 DEFERRED PAYMENTS SCHEDULE. If deferred payments are called for or allowed, the schedule for same shall be set forth.

8 ASSESSMENTS. If provisions for assessment of the limited partners are allowed, the method of assessment and the penalty for default shall be prominently set forth.

9 INVESTMENT OBJECTIVES AND POLICIES. Describe the investment objectives and policies of the program (indicating whether they may be changed by the general partner without a vote of the limited partners) and, if and to the extent that the sponsor is able to do so, the approximate percentage of assets which the program may invest in any one type of investment.

10 DESCRIPTION OF REAL ESTATE AND PROPOSED METHOD OF FINANCING. State the location and describe the general character of all materially important real properties now held or presently intended to be acquired by or leased to the program. Include information as to the present or proposed use of such properties and their suitability and adequacy for such use. Describe terms of any material lease affecting the property. Describe the proposed method of financing, including estimated down payment, leverage ratio, prepaid interest, balloon payment(s), prepayment penalties, due-on-sale or encumbrance clauses and possible adverse effects thereof and similar details of the proposed financing plan. A statement that title insurance and any required construction, permanent or other financing, and performance bonds or other assurances with respect to builders have been or will be obtained on all properties acquired shall be set forth.

11 "TRACK RECORDS." When required or permitted by the Administrator, shall contain the following information:

a. The previous syndication experience of the sponsor and other relevant parties shall be disclosed in the prospectus for all programs during the past five years which:

1   Involved a public offering registered under state or federal securities laws,

2   Involved a private or limited offering, the results of which are material to an informed investment decision by the investor.

b. The Administration may require information on previous programs including, but not limited to, the following:

1   Identification of the program, including the name and location.

2   The effective date of the offering, the date it commenced operations and the date of dissolution or termination or, if it is continuing, that fact.

3   The total amount of interests offered, the gross amount of capital raised by the program, and the number of participants.

4   The types of property acquired, by general classification, and cost separately stating the aggregate cash payment for noncapital items, such as prepaid interest, points, prepaid management fees, etc. whether new or used and depreciation rate used; date of purchase by program; the initial encumbrance, amount of reduction thereof, and whether fully amortized by equal payments over term or whether balloon payments or maturity will occur during contemplated holding period; the ratio of the sponsor's projected net operating income before debt service to the total purchase price for the property; and, if the properties have been sold, the date and results of sale in terms of whether the property was sold at a gain or loss taking into account recapture of depreciation and in terms of type of consideration received and the terms thereof.

5   Total dollar amounts of federal tax deductible items passed on to investors.

6   Cash distributions to participants segregated as to payments to participants from cash available for distribution, proceeds from sale and refinancing, reserves from the gross

amount of investment in the program, lease payments on net leasebacks and other sources.

7 Compensation to the sponsor, segregated as to type, to be received on disposition of the property.

8 Disclosure of any foreclosure or sale or conveyance in lieu of foreclosure of any prior program.

9 A comparison between all projected and actual results.

10 Such additional or different disclosures of the success or failure of the programs as may be permitted or required by the Administrator.

11 The following caveat should be prominently featured in the presentation of the foregoing information: "It should not be assumed that investors in the offering covered by this prospectus will experience returns, if any, comparable to those experienced by investors in prior programs."

c. Information required to be set forth in subparagraphs (5), (6), and (7) of subsection *b* above shall be supported in the application for qualification by an affidavit of the sponsor that the performance summary is a fair representation of the information contained in the audited financial statements or the federal income tax returns of the program.

12 OPERATING DATA. Furnish appropriate operating data with respect to each improved property which is separately described in answer to subsection 10 of Section VIII C.

13 THE PARTNERSHIP.

a. Date of Formation

b. Place of Formation

c. General Partners

d. Initial Partners

e. Address and telephone number of partnership and general partner.

f. Duration.

g. Information called for in items "*a* through *f*" hereof shall be given for any other programs, such as local programs operating property, in which the public program invests.

14 SUMMARY OF TERMS OF THE PARTNERSHIP.

a. Powers of the Sponsor

b. Rights and Liabilities of the Participants

c. Allocation of Distributions

d. Provisions for Replacement and Maintenance Reserves

e. Termination and Dissolution

f. Meetings and Reports

g. Amendment of Agreement

h. Provision for additional Assessments

i. Other Pertinent Matter

15 FEDERAL TAX CONSEQUENCES.

a. A summary of an opinion of tax counsel acceptable to the Administrator and/or a ruling from the Internal Revenue Service covering major tax questions relative to the program, which may be based on reasonable assumptions such as those described in Section IX F. below. To the extent the opinion of counsel or Internal Revenue Service ruling is based on the maintenance of or compliance with certain requirements or conditions by the issuer or sponsor(s), the Prospectus shall to the extent practicable, contain representations that such requirements or conditions have been met and that the sponsors shall use their best efforts to continue to meet such requirements or conditions.

b. Tax treatment of the program

c. Tax treatment of the participants

d. Allocation of depreciation, investment, credit construction interest, points, etc.

e. Method of depreciation, useful life, applicable recapture provisions and consequences thereof.

f. Method of allocation of losses or profits and cash distribution upon transfer of a partnership interest or the right to income.

g. Any other pertinent information applicable to the tax shelter aspects of the investment.

h. Possibility of requirement for filing tax returns with states in which properties are held.

16   LIMITED PARTNERSHIP INTERESTS.

    a. Amount
    b. Minimum purchase
    c. Assessability
    d. Transferability
    e. Voting rights

17   PLAN OF DISTRIBUTION.

    a. Discounts and commissions
    b. Estimated fees and expenses paid or reimbursed by program
    c. Indemnification provisions
    d. Terms of payment
    e. Identity of underwriter, managing dealer or selling agent
    f. Type of underwriting—best efforts or firm commitment
    g. Minimum and Maximum Sales
    h. Escrow Provisions
    i. Material Relationship of Underwriter to program, if any.

18   PENDING LEGAL PROCEEDINGS.   Briefly describe any pending legal proceedings to which the program or the sponsor is a party which is material to the program and any material legal proceedings between sponsor and participants in any prior program of the sponsor and describe any material legal proceedings to which any of the program's property is subject.

19   TRANSACTIONS WITH AFFILIATES.   Describe fully any transactions which have been in the past five years or which may be entered into between the program and any affiliate of the sponsor. Include a description of the material terms of any agreement between the program and any such affiliate. Where the sponsor sponsors other programs, describe the equitable principles which will apply in resolving any conflict between the programs.

20   INTEREST OF AFFILIATES IN PROGRAM PROPERTY.   If within the last years any affiliate had a material interest in any transaction with the sponsor or was previously in the chain of title or had a beneficial interest in any property to be acquired, this fact must be disclosed.

21 INTEREST OF COUNSEL AND EXPERTS IN THE SPONSOR OR PROGRAM.
Where counsel for the selling representatives or the sponsor are named
in the Prospectus as having passed upon the legality of the securities
being registered or upon other legal matters in connection with the
registration or offering of such securities, there should be disclosed in
the Prospectus the *nature and amount* of any direct or indirect interest
of any such counsel, other than legal fees to be received by such counsel,
in the sponsor. Any such interest received or to be received in connection
with the registration or offering of the securities being registered, including
the ownership or receipt by counsel, or by members of the firm participating in the matter, of securities of the sponsor or the program for services shall be disclosed. Employment by the sponsor, other than retainer
as legal counsel, should be disclosed in the Prospectus.

22 FINANCIAL STATEMENTS AND PROJECTIONS.　As provided elsewhere
in these regulations.

23 SUMMARY OF AGREEMENT OF LIMITED PARTNERSHIP.

24 INVESTMENT COMPANY ACT OF 1940.　Where beneficial interests of
a limited partnership are to be sold, treatment under the Investment Company Act of 1940 must be disclosed.

25 ADDITIONAL INFORMATION.　Any additional information which may
be material should be included; further, in furnishing the information
requested in the paragraphs listed above, the instructions for completing
Form S-11 for filing under the Securities Act of 1933 should be referred
to as a guide for the information to be furnished.

D　Projections

1 USE OF PROJECTIONS.　The presentation of predicted future results
of operations ("projections") of real estate programs shall be permitted
but not required. Such projections shall be included in the prospectus,
offering circular or sales material of the partnership only if they comply
with the following requirements:

a General.　Projections shall be realistic in their predictions and shall
clearly identify the assumptions made with respect to all material features
of the presentation. Projections should be prepared by a qualified person
or firm and that person or firm should be identified in the prospectus or
offering circular as being responsible for the preparation of the projections.

No projections shall be permitted in any sales literature which does not appear in the prospectus or offering circular. If any projections are included in the sales literature, all projections must be presented.

b *Material Information.*   Projections shall include all the following information:

1 Annual predicted revenue by source; including the occupancy rate used in predicting rental revenue

2 Annual predicted exepnses

3 Mortgage obligation—annual payments for principal and interest, points and financing fees; shown as dollars, not percentages

4 The required occupancy rate in order to meet debt service and all expenses; rental revenue shall also be predicted based on occupancy rates 10% below the break-even occupancy rate

5 Predicted annual cash flow; stating assumed occupancy rate

6 Predicted annual depreciation and amortization with full description of methods to be used

7 Predicted annual taxable income or loss and a simplified explanation of the tax treatment of such results; assumed tax brackets may not be used

8 Predicted construction costs—including disclosure regarding contracts

9 Accounting policies—e.g., with respect to points, financing costs and depreciation

c *Presentation*

1 *Caveat.*   Projections shall prominently display a statement to the effect that they represent a mere prediction of future events based on assumptions which may or may not occur and may not be relied upon to indicate the actual results which will be obtained.

2 *Format.*   The presentation of projections proposed in accordance with these standards shall be coupled with a summary of predicted results in the event of a material adverse change in one or more significant economic factors, e .g., the effect on partnership cash flow and rate of return of revenues of rental projects at rates 10% to 15% less than expected and in addition the effect of a level of operating expenses 10% to 15% greater than anticipated in the primary projections. A break-even point insofar as occupancy and expenses should be disclosed as should other relevant financial ratios.

3 *Additional Guidelines.* Explanatory notes describing assumptions made and referring to risk factors should be integrated with tabular and numerical information.

4 *Sale-leasebacks.* When a sale-leaseback is employed, the statement that the seller is assuming the operating risk and consequently may have charged a higher price for the property must be included.

d *Additional Disclosures and Limitations.*

1 Projections shall be for a period at least equivalent to the anticipated holding period for the property, or 10 years, whichever is shorter, but they shall definitely project a resale occurrence, including depreciation recapture, if applicable. The projected resale price must be reasonable.

2 Adequate disclosure shall be made of the changing economic effects upon the limited partners resulting principally from federal income tax consequences over the life of the partnership property, e.g., substantial tax losses in early years followed by increasing amounts of taxable income in later years.

3 Projections shall disclose all possible undesirable tax consequences of an early sale of the program property such as, depreciation, recapture or the failure to sell the property at a price which would return sufficient cash to meet resulting tax liabilities of the participants.

4 In computing the return to investors, no appreciation, so-called "equity buildup," or any other benefits from unrealized gains or value shall be shown or included.

2 *PROJECTIONS SHALL NOT BE ALLOWED FOR UNIMPROVED LAND.* Instead, a table of deferred payments specifying the various holding costs, i. e., interest, taxes, and insurance shall be inserted. However, where the program intends to develop and sell the land as its primary business, a detailed cash flow statement showing the timing of expenditures and anticipated revenues shall be required. Additionally, the consequences of a delayed selling progrgam shall be shown.

IX MISCELLANEOUS PROVISIONS

A Fiduciary Duty

The program agreement shall provide that the sponsor shall have fiduciary responsibility for the safekeeping and use of all funds and assets of the program, whether or not in his immediate possession or control, and that he shall not employ, or permit another to employ such funds or assets in any manner except for the exclusive benefit of the program.

B   Deferred Payments

Arrangements for deferred payments on account of the purchase price of program interests may be allowed when warranted by the investment objectives of the partnership, but in any event such arrangements shall be subject to the following conditions:

1   The period of deferred payments shall coincide with the anticipated cash needs of the programs.

2   Selling commissions paid upon deferred payments are collectible when payment is made on the note.

3   Deferred payments shall be evidenced by a promissory note of the investor. Such notes shall be with recourse and shall not be negotiable and shall be assignable only subject to defenses of the maker. Such notes shall not contain a provision authorizing a confession of judgment.

4   The program shall not sell or assign the deferred obligation notes at a discount to meet financing needs of the program.

C   Reserves

Provision should be made for adequate reserves in the future by retention of a reasonable percentage of proceeds from the offering and regular receipts for normal repairs, replacements and contingencies. Normally, not less than 5% of the offering proceeds will be considered adequate.

D   Reinvestment of Cash Flow and Proceeds on Disposition of Property

Reinvestment of Cash Flow (excluding proceeds resulting from a disposition or refinancing of property) shall not be allowed. The partnership agreement and the Prospectus shall set forth that reinvestment of proceeds resulting from a disposition or refinancing will not take place unless sufficient cash will be distributed to pay any state or federal income tax (assuming investors are in a specified tax bracket) created by the disposition or refinancing of property. Such a prohibition must be contained in the Prospectus.

E   Financial Information Required on Application

In any offering of interests by a real estate program, the program shall provide as an exhibit to the application or where indicated below shall provide as part of the Prospectus, the following financial information and financial statements:

1   CASH FLOW STATEMENT OF PROGRAM.   As part of the prospectus, if the program has been formed and owns assets, a cash flow statement, which may be unaudited, for the program for each of the last three fiscal years of the program (or for life of the program, if less) and unaudited statements for any interim period between the end of the latest fiscal year and the date of the balance sheet furnished, and for the corresponding interim period of the preceding years.

2   BALANCE SHEET OF PROGRAM.   As part of the prospectus, a balance sheet of the program as of the end of its most recent fiscal year, prepared in accordance with generally accepted accounting principles and accompanied by an auditor's report containing an unqualified opinion of an independent certified public accountant, and an unaudited balance sheet as of a date not more than ninety days prior to the date of filing.

3   STATEMENTS OF INCOME, PARTNERS' EQUITY, AND CHANGES IN FINANCIAL POSITION OF PROGRAM.   As part of the prospectus, if the program has been formed and owns assets, statements of income, statements of partners' equity, and statements of changes in financial position for the program for each of the last three fiscal years of the program (or for the life of the program, if less), all of which statements shall be prepared in accordance with generally accepted accounting principles and accompanied by an auditor's report containing an unqualified opinion of an independent certified public accountant or independent public accountant, and unaudited statements for any interim period ending not more than ninety days prior to the date of filing an application.

4   BALANCE SHEET OF SPONSOR.

1   Corporate Sponsor. A balance sheet of any corporate sponsors as of the end of their most recent fiscal year, prepared in accordance with generally accepted accounting principles and accompanied by an auditor's report containing an unqualified opinion of an independent certified public accountant or independent public accountant, and an unaudited balance sheet as of a date not more than ninety days prior to the date of filing. Such statements shall be included in the prospectus.

2   Other Sponsors. A balance sheet for each non-corporate general partner (including individual partners or individual joint venturers of a sponsor) as of a time not more than ninety days prior to the date of filing an application; such balance sheet, which may be unaudited, should conform to generally accepted accounting principles, shall be signed and sworn to by such sponsors and prepared by a certified public accountant. A representation of the amount of such net worth must be included in the prospectus, or in the alternative, a representation that such sponsors meet the net worth requirements of Section II B.

5   STATEMENTS OF INCOME FOR CORPORATE SPONSORS.   A statement of income for the last fiscal year of any corporate sponsor (or for the life of the corporate sponsor, if less), prepared in accordance with generally accepted accounting principles and accompanied by an auditor's report containing an unqualified opinion of an independent certified public accountant or independent public accountant, and an unaudited statement for any interim period ending not more than ninety days prior to the date of filing an application. The inclusion of such statements in the prospectus shall be at the discretion of the Administrator.

6   FILING OF OTHER STATEMENTS.   Upon request by an applicant, the Administrator may, where consistent with the protection of investors, permit the omission of one or more of the statements required by these regulations of the filing, in substitution thereof, of appropriate statements verifying financial information having comparable relevance to an investor in determining whether he should invest in the program.

F   Opinions of Counsel

The application for qualification and registration shall contain a favorable ruling from the Internal Revenue Service or an opinion of counsel to the effect that the issuer will be taxed as a "partnership" and not as an "association" for federal income tax purposes. An opinion of counsel shall be in form and substance satisfactory to the Administrator and shall be unqualified except to the extent permitted by the Administrator. However, an opinion of counsel may be based on reasonable assumptions, such as: (1) facts or proposed operations as set forth in the offering circular or prospectus and organizational documents; (2) the absence of future changes in applicable laws; (3) the securities offered are paid for; (4) compliance with certain procedures such as the execution and delivery of certain documents and the filing of a certificate of limited partnership or an amended certificate; and (5) the continued maintenance of or compliance with certain financial, ownership, or other requirements by the issuer or general partner(s). The Administrator may reqeust from counsel as supplemental information such supporting legal memoranda and an analysis as he shall deem appropriate under the circumstances. To the extent the opinion of counsel or Internal Revenue Service ruling is based on the maintenance of or compliance with certain requirements or conditions by the issuer or general partner(s), the offering circular or prospectus, shall contain repre sentations that such requirements or conditions will be met and the partnership agreement shall, to the extent practicable, contain provisions requiring such compliance.

There shall be included also an opinion of counsel to the effect that the securities being offered are duly authorized or created and validly issued interests in the issuer, and that the liability of the public investors will be limited to their respective total agreed upon investment in the issuer.

G Provisions of Partnership Agreement

The requirements and/or provisions of appropriate portions of the following sections shall be included in a partnership agreement: II. C.; IV. D.; IV. E.; IV. F; V. A.; V. B.; V. C.; V. D.; V. E.; V. F.; V. G.; V. H.; V. I.; V. J.; V. M.; VI. C.; VI. D.; VI. E.; VI. F.; VII. A.; VII. B.; VII. C.; VII. D.; VII. E.; VII. F.; VII. H.; VII. I.; IX. A.; IX. B. 4.; IX. C.; and IX. D.

Appendix H MAXIMUM AMOUNT TO PAY FOR $100 PER MONTH EQUAL PAYMENT AMORTIZING MORTGAGE

Months of Yield	10%	15%	Yield Desired 20%	25%	30%
12	11.374508	11.079312	10.795113	10.521420	10.257765
24	21.670855	20.624235	19.647986	18.736585	17.884986
36	30.991236	28.847267	26.908062	25.151016	23.556251
48	39.428160	35.931481	32.861916	30.159427	27.773154
60	47.065369	42.034592	37.744561	34.070014	30.908656
72	53.978665	47.292474	41.748727	37.123415	33.240078
84	60.236667	51.822185	45.032470	39.507522	34.973620
96	65.901488	55.724570	47.725406	41.369041	36.262606
108	71.029355	59.086509	49.933833	42.822522	37.221039
120	75.671163	61.982847	51.744924	43.957406	37.933687
132	79.872986	64.478068	53.230165	44.843528	38.463581
144	83.676528	66.627722	54.448184	45.535414	38.857586
156	87.119542	68.479668	55.447059	46.075642	39.150552
168	90.236201	70.075134	56.266217	46.497454	39.368388
180	93.057439	71.449643	56.937994	46.826807	39.530361
192	95.611259	72.633794	57.488906	47.083966	39.650797
204	97.923008	73.653950	57.940698	47.284757	39.740348
216	100.015633	74.532823	58.311205	47.441536	39.806934
228	101.909902	75.289980	58.615050	47.563949	39.856445
240	103.624619	75.942278	58.864229	47.659530	39.893259
252	105.176801	76.504237	59.068575	47.734160	39.920632
264	106.581856	76.988370	59.236156	47.792431	39.940985
276	107.853730	77.405455	59.373585	47.837929	39.956119
288	109.005045	77.764777	59.486289	47.873455	39.967372
300	110.047230	78.074336	59.578715	47.901193	39.975739
312	110.990629	78.341024	59.654512	47.922851	39.981961
324	111.844605	78.570778	59.716672	47.939762	39.986587
336	112.617635	78.768713	59.767648	47.952966	39.990027
348	113.317392	78.939236	59.809452	47.963275	39.992584
360	113.950820	79.086142	59.843735	47.971325	39.994486
372	114.524207	79.212704	59.871850	47.977611	39.995900
384	115.043244	79.321738	59.894907	47.982518	39.996951
396	115.513083	79.415671	59.913815	47.986350	39.997733
408	115.938387	79.496596	59.929321	47.989342	39.998315
420	116.323377	79.566313	59.942038	47.991678	39.998747
432	116.671876	79.626375	59.952466	47.993502	39.999068
444	116.987340	79.678119	59.961018	47.994927	39.999307
456	117.272903	79.722696	59.968032	47.996039	39.999485
468	117.531398	79.761101	59.973784	47.996907	39.999617
480	117.765391	79.794186	59.978500	47.997585	39.999715

INDEX